WITHDRAWN
UTSA LIBRARIES

European Monographs in Social Psychology
Account episodes
The management or escalation of conflict

European Monographs in Social Psychology

Executive Editors:
J. RICHARD EISER and KLAUS R. SCHERER
Sponsored by the European Association of Experimental Social Psychology

This series, first published by Academic Press (who continue to distribute the numbered volumes), appeared under the joint imprint of Cambridge University Press and the Maison des Sciences de l'Homme in 1985 as an amalgamation of the Academic Press series and the European Studies in Social Psychology, published by Cambridge and the Maison in collaboration with the Laboratoire Européen de Psychologie Sociale of the Maison.

The original aims of the two series still very much apply today: to provide a forum for the best European research in different fields of social psychology and to foster the interchange of ideas between different developments and different traditions. The Executive Editors also expect that it will have an important role to play as a European forum for international work.

Other titles in this series:

Unemployment by Peter Kelvin and Joanna E. Jarrett
National characteristics by Dean Peabody
Experiencing emotion by Klaus R. Scherer, Harald G. Wallbott and Angela B. Summerfield
Levels of explanation in social psychology by Willem Doise
Understanding attitudes to the European Community: a social-psychological study in four member states by Miles Hewstone
Arguing and thinking: a rhetorical approach to social psychology by Michael Billig
The child's construction of economics by Anna Emilia Berti and Anna Silvia Bombi
The political system matters. Social psychology and voting behaviour in Sweden and the United States by Donald Granberg and Sören Holmberg
Non-verbal communication in depression by Heiner Ellgring
Social representations of intelligence by Gabriel Mugny and Felice Carugati

Supplementary volumes:
Politics, power and psychology: views from working-class youth in Britain by Kum-Kum Bhavnani

Account episodes
The management or escalation of conflict

Peter Schönbach
Ruhr-Universität, Bochum

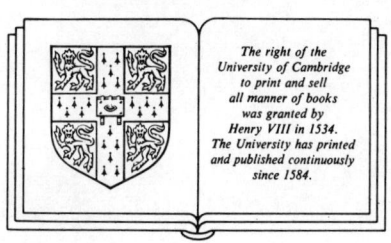

Cambridge University Press
Cambridge
New York   Port Chester   Melbourne   Sydney

Editions de la Maison des Sciences de l'Homme
Paris

Published by the Press Syndicate of the University of Cambridge
The Pitt Building, Trumpington Street, Cambridge CB2 IRP
40 West 20th Street, New York, NY 10011, USA
10 Stamford Road, Oakleigh, Melbourne 3166, Australia
and Editions de la Maison des Sciences de l'Homme
54 Boulevard Raspail, 75270 Paris Cedex 06

© Maison des Sciences de l'Homme and Cambridge University Press 1990

First published 1990

Printed in Great Britain at the University Press, Cambridge

British Library cataloguing in publication data
Schönbach, Peter
Account episodes. – (European monographs in social psychology)
1. Social responsibility
I. Title II. Series
303.4

Library of Congress cataloguing in publication data
Schönbach, Peter
Account episodes / Peter Schönbach.
   p. cm. – (European monographs in social psychology)
Includes index.
ISBN 0 521 35017 4
1. Social ethics. 2. Responsibility. I. Title. II. Series.
HM216.S285 1990
303.3'72 – dc20   89-35774 CIP

ISBN 0 521 35017 4
ISBN 2 7351 0329 3 (France only)

Dedicated to my wife,
Ruth Schönbach-Privat

Without her manifold
support this book
would not exist

Contents

Acknowledgements	page ix
1 The task	1
1.1 Demands for accountability	1
1.2 The structure of account episodes	10
1.3 Functions of account episodes	13
1.4 Basic questions and some specifications	16
1.5 Fundamental obstacle, multiple approximations	17
2 Theoretical guidance	20
2.1 Basic control–theoretical assumptions	20
2.2 A network of escalation	28
2.3 Supplementary speculations	38
3 Study designs and procedures	44
3.1 Common design features	44
3.2 Vignettes of failure events	45
3.3 Reproach phase studies	49
3.4 Account phase studies	54
3.5 Evaluation phase studies	60
3.6 Studies on the meaning of responsibility	65
4 Category systems and codings	68
4.1 Reasons, problems and strategies of category constructions	68
4.2 A taxonomy for reactions of actors during account phases	75
4.3 A taxonomy for reactions of opponents during phases of reproach and evaluation	86
5 Reproach phase results	91
5.1 Effects of severity of failure on severity of reproach	91
5.2 Effects of gender on severity of reproach	95
5.3 The meaning of responsibility for men and women – an excursus	113
5.4 Control needs and severity of reproach	117

6	**Account phase results**	121
	6.1 Effects of severity of reproach on defensiveness of accounts	121
	6.2 Effects of gender on defensiveness of accounts	127
	6.3 Sense of control, self-esteem and defensiveness of accounts	137
	6.4 Severity of failure and defensiveness of accounts	149
7	**Evaluation phase results**	152
	7.1 Defensiveness of accounts and negativity of evaluation	152
	7.2 Effects of gender on negativity of evaluation	161
	7.3 Sense of control, self-esteem and negativity of evaluation	166
	7.4 Severity of reproach and negativity of evaluation	173
8	**Inferences**	175
	8.1 Synopsis	175
	8.2 Transphase perspectives	176
	8.3 Tasks for the future	181
	Appendix A Taxonomy for account phases	188
	Appendix B Taxonomy for reproach and evaluation phases	196
	Notes	204
	References	208
	Name index	217
	Subject index	220

Acknowledgements

Many people have helped me with the research programme on which this monograph is based. Diploma students and seminar participants involved in specific projects are too numerous to list; they will be named in due course in notes of acknowledgement appended to the presentations of those projects. Yet some of these students have been employed as research assistants on more than one project. I would particularly like to mention Petra Kleibaumhüter, who has been involved in our account episode research for more than four years; her excellent contribution to several studies, particularly her data analyses, have been invaluable. I am grateful too for the splendid work provided, in rough chronological order, by Petra Flaßhove, Rudolf Schiffmann, Annegret Heynen, Barbara Birkendorf, Susanne Bubber, and also by Gabriele Wilke, technical assistant on our permanent staff.

Margret Ernsting did the typing of drafts and revisions with great skill and care and untiring patience, this time after having adapted to computer-aided text-processing. Brigitte Reckeweg very efficiently came to her and my succour not only in times of emergency. Günter Keim, with his remarkable talent and experience, once more took charge of drawing and photographing the figures.

My two senior co-workers at the socio-psychological section, Wolfgang Heinemann and Ulrich Wagner, although not immediately involved with the account episode research, have been providers of most welcome stimulating and/or critical feedback over the many years of our association, and more recently they were joined in this role by Andreas Zick. Of course, many other friends and colleagues have taken part in helpful discussions of our programme; I can mention only two, Amélie Mummendey and Robert A. Wicklund, as representative of our Münster–Bielefeld–Bochum group.

Finally, I should like to thank the editors of the European Monographs in Social Psychology and the staff of Cambridge University Press for their interest, encouragement, good counsel and most congenial cooperation in carrying this book into print and publication.

1 The task

1.1 Demands for accountability

It has been the custom for a number of years for the Chancellor of the Federal Republic of Germany to speak to the public on television on New Year's Eve. As expected, Chancellor Helmut Kohl appeared on the screen on 31 December 1986 at 20:05, right after the main news broadcast of the day on the ARD station; yet to everybody's amazement he did not inaugurate the year 1987 but referred to 1986 starting its course. Instead of the prerecorded message for 1987 somebody at the Norddeutsche Rundfunk (NDR), the station in charge of the transmission, had put on last year's tape.

This event immediately turned into a sensation. It caused much turmoil and confusion. It was a source of hilarity for many listeners, and of great vexation to many others, notably in the federal government and in the Chancellor's party, the CDU. Straightaway there was much concern about the political damage which this exchange of the tapes might entail, damage not only to the prospects of the CDU in the impending election to the Bundestag, but damage also to the dignity of democratic rituals and to the institution of the Federal Chancellor as such, as columnist Mathias Schreiber of the *Frankfurter Allgemeine Zeitung* (3 January 1987) feared. Gerold Tandler, secretary-general of the CSU, the Bavarian sister party of the CDU, announced his conviction that the exchange of the tapes had not just been a blunder, but a planned sabotage in order to expose Helmut Kohl to ridicule. A speaker of the Social Democrats, on the other hand, considered the whole affair as 'much ado about nothing' and spoke of artificial excitement (*Westdeutsche Allgemeine Zeitung*, 2 January 1987).

Naturally, there was very strong pressure on the NDR to render an account of what had happened, and much investigation and soul-searching took place. The upshot of it was an official statement from the NDR, together with a renewed apology to Chancellor Kohl and the public, that the mistake had been due to a concatenation of unfortunate circumstances coupled with human failure; deliberate action could be excluded with certainty. The Chancellor accepted the apology; his correct speech had already been broadcast one day later, on 1 January, and the comparison of the two versions invited further, mostly satirical, comments, but rather soon the media lost interest and turned to other events. On 19 January 1987 the *Westdeutsche Allgemeine Zeitung*, rather as an afterthought, carried a very short and rather cryptic message that the head of the NDR, Intendant Räuker, had announced 'consequences of a labour legislative nature' but said that no 'heads should roll'.

Two aspects of the affair are noteworthy for my topic: (1) the elusiveness of 'responsibility' in this as in so many other cases, and (2) an excessive search for culprits. What apparently had happened was this, according to the *Frankfurter Allgemeine Zeitung* of 3 January 1987. Journalists at the Westdeutsche Rundfunk in Cologne had requested the old 1985/86 tape, but had returned it unused to the Norddeutsche Rundfunk in Hamburg. There it did not reach the archives, but ended up in the editorial office and was on hand in the transmission room at the crucial moment. This old 1985/86 tape was not clearly labelled, and the assistant in charge, who had forgotten or did not realize that the correct 1986/87 speech was part of a library tape, mistook the old 1985/86 tape for the right one and put it on. The error was noticed at the NDR right away, but it could not immediately be rectified because the correct 1986/87 speech of the Chancellor could not quickly be located on the library tape.

A chain of unfortunate circumstances and a marvellous example of diffused responsibility, indeed. Who was to blame? The most visible target is the hapless assistant who put on the wrong tape. But then it had been on hand; it was labelled 'Neujahrsansprache des Bundeskanzlers', and only a close look would have revealed that this tape was recorded in December 1985. Most likely, the assistant's expectation, engendered by the whole setting, prevented the registering of that inconspicuous yet crucial detail. Ever since the days of Bartlett (1932) social psychologists, and many others of course, realize that such errors in social cognition, errors that accord with one's expectations, are a pervasive human frailty. So we should sympathize with Intendant Räuker's moderation; yet many public voices would not agree.

The search for those responsible did not stop in the transmission room. On 2 January 1987 the *Westdeutsche Allgemeine Zeitung* reported on the front page a statement of the government's press secretary on New Year's Eve that the event could not be explained away as a technical failure. Those responsible should be held accountable. Right beside this text the newspaper carried a photograph with the caption 'Responsible at the NDR: programme director Rolf Seelmann-Eggebert'. This juxtaposition implicates Mr Seelmann-Eggebert, and some readers may even have inferred that this man was responsible for a conscious exchange of the tapes. More soberly, we may ask in what way a programme director might be held accountable for a failure event such as the one described. Can he be expected to supervise the selection and insertion of every tape to be broadcast? Evidently not. Can we put the blame on him that the returned 1985/86 tape was not immediately sent to the archives? Again no, I would think. Should he have had enough foresight to rule against the use of a library tape in such a case because of some possible trouble? I am not familiar with the conventions and technical procedures at a television station, but once more I would hesitate to say yes. So, what kind of responsibility is it that the programme director could be charged with? Is it the supervisor's role responsibility which requires him to take the blame and to suffer sanctions for his subordinates' negligence or, in the final analysis, for human frailty?

Much more outspoken in his criticism and in his demand for accountability was Mathias Schreiber of the *Frankfurter Allgemeine Zeitung* in the article of 3 January 1987 already mentioned. He declared: 'Responsibility for programmes should not be "divided up" in such a way that it leaves grey areas.' He conceded that such a blunder could also, once in a while, happen in the editorial office of a newspaper, but added that 'these editorial offices compete with a large enough number of others, and this competition automatically provides for reciprocal corrections'.[1]

In the case of television chartered under public law with no comparable competition, Mr Schreiber continued, there are hardly any such corrective mechanisms. Therefore particularly strict standards are required in view of this broadcasting monopoly. And a horrified Mr Schreiber concluded his article with the sentence: 'Seen in this light, the fact that the person responsible cannot be found is almost eerie.'[2]

No doubt the broadcast of the wrong speech was a deplorable failure. But again, what, in practical terms, could be done in order to meet Mr Schreiber's moralistic demands? Together with his apology to the Chancellor and to the public, Intendant Räuker of the NDR promised to take steps to ensure that such mistakes would be prevented in the future. A bold promise indeed.

The case just described is not exceptional. The elusiveness of responsibility, and yet the intensive, and sometimes frantic, search for those responsible has been a pervasive human phenomenon through the ages. Why?

Trying to assemble a tentative partial answer I would suggest as a basic ingredient the desire to have control over one's physical and social environment. I shall have more to say about this control motivation in the next chapter – that on theoretical guidance – and there I shall also refer to relevant publications.

Because of this fundamental desire for at least some control over the environment, we want this world of ours to be an orderly one, and many of us at least, as Lerner (e.g. 1980) has proposed, also want it to be, and would like to see it as, a just world. These needs for orderliness and justice entail several other needs and normative expectations. One of them, I think, is our strong desire for openness and reliability in those with whom we have to interact, as well as in those who have some higher-order control over us, whom we cannot reach in any direct way.

A partial replication (Schönbach 1972) of Anderson's (1968) study on the likableness ratings of 555 personality trait words using a subset of 100 terms from Anderson's list translated into German and rated by 170 students of an introductory social psychology course at the University of Bochum produced, in striking similarity to Anderson's results, very high ratings of traits belonging to the trustworthiness syndrome. Within the subset of the 100 trait words rated in both studies, *sincere, trustworthy* and *dependable* achieved ranks 1, 2 and 3 with Anderson's 100 student respondents; the German equivalent terms *aufrichtig, vertrauenswürdig* and *zuverlässig* achieved ranks 3, 4 and 7 in our study. The opposite terms *insincere* and *phony* received ranks 98 and 100 in the American data set, and the corresponding German terms *unaufrichtig* and *falsch* ranked 96 and 99; these were in close proximity to *cruel* (rank 99) in the American set and *grausam* (rank 100) in the German one.

Freedman, Carlsmith and Sears (1970, pp. 76–7) called attention to Anderson's data: 'One of the most striking results of the study was that apparently the trait most valued by college students in the 1960s was sincerity. Of the eight top adjectives, six – sincere, honest, loyal, truthful, trustworthy, and dependable – related to sincerity in one way or another. Similarly, the adjectives rated lowest were liar and phony, with dishonest being close to the bottom.'

Freedman, Carlsmith and Sears offered no further comment. In the light of the similarity of Anderson's and our own data with respect to the high value accorded to sincerity and trustworthiness I suggested in my replication report 'that this finding provides indirect support for interaction theories of the self, e.g. Secord and Backman, 1961. If not only behavioral stability but also the formation and maintenance of the self-concept depend on congruent interactions with others, then indeed the desire for sincerity in others must be a strong and universal need' (Schönbach 1972, p. 332). Today I would extend this reasoning and regard the social process of self-formation and self-maintenance as but one aspect, albeit a centrally important one, of a pervasive striving for the gaining or regaining of some sense of control in every situation; and I think that it is this fundamental motivation of ours which is served in the first place by trustworthiness and predictability in a person with whom we have to interact. The relationship between sense of control and self-esteem will be discussed in greater detail in the next chapter.

The desire for openness and reliability in others is particularly urgent whenever something seems to have gone wrong, when in our view the orderly course of the world has been interrupted and we have to rely on those others to mend the rupture, or to render a plausible account as a first step in restoring order and justice, if not as a relieving message that nothing out of order has occurred after all. The concept of 'account' is to be understood as a special kind of explanation: an account is an answer to an explicit or implicit question guided by a normative expectation.

Because of the joint needs for order and justice the title of this section 'Demands for accountability' has a double meaning. (1) We wish the events in our world to be accountable in the sense of being understandable and of conforming to normative expectations. But whenever the course of events seriously fails to meet this desire we (2) strongly wish for somebody to be available who can be held to render an account and to be liable for negative sanctions if the account is not forthcoming or is found to be wanting. The demand for accountability in this latter sense – the demand and search for persons to be held accountable – may be considered as a second line of defence of the notion of orderliness and justice in the world, and it is this second aspect with which my treatise will mainly be concerned. The demand for, and the giving and receiving of, an account is, roughly speaking, what I call an account episode. A more detailed description of such episodes will be given in the following section.

The institutional paradigm of account episodes is, of course, legal procedure. Since the days of antiquity the rule 'Audiatur et altera pars!' holds.[3] But the domain of account episodes extends far beyond the boundaries of law. In every society known from history a generally shared vital interest in reducing stress and strain for its members as they engage in the management of intrasocietal conflict can be recognized. Primitive forms of conflict behaviour such as immediate retribution after an offence without prior questioning have been outlawed and have become the exception everywhere. Instead, intervening phases of challenge and account have become normative not only in the domains of law, but also in everyday life.

Normative expectation need not always be held consciously. It rather seems that, as a rule, the flow of conduct in verbal interactions focusing on conflicting views is markedly influenced by behavioural scripts (Schank and Abelson 1977). Bennett (1980), for instance, pointed out that a person B's challenge addressed to person A with respect to an issue X implies the rule (1) that A does reply to the challenge and (2) that this reply does in some way refer to X. A's failure to meet this expectation is likely to incur in the challenger B, as well as in bystanders, an increment in any tendency towards a negative judgement of A's views and deeds, regardless of any pre-established justifiability of A's conduct or position with respect to issue X. On the other hand, if A does reply within the wide frame just mentioned, even if this reply does not fulfil the specific desires of B, A has thereby invoked a general expectation in his or her favour, namely to have the view expressed in the reply considered by B, and/or by third parties, before any final verdict is issued. Thus, if the interaction between A and B happens to be an account episode, then a minimum necessary, but certainly not sufficient, condition for a beneficial outcome is thereby established. McLaughlin, Cody and Rosenstein (1983) present data concurring with this view.

Institutionalized phases of challenge and account, partly guided by behavioural scripts, seem to fulfil a double purpose in the service of stress reduction: (1) they may help to reduce the conflict potential inherent in a direct, unmitigated confrontation of claim and counterclaim, and (2) because of the scripted conduct components, they diminish the effort that has to be put into the negotiation of conflict and its resolution.

The considerations just presented make it clear why account episodes stand an appreciable chance of running a fairly smooth and satisfactory course. Nevertheless, as we all know, such episodes often end up in, or are replaced from the very beginning by, bitter strife. In many such cases the views on accountability are not shared by the participants, and the reasons for such a discrepancy will be the main concern of this monograph.

There are, of course, those instances in which the interests of the interactants collide head on, with no room for reconciliation by negotiation. I will have little to say about such instances. However, there are many other cases in which a resolution of conflict by way of an account episode seems to an impartial observer an achievable outcome, and yet it does not occur. In order to deal with such cases I turn once more to the linkage, and discrepancy at the same time, between diffusion and elusiveness of responsibility on the one hand, and the intensive, and quite often relentless, search for culprits on the other. In this context a brief discussion of the concepts of cause and responsibility is now in order.[4]

Human beings, as a rule, have a simplified view of causality. There is a widespread stubborn disposition to segment a complex flow of events into single cause–effect units or, at best, to consider causal structures in complex processes as unidirectional chainings of cause–effect links, perhaps with several such chains converging towards some ultimate effect. Under the influence of such a disposition many of us either fail to see, or are reluctant to bring into full view, what is the usual state of affairs with any social process of some scope: intricate interactions of many factors; bidirectional, or rather multidirectional, reciprocal influence lines; negative and positive feedback loops, sometimes integrated into complex hierarchical structures. Simplified linear causal thinking in the face of more complex causal structures appears in many different forms. I shall limit myself to just a few examples that are particularly pertinent to my topic.

One important embodiment of linear causal thinking can be seen in the

Demands for accountability

famous distinction between actors' and observers' causal attributions which Jones and Nisbett (1971) highlighted. The actor's basic tendency to interpret his or her behaviour as an appropriate reaction to situational determinants, and the observer's basic tendency to view this very same behaviour as originating from the actor's pervasive dispositions are, of course, both one-sided. They fail to take into proper consideration the interplay between situational and dispositional factors, let alone feedback cycles such as the selection or change of situational contexts due to dispositional preferences, which in turn leads to an increase in the dominance and salience of those dispositional factors.

Jones and his co-workers see the dispositional as well as the situational attribution tendency as guided and limited by the specific experiences (or lack of experiences) of actors and observers in the past and by their current different perspectives on the act in question. However, they (e.g. Jones and McGillis 1976) also regard each of these two attribution tendencies as being in the service of a specific control need. Actors do not like to see themselves as being pushed by pervasive dispositions, nor, of course, as irresistibly drawn by situational forces. But they can well preserve a sense of being in control by picturing themselves as sensibly reacting in differential ways to this or that situational constellation. Observers, on the other hand, can maintain or regain some sense of control by attributing any behaviour of the actor, even unexpected and obnoxious conduct, to some stable and hence predictable disposition. Obviously, this view is close to my own and has been encouraging for my thinking about the determinants of account episodes. Let us take an actor and an observer from Jones and Nisbett's frame and join them as opposing participants in an account episode in which some deed, or omission to act, on the part of the actor has violated a normative expectation held by the observer. Their different attributional perspectives, due in part to limited views of linear causal processes, posit yet another hindrance to an amicable outcome of such an account episode.

A decade before Jones and Nisbett's (1971) influential paper, when attribution theory and research were still in their very early days, the political scientist and social psychologist Raymond A. Bauer (1961) described essentially the same difference between the perspectives of actors and observers in his discussion of problems of perception and the relations between the United States and the Soviet Union. Bauer stated that each side, Russians and Americans alike, would see their own policies primarily as judicious reactions to political events and situational contingencies, and sometimes as diverted by errors and misperceptions. However, such knowledge and perspectives would not enter into the evaluations of the policies of the other side. Instead of allowing for reactive moves, misperceptions and blunders in the other camp's policies, each side would be prone to overrationalize the other side's position, and to see its political and military moves as the result of long-range strategies. And such views would then in turn provide further justification for each side to increase its own defensive efforts without due regard to the interpretation of such moves by the other camp, and thus contribute to the spiralling escalation of tension, distrust and rearmament, with its many burdens.

Bauer wrote his paper at the height of the cold war between East and West. Nowadays there are definite signs of a more sophisticated understanding and appreciation in the Soviet Union and the United States of each other's experiences, actions and reactions. Yet the basic discrepancy involved in viewing one's own policies within a framework of contingencies in contrast to emphasizing the long-range plans and strategies of the other side is still clearly visible in both camps.

Of course, I do not wish to imply that the complexities of the relationship between the United States and the Soviet Union and its attendant high-level policies could in an explanatory scheme be reduced to the divergence between basic attribution tendencies of individual actors and observers. Such attribution tendencies are presumably contributing factors among other major ones such as the conscious pursuit for internal and third-party consumption of the (however dubious) benefits of portraying the agents of the other superpower as forever scheming strategists with lasting evil intentions, and one's own policies as restrained and merely defensive countermoves. Another factor may be sought in the role requirements of the intelligence agencies and security advisers on both sides. They understandably see it as their task to be highly vigilant, to spot any dangerous development in the other side's policies at its very beginning and to risk a type I error of false alarm rather than a possibly fatal type II error of failing to recognize a decisive turn. Such a professional attitude is, of course, bound to stress coherence, rationality and strategic planning rather than blunders, confusions and coincidences. It is, within limits, a legitimate attitude, considering the forces of defensive avoidance that are also at work in political and military establishments and that have made possible many disasters such as the Japanese surprise attack on Pearl Harbor in the Second World War (Janis and Mann 1977). However, the professional perspectives and subsequent activities of intelligence agencies and security advisers are often under a decidedly insufficient counterbalancing control and thus dangerously free to direct policies, as Janis and Mann (1977) and Janis (1972) have amply documented and as the Iran–Contra scandal of the Reagan administration has once again exemplified.

The point I want to make with respect to Bauer's discussion of the problems of perception in Russian as well as American political circles is this. Whatever determinant one may plausibly assume to contribute to the discrepancy between the dominant views of one's own as opposed to the other side's political actions, they all clearly show the marks of an imbalance that is due to restricted linear causal thinking; and all these forces imply very one-sided demands for accountability.

Many more testimonials of insufficient, segmented, unidirectional causal thinking could be invoked from studies on social interactions and attributions,[5] but I shall limit myself to just one more illustrative case that highlights the precarious conceptual relationship between cause and responsibility and the related difficulties and simplifications in responsibility attributions.

Rupert Riedl (1984, pp. 184ff) once confronted a group of ecology students with a questionnaire about river pollution emanating from a paper mill. Aided by a list of 14 possible individual or institutional originators of, or contributors to, the pollution, the students were to solve the question of guilt. Many of the students had remarkably little difficulty in pinpointing a central culprit. They designated primarily the paper mill's director or else the Minister of Constructions. Captivated by a narrowly conceived originator principle they did not pay attention to the many impelling and limiting forces acting on the individuals involved, even though many such forces had explicitly been suggested in the list given to the students.

Riedl, a prominent proponent of an evolutionary theory of knowledge (e.g. 1981),[6] considers such attribution tendencies to be largely due to an inherited disposition towards short-term linear causal thinking which focuses on the immediate *causa efficiens* to the neglect of other vital causal conditions. Despite the insights and teachings of scholars like Wiener, Bertalanffy, Ashby and others on cybernetics and systems theory, we all suffer, according to Riedl, not from a cultural, but from a genetic lag, so to speak. The anthropological disposition to seize upon short, linear causal chains in judging the environment was eminently suitable and efficient in most circumstances in prehistoric times, and it had, of course, evolved because of its very fitness for aiding the survival and improvement of the human species. However, with the rapid advances and changes in historic times, and in particular with respect to the alarming acceleration in the growth of the scope, differentiation, interconnectedness and speed of all societal events in this century, this previously adaptive way of causal thinking has become outmoded and detrimental for judgements in many situations – not least in episodes of some complexity involving the demand for, and the giving and receiving of, accounts of failure events.

Whatever the origins of linear causal thinking, its ubiquity as a habit with all too few exceptions at all levels of social complexity is a glaring fact and, I believe, a detrimental factor for evaluative judgements in two respects. (1) Such simplified causal thinking will often not adequately grasp the complexity of a situation, and even opponents of some good will towards each other in a normative argument will often be put at cross purposes because of their limited causal views. (2) Furthermore, baffled or frightened by the dimly perceived complexity of an issue, those tentatively willing to expend the effort required for differentiation and integration may fall back on, and cling to, the comfortable habit of thinking in terms of single, short causal chains.

There seems to be yet another, albeit related, obstacle to the *rapprochement* of opposed agents in an account episode. Responsibility is not only elusive as an attribute to be assigned to this or that agent; it is, first of all, elusive as a concept to be grasped (see also Shaver 1985, p. 155). In two of our studies (see section 5.3) many respondents were baffled by the question of what it means to say that somebody is responsible for something, and they found it cumbersome to arrive at an answer. It seems that the multidimensional nature of the concept 'responsibility', for example answerability for any causal connection with a failure event versus liability for restitution, compensation and/or sanction (see Brickman et al. 1982), is basic to the cognitive difficulty with the meaning of 'responsibility'. In the two studies just mentioned we found that men and women emphasized different aspects of responsibility. I shall return to this point in section 5.3.

In sum, there are strong demands for accountability after many failure events, yet these demands and their corresponding expectations are not easily met for various reasons. In this introductory section I have sketched some of these reasons, slightly emphasizing the cognitive factors. Much more will have to be said about the motivational factors in the chapter on theoretical guidance. However, I hope I have provisionally justified my interest in account episodes and my conviction that they need and deserve extensive, systematic research.

1.2 The structure of account episodes

From the very beginning of my work on account episodes in 1975 I was convinced that it would not do to concentrate, however provisionally, on just one phase of the process – say, the demand for an account, or else the offering of accounts. I have always thought it necessary to keep at least a minimally extended series of events and interactions in perspective, even though it would not be possible to capture the essence of any such interaction sequence with one big study, especially in the early stages of research.

It would appear that only very few researchers in this area have tried to realize one way or another a longitudinal strategy. For a long time the remarkable empirical study by Blumstein et al. (1974) remained a rare exception. More recently, McLaughlin, Cody and their co-workers offered much welcomed support with a series of important studies (McLaughlin, Cody and O'Hair 1983; McLaughlin, Cody and Rosenstein 1983; Cody and McLaughlin 1985; McLaughlin, Cody and French 1989).

The structure of account episodes

Obviously, one must limit one's scope. In observing and analysing episodes concerning accountability with respect to some questionable conduct one must excise them from the never-ending complex stream of events in the real world and thereby furnish them with a beginning and an end. The same holds true for any experimental construction of such episodes. I had little doubts about the beginning. The failure event, whatever its own antecedents, seems to be a quasi-natural starting point because it is mainly this event, the disturbance of an unquestioned flow of events, which sets in motion the specific behaviours to be investigated. I was less certain about where to end my pursuit of the consequences. With an eye on court procedures, I settled for the verdict which the challenging party issues, after the perpetrator has been given a chance to render an account of his or her alleged misconduct. One could, of course, extend one's scope to include the perpetrator's reaction to the challenger's verdict in order to arrive at a prediction of the future state of the relationship between these two agents. However, the additional effort required by such an extension did not seem warranted. Knowing the specific type of account offered by the (true or falsely accused) 'perpetrator' *and* the challenger's subsequent verdict, one can, I believe, usually form a pretty good guess about the inclinations of both agents with respect to the further course – mitigation or aggravation – of the conflict engendered by the failure event. These, then – failure event and quasi-final verdict of the challenger or opponent – are the boundary regions of my domain of discourse in this report.

Account episodes can be viewed as a succession of stages of events. At any given stage the potential range of events is already formidable, and the potential variety of complete account episodes, due to the combination of those single-stage variances, appears to be almost limitless even though some constraints from one stage to the following ones may be assumed. In order to provide some limitation on this variety as well as a framework for theoretical constructions, it proved useful to postulate the following basic model of an account episode (see also figure 1), in which two agents, an 'actor' and an 'opponent', engage in an interaction across four phases:

1. *Failure event.* The actor is, rightly or wrongly, held at least partly responsible by the opponent for a failure event, that is the violation of a normative expectation held by the opponent. This can either be an acted offence, or the omission of an obligation.
2. *Reproach phase.* Frequently the opponent reacts to the failure event with some kind of a reproach, ranging from a raised eyebrow or a seemingly innocuous *why*-question to most violent vituperations. However, instead of, or in addition to, a reproach, the opponent may also offer other responses, such as an expression of sympathy or compassion, during this phase, or may genuinely ask without any negative insinuation why the failure event occurred.

3. *Account phase.* The actor's reaction to the opponent's utterance is often an account in the narrow sense – an excuse or a justification; hence the label account phase for this stage of the interaction. Other prominent types of reaction during this phase are concessions of one's own responsibility or guilt, or else some direct or indirect refusal to offer an account or to admit one's responsibility.
4. *Evaluation phase.* Eventually, either right after the actor's account, concession or refusal, or after some more altercations between the two agents, the opponent will come to an evaluation of any or all of the following: the account or account substitute, the failure event in the light of the account, and the actor's personality in the light of both failure event and account.

The basic pattern just described is, of course, often modified in various other forms of account episodes; for instance, it may be shortened or expanded. The dotted arrows in figure 1 indicate some of these variants.

If an actor realizes right after the failure event that he or she has committed a grave mistake, then he or she may hasten to offer an account or an account substitute, without waiting to be challenged by an opponent. In this case a reproach phase may be superfluous and will then not occur. The same holds true in those situations in which an actor anticipates a challenge or reproach even before the act that might be interpreted as a normative violation, and tries to obviate such a challenge by a disclaimer (Hewitt and Stokes 1975; see also Brown and Levinson 1987). In both these cases, however, the very fact that the actor hastens towards an account and thereby tries to forestall a reproach clearly indicates that the basic account episode pattern, including a reproach phase, is present in his or her mind as a model.

In another account episode variant the very account phase is bypassed. This happens, for instance, when the opponent is so enraged by the failure event and the actor's perceived involvement in it that the opponent refuses to listen to anything the actor might have to say. Reproach and vituperation inevitably entail the final verdict; but again, both agents are most often aware that something is missing. Here too the basic pattern serves as a model, although with different perspectives for actor and opponent. For the actor, the basic pattern makes salient the denied opportunity to render an account and enhances the sense of frustration. For the opponent, his or her deviation from the basic pattern may reflect the severity of the actor's offence that justified the refusal to listen.

The arrow in figure 1 which points from the account phase back to the reproach phase should serve as a reminder that the basic account episode pattern often expands into a lengthy altercation before the opponent's (quasi) final verdict if the actor responds to the challenge or reproach with an

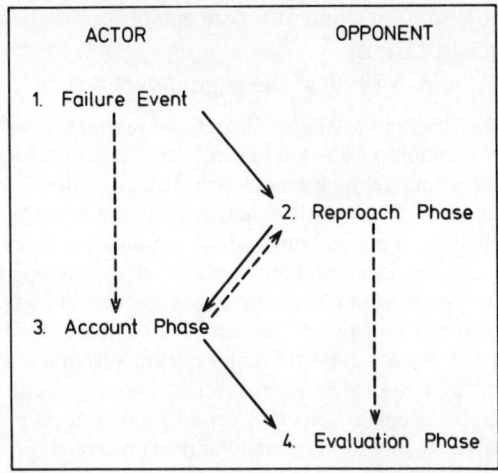

Figure 1. Basic pattern of an account episode and some variants

unsatisfactory account or even a counter-reproach and thereby elicits further, perhaps more acrimonious, attacks from the opponent.

There are still other forms of expansion of the basic pattern. Account episodes occur at all levels of social complexity and scope. The two agents may be single persons such as husband and wife engaged in a minor quarrel that is quickly overcome. At the other extreme, for instance in high-level diplomatic negotiations, there may be two or more groups of agents who take, and often quickly shift, the roles of actors and opponents. Maynard (1984), in his book on inside plea bargaining, presents complex forms of account episodes with principal and deputy agents and multiple interaction loops. A famous case in point has been the Iran–Contra scandal of President Reagan's administration. The word 'episode' would be a misnomer in view of the scope and complexity of this affair, with its large cast of actors and opponents and its far-reaching repercussions. Nevertheless, the core elements of the basic account episode pattern can be clearly identified at crucial points in the course of events. Snyder and Higgins (1989), in their incisive analysis of President Reagan's 4 March 1987 speech on the Iran arms scandal, present a beautiful example of account phase behaviour.

1.3 Functions of account episodes

Account episodes are special cases of 'aligning actions' (Stokes and Hewitt 1976). They share membership in this superordinate category with Mills' (1940) 'motive talk', Goffman's (1971) 'remedial interchanges', McHugh's

(1968) 'definition of the situation', and the concept of 'quasi-theorizing' proposed by Hall and Hewitt (1970).

Stokes and Hewitt (1976, p. 838) describe aligning actions as

> largely verbal efforts to restore or assure meaningful interaction in the face of problematic situations of one kind or another: Activities such as disclaiming, requesting and giving accounts, constructing quasi-theoretical explanations of problematic situations, offering apologies, formulating the definition of a situation, and talking about motives illustrate a dual process of *alignment*. First, such activities are crucial to the process in which people create and sustain joint action by aligning individual lines of conduct when obstacles arise in its path. Second . . . aligning actions can be shown to play a major part in sustaining a relation between *culture* and *conduct*, in maintaining an alignment between the two in the face of actions that depart from cultural expectations or definitions of what is situationally appropriate.

This general statement about the dual process of alignment fully applies to our specific domain. Account episodes fulfil a crucially important linkage role for large-scale societal processes as well as for the individuals involved in such episodes. This is mainly due to the fact that account episodes encompass both the origin of a conflict engendered by the violation of a normative expectation and – if things go well – the solution or mitigation of this conflict, or else its exacerbation. Due to this fact one may recognize account episodes as important mediators of social stability as well as of social change.

For instance, stability in a positive sense is maintained or restored if a thoughtful reproach is successful in eliciting from the actor a genuine expression of regret plus vivid efforts to make amends which consolidate the endangered relationship between actor and opponent. The same effect may also be achieved if the actor, to the opponent's relief, convincingly accounts for his or her part in the failure event.

Positive social change – progress – may ensue if the opponent's challenge leads to truly innovative actions of the actor, and in such cases a beneficial stability of interpersonal or intergroup relationships may be closely linked to beneficial changes of behaviour and beneficial effects on the environment.

On the other hand, there may also be social change for the worse. This will happen, for instance, if the actor's reaction during the account phase is so unsatisfactory for the opponent that a disruption of a previously viable relationship between them becomes inevitable and entails a serious disturbance of their common (or particular) social environment too.

Finally, social stability may turn into detrimental stagnation if an account episode ends in a stalemate of reproach and counter-reproach with no room for liberating action. Until the late 1980s we have witnessed such a state of affairs for decades in a long series of futile episodic attempts by the superpowers to halt the arms race. And, once more, aspects of social change

Functions of account episodes

and aspects of 'stability' – disruption and stagnation in this case – may be closely linked.

It is in such links between stability and change, whether positively or negatively valued, that one can also most clearly recognize points of connection between the two strands of the dual process of alignment or misalignment between (1) culture and conduct and (2) between the individuals actively engaged in an account episode. The disruption at the interpersonal level between the participants of an unsuccessful account episode may entail stagnation not only at this level but also stagnation and misalignment between generally shared normative expectations as well as action barriers at the socio-cultural level. This is particularly the case if the participants in account episodes with changing roles of actor and opponent are representatives of distinct political, religious or otherwise important affiliations.

Misalignments at both levels are deplorably frequent as we all know. I believe that one important causal condition for this phenomenon rests in the fact that within the dual process of alignment or misalignment at the socio-cultural and interpersonal levels, a second duality of process takes place, mainly at the interpersonal level, in most if not all account episodes. In both actors and opponents one may in a sense distinguish frontstage and backstage intention and behaviour. In the foreground, the interactions of actors and opponents are mostly concerned with the management of the conflict engendered by the failure event. In the background, however, but sometimes also clearly coming to the fore, a concomitant interaction process evolves which focuses on a negotiation of identities in the service of preserving (if not enhancing) self-esteem. Scott and Lyman (1968), in their seminal paper on accounts, already clearly state that 'every account is a manifestation of the underlying negotiation of identities' (p. 59, italics omitted), and they elaborate that such negotiation is often carried out by skilful ploys of identity assumptions and altercasting. Scott and Lyman emphasize the benefits of such identity negotiations for the overt purposes of the participants in the giving and receiving of accounts. They say (1968, pp. 58–9) that 'Each of the interactants has a stake in the negotiations since the outcomes of the engagement will often depend on these pre-established identities.' This I can readily accept; but I would add that the negotiation of identities in the service of maintaining or restoring self-esteem often becomes the primary purpose for one or both interactants of an account episode, relegating the concrete conflict issue to a position of secondary importance. I shall have more to say about this in the following chapter. At any rate, I believe that it is primarily the difficulty of competitive negotiations of personal and social identities (Tajfel and Turner 1979) in the service of self-esteem which decisively contributes to the frequent miscarriage of account episodes at the interpersonal level, and thereby also to misalignments at the socio-cultural level. I should add, though, that in my view such a competitive negotiation of identities gains its full force only because of its close linkage to a fundamental need for control over self-relevant events in the environment. I shall elaborate on this point too in the following chapter.

1.4 Basic question and some specifications

Account episodes are either accomplished or they founder. An account episode may be said to be successfully accomplished if the interaction between actor and opponent is of such a nature that the conflict engendered by the failure event is resolved or at least noticeably diminished. An account episode shall be deemed to have foundered if the conflict entailed by the failure event is not resolved, and is perhaps even exacerbated, by the interactions from the reproach phase to the final stage of evaluation.

Our basic question has been this. Under which conditions is an account episode likely to be accomplished, and under which other conditions is such an episode likely to founder? Obviously this basic question, in order to become researchable, has to be detailed and pursued in its many ramifications to the point of testable hypotheses. The first step in this direction is a further specification of the concepts of 'accomplishment' and 'foundering', as has already been indicated in the preceding section.

'Accomplishment' may mean that the opponent's challenge and reasoning induces the actor to accept responsibility for the failure event and to react with appropriate concessions, modified perhaps by an acceptable excuse. At any rate, a successful account in this sense reassures and mollifies the opponent and induces the latter in turn to pass a relatively mild judgement on the failure event, coupled with a comparatively positive evaluation of the actor's character. But accomplishment may also mean that the actor succeeds during the account phase in convincing the opponent of the untenability of his or her reproach, so that such an opponent also concludes the account episode with relief and a favourable evaluation of the actor.

'Foundering', then, means the opposite of both solutions just described. It is neither the case that the opponent succeeds in eliciting from the actor signs of regret and a willingness to make amends, nor that the actor is able to provide an account that could bring the opponent round to a more favourable evaluation of the affair. The episode ends in a clearly negative verdict on the part of the opponent, and the relationship between actor and opponent suffers appreciably, if it is not altogether disrupted.

It should be noted in passing that the accomplishment and foundering of account episodes are here defined exclusively from the perspective of actors and opponents actively engaged in such episodes. Nothing is said about the reactions of their social environments. As a rule an account episode successfully accomplished between an actor and an opponent also benefits their social environments and ultimately society at large. However, there are exceptions, notably the case of collusion between opponent and actor, (Snyder and Higgins 1988). In principle, every account episode is a situation of mixed motives – antagonistic and cooperative – on each side of the issue. In reality too, in the interest of reducing stress and strife, opponents often, and quite legitimately, try to build bridges for the actor to cross. However, if the circumstances have forced a person into the role of an opponent *vis-à-vis* an actor with whom he or she secretly shares moral or material interests to the exclusion of third parties, then the reproach is likely to be less forceful than it might be, and any seemingly reasonable account is readily accepted, with society being the loser. After having clarified this point I am happy to say that such borderline cases of 'accomplishment' will not trouble us any further in this report.

With the meaning of the accomplishment and foundering of account episodes thus specified, the basic question may now be elaborated. Which types of reproach and which types of account, each one by itself or in specific conjunctions, have an influence on the probability of an account episode's accomplishment being appreciably increased, or else markedly diminished? After which kinds of failure event are such effects particularly strong? Do we, in addition, have to pay attention to interactions of these process variables with dispositional variables, and if so, to which ones in actors and opponents? A host of hypotheses may be derived from these questions; I shall present some of them in chapter 2.

1.5 Fundamental obstacle, multiple approximations

The specifications of the basic question underline my previous contention that an exclusive concern with only parts of the account episode domain will not do. All four stages and the interaction sequence as a whole have to remain in focus for theoretical constructions and for subsequent empirical research as well, even though any particular study may be concerned with just one limited subsample of the process. However, this demand confronts the researcher with a fundamental obstacle to any nomothetic ambition.

The postulation of a basic model of account episodes was just a first step in trying to cope with the almost limitless variety of phenomena and events in this domain of discourse. Yet, even within the confines of our basic model with but four stages of interaction, there are enough entrance points for large variations to occur on many dimensions, so that even account episodes close to the basic pattern are likely to become highly singularized; any attempt to pursue and capture their essence is in constant danger of falling behind the rapid unfolding of variety, and nomothetic ambitions are always liable to degenerate into idiographic sketches.

Obviously, it is not possible to solve this dilemma at a stroke. There can only be approximations, and they have to take several different routes for the boundaries of uncertainty to be pushed back to any appreciable degree. Three strategic decisions in fact defined the subtasks by which I hoped to approach an answer to the basic question about the outcome of account episodes.

1 The first subtask was the search for theoretical guidance on the generation of testable hypotheses about factors that are relevant for the accomplishment or foundering of account episodes. It has been my conviction that this theoretical frame would have to encompass main effects as well as interactions of three types of factors: (1) situational constraints, (2) process variables and (3) the personal dispositions of actors and opponents. Otherwise there would be little hope of tackling the longitudinal structure of account episodes and its inherent difficulty of almost limitless variance. In order to arrive at such a heuristic frame and the subsequent derivation of hypotheses I have found it most useful to employ and develop theoretical notions of control needs that are linked to self-esteem and self-protection.

2 The second subtask was the construction of category systems for the classification of events in all four phases of an account episode. I must confess that not very much progress has been made so far with respect to the categorization of failure events, but fairly elaborate taxonomies do now exist for the coding of an opponent's reaction during the reproach phase and again during the evaluation phase, as well as for the reactions of actors during the account phase. In our empirical studies we have also extensively used scales and multiple-choice questions given to our respondents in their roles as actors and opponents. But it seemed necessary to go beyond such precoded measures. It is my impression that all of us who work in this field still have a long way to go. Thus it would be dangerously premature to rely exclusively on measures which, of necessity, strongly reflect one's particular and limited theoretical predilections. The scope must be wider, leaving room for explorations beyond hypothesis-testing in a conventional sense. Therefore one ought to take notice of what actors and opponents think and say in their own words. Yet, in order to avoid the morass of unmanageable variance and specificity, and for the sake of the quantitative machinery of any analysis of some nomothetic ambition, one has to strike a compromise. The best location of such a compromise between richness and structure seems at present to be a set of category systems which meets the following criteria. Each taxonomy within this set should be specifically applicable to a distinct situation or phase within the complete episode, yet of such a wide scope that it could encompass every potentially relevant event in this situation or phase. The basic categories of such a taxonomy should be sufficiently numerous and detailed

for it to be possible to go a long way towards capturing the specificities of an actor's or an opponent's reaction. However, these basic categories should be ordered and grouped in such a way that it would be easy to combine them in superordinate categories at several levels if theoretical considerations or sample size suggested such a procedure. Chapter 4 and appendices A and B present the category systems and my reasoning concerning their construction and use.

3 The third subtask was the design and execution of a series of empirical studies which could form a network with 'vertical' as well as 'horizontal' linkages. It seemed advisable to start our research programme with studies which would each be devoted to a single phase instead of pursuing right from the beginning a strategy of simulating whole account episodes, a strategy which would have been overly ambitious and would have entailed a high risk of failure considering our initial lack of knowledge about crucial turning points in account episodes. Our single-phase studies were designed to help us gain this very knowledge for the sake of future simulation studies across all four account episode phases. For this purpose the overall design of the research programme had to provide various matching features across the studies. For instance, if one study might require the participants to role-play an opponent during the reproach phase after a given failure event, another study might request the participants to take the role of an actor involved in the same failure event. This is what I mean by 'vertical linkage' between two studies. These vertical matchings across two or more phases were supplemented by horizontal matchings within a given phase, that is the addition of systematically extended or otherwise modified replications of the initial study devoted to that phase.

Chapter 3 describes the designs and procedures of our empirical studies, chapters 5, 6 and 7 present the results phase by phase, and chapter 8 discusses the inferences to be drawn from a transphase perspective, as well as the challenges and tasks that remain for the future.

2 Theoretical guidance

2.1 Basic control – theoretical assumptions

Account episodes are multilayered processes. Scott and Lyman (1968) have already pointed out that, along with the interactants' joint or separate attempts to cope with the specific conflict at hand, the giving and receiving of reproaches and accounts implies a negotiation of identities in the service of preserving, if not enhancing, self-esteem. To this view I would add the suggestion that there is a third process closely connected with the negotiation of identities that is carried through most, if not all, account episodes: a negotiation of aspirations and feelings of control competencies in general, beyond the coping attempts concerned with the specific problem at hand.

Many authors have previously observed a close linkage between self-esteem and sense of control in other contexts. I shall, by way of example, name only a few. The earliest proponent within psychology was Alfred Adler (1929) in his thinking on compensations for feelings of inferiority. Robert White (1959), in a similar vein, argued in favour of a competence motivation independent of basic drives such as hunger or thirst, and he saw a person's self-esteem strengthened if that person could satisfy his or her competence motivation by gaining some sense of control over the environment. Abramson, Seligman and Teasdale (1978), in their theory of helplessness and depression, emphasized the converse process, the loss of self-esteem due to prolonged experiences of inadequate coping and helplessness. Dörner et al. (1983) regarded self-confidence as an antecedent condition with beneficial effects on solving complex cognitive tasks, in this case requiring the participants in a computer simulation to keep highly interconnected processes in an urban community under control. Self-confidence, according to Dörner, assured the flexibility and readiness to explore alternatives – a flexible curiosity that was a prerequisite for solving the task at hand and the very opposite of narrow, cause-and-effect investigation.

These authors paid attention mainly to one of the two possible causal directions between self-esteem and sense of control. Other researchers have emphasized the bidirectional nature of the relationship between these two self-relevant evaluative cognitions, and this point of view also plays a central role in my thinking about the demand for, and the giving and receiving of, accounts. Aronson and Bridgeman (1981), in relation to their work with jigsaw groups set up to improve the status and achievement of minority children, surveyed the educational domain and concluded (p. 337): 'There is ample evidence for a two-way causal connection between performance and self-esteem.' Snyder, Higgins and Stucky (1983), in their treatment of self-handicapping, concur with Bandura's (1977) view that 'one's beliefs about his or her ability to achieve desired outcomes in life derive from experiences of being able to deal effectively with situations. Avoidance of opportunities to develop effective coping skills can only lead to lowered feelings of self-efficacy and increased avoidance' (Snyder, Higgins and Stucky 1983, p. 194), and they summarize the observation of Zimbardo and Radl (1981) on the cyclical nature in problems in terms of shyness: 'Shyness breeds avoidance, which results in lost opportunities to develop self-esteem, which begets increased shyness, and so on' (ibid., p. 193). Very similar feedback loops are described in detail in Hyland's (1987) control theory of depression and he concluded: 'Depression becomes a vicious circle' (p. 116). Taylor (1983) and Snyder and Higgins (1988) have come to similar conclusions.

Carver and Scheier (1981) offer probably the most extensive theoretical treatment of feedback linkages between self-esteem and control behaviour and experience. Their central concept is that of a hierarchy of control systems consisting of nested feedback loops, where the output at a higher level constitutes (and sometimes changes) the standard for the feedback loop at the next lower level. For instance, in their illustrative example of 'making coffee' Carver and Scheier (1981, p. 133) set at the highest level the principle 'Be a gracious person', which provides the standard for the next lower level, the programme 'Provide guests with refreshments', which in turn constitutes the standard for the next level, the sequence 'Measure coffee', and so forth. Feedback for every level is provided via the behavioural effect on the environment and the analysis of the sensory input stemming from the environment's reaction. Self-esteem is placed by Carver and Scheier at the highest superordinate level of such a hierarchy. Quoting (p. 257) Powers (1973, p. 171) they state: 'Human beings seem to perceive unity in a collection of moral, factual, or abstract principles', and they add in their own words the suggestion: 'One such system concept . . . is the sense of coherence and adequacy associated with the self. This is a superordinate standard, to which one's present state can be matched by the specification of principles, which lead to the specification of programmes of action, and so on. Perhaps the process of keeping discrepancies small with regard to this particular superordinate standard is what we have been calling self-esteem maintenance, or egotism' (ibid.).

Clearly, this conception implies a strong asymmetry of status and importance, even though self-esteem and control actions do influence each other through the feedback hierarchy just described. All control behaviours and experiences at various levels of specificity are ultimately seen as servants of self-esteem. I am not sure of this asymmetry, and neither is Hyland (1987, p. 110). Could it not be that the superordinate standard of 'coherence and adequacy associated with the self' is not the ultimate goal but rather a means in the service of a general feeling of being in control, which in turn facilitates the judicious and efficient use of various control strategies? Tedeschi and Norman (1985), Arkin and Baumgardner (1986) and Greenberg, Pyszczynski and Solomon (1986) have all dealt with this question.

Doubts about the dominant role assigned to self-esteem by Carver and Scheier (1981) arise also from an evolutionary perspective. It seems clear to me that the disposition to reflect upon and evaluate the self is a rather late product of the phylogenetic development of the human species. Many of our various capacities and propensities towards control-oriented behaviour must have evolved much earlier. Such temporal priority does not, of course, preclude the possibility that in the course of evolution the need for self-esteem gained a reasonably stable supremacy in a hierarchy of cognitive and behavioural regulators. On the other hand, one can easily conceive of many threatening situations in which a phylogenetically more basic need and disposition to maintain or regain control over the events in the physical or social environment is likely to be of paramount importance, an importance to which all other regulatory components, including self-evaluation with respect to one's potential, are subordinated. At any rate, it seems prudent for my purpose to refrain from postulating a stable hierarchy of the reciprocal causal linkages between control dispositions and behaviours on the one hand and self-esteem on the other. This, then, is my first basic assumption:

(1) There exists a reciprocal relationship between a person's sense of having control and his or her self-esteem such that a subjective feeling of lack or loss of control will result in a lowering of self-esteem, and a reduction in self-esteem, for whatever reasons, will engender or strengthen feelings of lack or loss of control.

Nothing is implied here about the strength of such a secondary influence. I would guess that a reductive influence on the first component does not fully carry through to the second one, rather that there is some slippage, or else some protection of the second component, be it self-esteem or sense of control, that to some extent diminishes the secondary impact.

Before I proceed to my second basic assumption I should like to add a few more comments on the evolution of control dispositions in the human species. Encouragement to pay attention to this aspect comes from various quarters. Proponents of an evolutionary epistemology (e.g. Popper 1972; Campbell 1974; Lorenz 1973; and Riedl 1981, to name but a few) consider the very essence of evolution as a knowledge-gaining process, that is evolution is seen as a 'growing hierarchical system of plastic controls' (Popper 1966, p. 23; quoted by Campbell 1974, p. 419). Festinger (1983, p. 113) also sees the disposition to control as a central trait and force of the phylogenetic as well as of the historic development of the human species: 'Man, that imaginative animal, had for many, many hundreds of thousands of years sought ways not only to exploit his environment but also to control it, to change it at will, or to protect himself from it if he could not change it . . . My image of man convinces me that he must have tried to control just about everything – and he still does.'

As we all know, each animal species that exists today has achieved some measure of control over the vicissitudes of its environment by efficient modes of accommodation. Only our own species has moved far beyond such levels of control in the course of its evolution by developing capacities and motivations not only of accommodation but also of assimilation of parts of the environment to our needs. We can and do change nature, and we transform our social environments as well. Festinger also emphasized this principal difference and deplored in an earlier paper (1981, pp. 313–14) that to his knowledge 'we have never adequately studied the specificity of the human evolution [which] seems to have fostered the inclination to control the environment, to control other animals, and even to control other humans'.

I believe that the enormous, if partially dubious, achievements of the human species in gaining control over its environments have become possible only through a dual course of evolution with positive feedback linkages between its two strands. One of these strands has been the development of very many specific techniques and mechanisms of control, preserved or modified and transmitted from generation to generation. The other strand, I believe, has been the evolution of a genetically based general readiness to learn techniques and mechanisms of control, similar in its uniqueness to the inborn readiness of human beings to acquire language, given a minimum of appropriate stimulation.[7]

The notion of a general readiness to learn techniques and mechanisms of control implies a double meaning of the term 'readiness', referring both to the capacity and to the motivation to learn quickly and easily a wide variety of control techniques and mechanisms functioning either alone or as interlocking and mutually supportive components within higher-order control strategies. Techniques of directly influencing the course of events may, for instance, be backed up by ways and means of maintaining a certain degree of constancy, of keeping the variations in one's environment, and in oneself, within manageable limits. The maintenance of self-esteem by various modes of stabilization or enhancement of one's judgement about oneself, 'symbolic self-completion' as Wicklund and Gollwitzer (1982) call it, is in my view the most important back-up strategy in the service of relative constancy. The man who knows his worth and is confident of himself has clearly more degrees of freedom to cope with the exigencies of his environment than the man who is not sure of himself and always frets about the impression he makes on other people. Moreover, the fact of having succeeded in some coping attempt is likely to bolster one's self-esteem, and a failure to achieve some attempted measure of control is apt to diminish confidence and to lower one's level of self-esteem.

In the present context I need not dwell upon the enormous range of imaginative techniques of primary and secondary control (see, for instance, Rothbaum, Weisz and Synder 1982; Langer 1983; and Osnabrügge, Stahlberg and Frey 1985). One distinction, however, should be mentioned as it is highly relevant for our domain of discourse; it is related to the two fundamental strategies of accommodation and assimilation.

A comprehensive definition of control, which encompasses both accommodative and assimilative performances, may be stated as follows:

> To execute control means to bring into full or partial alignment states and events of the environment, on the one hand, and one's own expectations on the other.

Modifications that are necessary to achieve such alignments imply as a prerequisite either a degree of competence that enables the would-be controller to change the environment and assimilate it to his or her expectations and wishes, or they imply a matching of two prerequisites: (1) sufficient flexibility to adapt one's expectations and wishes to the environment, and (2) a sufficient degree of constancy in the environment, so that the remaining environmental variability does not overtax the would-be controller's accommodative capacity.[8]

The need for constancy and the need for competence are two fundamental manifestations of the need to control. They are complementary needs, to be sure. Efforts to change the environment may not succeed unless some constancy in the environment, as well as in the self, is guaranteed. Yet the active exertion of one's competence will also often be necessary in order to ensure the desired degree of constancy in the environment. Much skill and labour has to be invested in order to erect the dam which prevents the river from flooding the crop. Nevertheless, despite the close linkage between these needs for constancy and competence, they are distinguishable, and one can easily imagine various situations in which one or the other need becomes the dominant motive and regulator.

In our domain, for instance, one may hypothesize that the need for competence becomes particularly strong in an opponent during the reproach phase, in his or her endeavour to set things right after the disturbance created by the failure event. The need for constancy may in turn become highly salient for many actors during the account phase after an alarming reproach that foreshadows yet more violent reactions from the social environment. Alternatively, it is quite conceivable that for some, or many, opponents the need for constancy also becomes most urgent after this or that failure event has seriously shaken their belief in a just and orderly world (Lerner 1980). Furthermore, we should entertain the possibility that for some persons, even distinct categories of persons, the need for constancy is habitually stronger, despite fluctuations, than the need for competence, whereas for other individuals or groups of persons it may be the other way around. Finally, should we take a heuristic lead from the plausible assumption that accommodative skills, and hence also the need for constancy, evolved earlier than assimilative capacities and the need for manifesting and improving competence?

Whatever its roots, the need for constancy apparently plays a major role in account episodes. Kelley (1979), in his book on the structures and processes of personal relationships, reported data that are clearly symptoms of a pervasive need for constancy control – predictive control in particular in such relationships. In a classification of problems reported by heterosexual couples (ibid., p. 19) complaints about carelessness, sloppiness or impulsivity in the partner rank highest in frequency if the data from two studies are combined. Another indication may be seen in the emphasis placed by Kelley's respondents on the continuation of certain desirable behaviours and attitudes in the partner as compared to any wishes concerning the start, or else the termination, of certain other behaviours or attitudes (ibid., p. 97).

Of course, with the reasoning just presented I do not wish to diminish the importance also of the need for competence for the participants in account episodes as well as in other types of interaction. Our control competencies are enormous, and they have furnished us with marvellous achievements. Yet these very achievements have created new problems of such a scope and complexity that our present coping skills and strategies seem dangerously insufficient. We all know this, or should know it (see Council on Environmental Quality and the US State Department 1980). The root of the newly created problems in this modern world of ours may be described in one sentence: we rely too much on our control competencies! Janis (1986) has recently given a vivid example from the political arena with what he calls the 'can do!' directive in international crisis management.

Riedl (e.g. 1981) maintains that our inborn teaching masters, acquired in the course of evolution, still predispose us to learn with ease a concept of linear causality – notions of short, unidirectional causal chains – and to employ such notions in executive actions. For hundreds of thousands of years this disposition towards executive causality has been very successful in accommodative and, more importantly, in assimilative coping with the dangers of the world. Festinger (1983) reminds us that until very recently, 8500 BC perhaps, groups of human beings living together rarely consisted of more than 40–50 members. This one fact may suffice to illustrate the untarnished survival and improvement value of executive causal thinking and acting – until that date. One might say, in a way, that there simply was no critical mass for the development of self-perpetuating processes with dangerous feedback cycles.

Since 8500 BC the world has been changed by the human species at a breathtaking, accelerating rate, but it seems that, due to the genetic anchorage of our cognitive and behavioural capacities, the development of modes of thinking and acting in the average single human agent does not keep up with the explosive evolution of our habitat. Systemic thinking, which should replace executive causality (e.g. Riedl 1981), and new future-oriented norms of responsibility (Jonas 1979) and their concerted implementation are hard to come by.

I shall now, after this excursion with some evolutionary vistas, return to my main line of argument and proceed to the next basic assumption. Frequently, account episodes are not only threatening events for both actor and opponent, but also embarrassing for both of them. The threatening aspects are fairly obvious. The failure event is likely to diminish the opponent's sense of control, and hence also indirectly (or else directly) his or her self-esteem as well. Likewise, an untoward reaction of the actor during the account phase may engender or intensify such feelings of loss of control and self-esteem on the part of the opponent. The actor in turn may experience very similar effects – either from fully realizing the negative implications of the failure event and/or from being confronted with a severe reproach attacking directly either his or her control competencies or self-esteem, or both.

Such feelings of loss of control and self-esteem may be aggravated if the account episode *per se*, apart from the specific issue at hand, is embarrassing for the participants; and I would think that this is often the case. The opponent may feel ill at ease in the face of the role demand to come forth with a reproach. Similarly, the actor may feel awkward when realizing that he or she will be expected (and asked) to render an account of the failure event. I presume that apprehensions of this sort render both participants of an account episode particularly vulnerable to threats directed at their sense of control and their self-esteem. Account episodes are predicaments. Schlenker (1980) extensively discusses the embarrassment which those in predicaments experience, as well as the self-serving efforts that ensue from such embarrassment, and I fully agree with his views. This, then, in short, is my second basic assumption:

(2)   Account episodes are likely to confront both actor and opponent with situations in which their feelings of control and self-esteem are highly vulnerable.

The specific vulnerability of cognitions of control competencies and self-worth in the context of account episodes may be a partial determinant of certain maladaptive reproaches and accounts, particularly the latter. It is amazing to see how often people, in giving an account of their actions, in no way respond to the needs of those expecting the account. Frequently one has the impression that a defiant actor is not really talking to his or her opponent but, rather, in an attempt at self-reassurance, to his or her own ego. Moreover, such egocentric accounts often show the marks of a hasty, shortsighted defence strategy which easily exposes the actor to further attacks. The mass media have furnished us with many examples from the political sphere. The most obvious one in recent history was probably President Nixon's behaviour after the Watergate affair (see Janis (1982) for this and several other cases, and see Wicklund and Gollwitzer (1982) with respect to the social insensitivity of self-symbolizers).

It seems to me that the tendency to such hasty and shortsighted egocentric accounts is partly due to the specific vulnerability of actors in account episodes. Furthermore, I believe that the corresponding vulnerability of opponents facilitates the tendency to make similarly hasty and shortsighted egocentric reproaches that do not leave any room for the actor to make an adaptive response during the account phase short of complete surrender. Finally, the tendency to such egocentric reactions might also be fostered in both actors and opponents by a basic disposition to satisfy their need for control with actions that follow an ingrained pattern of executive causal thinking and hence often manifest themselves in comparatively simple, shortsighted and one-sided 'can-do' behaviours. At any rate, this is my third basic assumption:

(3)   Both reproaches and accounts, particularly the latter, are often made in a hasty and shortsighted egocentric manner that does not take into consideration the need of the other participants(s) in the account episode to maintain self-esteem and a sense of control.

If egocentric reproaches (and evaluation tendencies) meet with egocentric accounts, then an escalation of conflict and ill feeling is a likely consequence, and the interactive structure of an account episode is, of course, conducive to such a clash. Therefore I propose as my fourth, and most central, assumption:

(4)   Due to a likely convergence of the structural constraints of account episodes and the egocentric dispositions of the participants the probability of conflict escalation in the course of such an account episode ending in its foundering is appreciably high.

28 *Theoretical guidance*

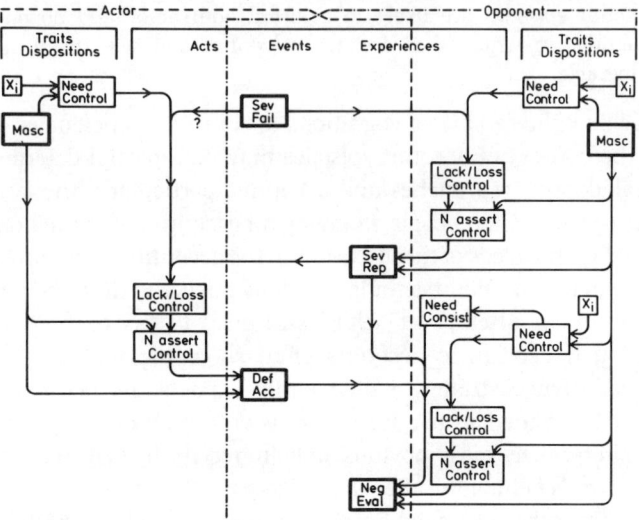

Figure 2. A theory of escalation in account episodes

2.2 A network of escalation

The elaboration of the escalation assumption just stated entails a constellation of several situational and dispositional factors and their sequential and simultaneous interplay. The main components of this network of events will be stated in the form of ten hypotheses. Figure 2 presents a synopsis of these hypotheses and their theoretical embedding.

Some explanations
For each of the principal participants of an account episode – actor and opponent – a distinction is made in figure 2 between enduring traits and dispositions, on the one hand, and momentary acts, events and experiences, on the other. Within the span of the latter there exists a partial overlap between the actor's and the opponent's domain. The overlap is partial in a double sense: (1) normally not all actual experiences such as feelings of lack or loss of control (Lack/Loss Control in figure 2) on the part of the opponent are shared by the actor, and vice versa; and (2) naturally the participants' experiences of one and the same event, for example an offence, differ according to their roles in it – the actor seeing it with the eyes of the (real or falsely accused) perpetrator, the opponent perhaps suffering from the offence as its immediate target or secondary victim, or regarding it as a bystander.

The central part of figure 2, specifically marked as the partially common domain of the actor's and the opponent's experiences, contains the four phases of an account episode of basic structure, the labels in the four boxes representing the principal ingredients of the process hypotheses. These hypotheses state that the severity of the failure event (Sev Fail) has, within limits, a strengthening effect on the severity of the opponent's reproach (Sev Rep); that by and large a more severe reproach will strengthen any tendency on the part of the actor to be defensive during the account phase (Def Acc), and that such defensiveness in turn is likely to increase any propensity of the opponent towards a negative evaluation (Neg Eval) of the account and/or the failure event and/or the actor. A more precise formulation of these hypotheses, including the intervening control-relevant variables, will follow on pp. 34–7.

An arrow leading from a box A to another box B represents the hypothesis that an increase in the magnitude of variable A leads, within limits, to an increase in the magnitude of variable B. The cautionary reminder 'within limits' has to cover many different possible restrictions on the assumed validity of the hypothesis. It may mean that the stated relationship holds only for a limited span within the total potential range of the antecedent variable A, or alternatively for a similarly restricted range of variable B, or under both these conditions. The phrase 'within limits' is also meant to imply that possibly certain situational or dispositional context conditions have to be fulfilled for the stated relationship to become manifest.

Two arrows leading from a box A and a box B, respectively, in a parallel fashion (↓↓) to a third box C are to be understood as indicating additive effects, in the manner just stated, from A and B on C. Two arrows leading from A and B to C, and converging in this course (↘↙), represent a case of multiple necessary causation. For instance, I would expect that an increase in the severity of the failure event experienced by the opponent would only have an increasing effect on the opponent's feeling of lack or loss of control if the opponent's need for control at the same time surpassed a certain minimum level. Conversely, I would also expect that an increase in the opponent's need for control would only enhance his or her feeling of lack or loss of control if the presence of such a feeling had been established in the first place by a failure event of non-negligible severity.

All theoretical components corresponding to independent and dependent variables are boxed in boldline frames in figure 2, whereas intervening variables, whether measured or not, appear in thinly lined boxes.

The term masculinity (Masc) in figure 2 stands for the contrast of male versus female actors or opponents. Further theoretical and empirical work should move beyond this basic dichotomy and consider 'masculinity' as a cognitive perspective in males which emphasizes or exaggerates or even falsely construes a sexual dimorphism on one or more of bodily, cognitive or emotional dimensions and attaches more positive values to the male forms than to the female ones.

This definition, which is related to, but not identical with, previously espoused concepts of masculinity versus femininity (e.g. Bem 1974; and Spence and Helmreich 1978) would allow for 'masculinity' to manifest itself in varying multidimensional degrees. The adoption or construction of adequate measurement instruments should not be too difficult in view of the existing body of research just mentioned (see also Runge et al. 1981; and Feather 1985).

For the time being, though, considering the studies just quoted, it seems reasonable to assume that on the average within a group of men a 'masculine' perspective, as defined above, is still more prevalent than in a group of women, despite some signs of an emergent convergence of male and female role perspectives (e.g. Spence, Deaux and Helmreich 1985).

The boxes labelled Need Control in figure 2 represent the fundamental motivational disposition introduced in the preceding section, that is the assumed pervasive need to have and to exercise at least a minimally adequate, primary or secondary, type and degree of control over the course of self-relevant events. I assume that many factors, besides masculinity, have some influence on the magnitude of the need for control, but for the time being I shall leave these factors unspecified and shall designate them with the label X_i. Furthermore, I believe that despite considerable variance in the magnitude of the need for control within any given population, this control need is appreciably strong in all or almost all members of that population (see above, p. 22).

The remaining intervening variables are quickly elucidated. The label Lack/Loss Control stands for the subjective feeling of a lack of control over self-relevant events or of a loss of such control. Presumably the occurrence of such a feeling depends on some threatening event – for instance, in the case of the opponent, on an appreciably severe failure event. The strength of such feelings of lack or loss of control I believe to be influenced by several factors, with the magnitude of the need for control playing a central role.

As depicted by figure 2 feelings of lack or loss of control are seen as the principal mediator between preceding events and dispositions, on the one hand, and the need to assert, or reassert, control over self-relevant events (N assert Control), on the other. The remaining intervening variable to be explained is a loan from dissonance theory (Festinger 1957). The need for cognitive consistency (Need Consist) or consonance in the opponent is introduced because it may contribute to the escalation of events towards negative evaluations by the opponent if he or she feels committed to a severe reproach just uttered.

The reader may wonder why self-esteem, figuring so prominently in my basic assumptions, does not appear in the flow chart. This omission is simply due to reasons of convenience. The figure would have become unbearably overloaded had I also tried to incorporate the self-esteem labels corresponding to the control-relevant variables. But I do of course believe that, wherever the need for control is affected, then so is, to some extent at least, self-esteem, and vice versa; and the postulated reciprocal relationship between control-relevant cognitions and self-esteem is also assumed for the stage of lack or loss experiences and the subsequent counteractive motivation.

After these explanations I shall now turn to the presentation of the hypotheses incorporated in figure 2. I shall state the hypotheses in their currently testable form, with some comments added. The hypotheses will be grouped according to their respective focus, that is (1) reproach phase, (2) account phase and (3) evaluation phase. The cautionary phrase 'within limits', mentioned and detailed above, applies to all the predictions that follow, but in order to avoid tedious repetition I shall henceforth omit this phrase. Likewise, the qualification 'on average' will be expressed just once in the first hypothesis; but it should be kept in mind as an unwritten companion of all subsequent hypotheses as well. Obviously, we can do no more than predict, and contrast, average tendencies within two or more groups.

Hypotheses on reactions of the opponent during the reproach phase

Failure events may be distinguished according to their severity. In the present context the term 'severity of failure' refers to one or both of the following two aspects. (1) Given that an opponent holds two different normative expectations that are of unequal importance for him or her, if the more important one of these expectations is violated by a failure event, then this failure will be considered more severe than the complementary case of a violation of the less important normative expectation. (2) A given normative expectation held by an opponent may be completely or only partly violated by a failure event; the more incisive the violation of the expectation the more severe the failure in the opponent's judgement. In the famous line of research started by Elaine Walster's (1966) experiment on the assignment of responsibility for an accident, attention has been focused on the severity of the consequences of the failure event, that is on the degree of damage to a victim. This aspect is not directly implied by my use of 'severity of failure' in this report. Severity of consequences may come into play, though, if a failure event with (perhaps unusually) severe consequences is in retrospect seen as particularly severe with respect to the normative expectations held by the opponent. According to the severity of failure the opponent's reactions presumably will be more or less severe, and by this I mean more or less punitive, hostile or derogatory. On this basis I am ready to state the first hypothesis:

> *Hypothesis 1.1.* The greater the severity of a failure event, the more severe will be, on average, the opponent's reaction towards the actor during the reproach phase.

Figure 2 shows the relationship between severity of failure event and severity of reproach phase reactions to be mediated by two intervening steps. Given that the opponent's general need for control exceeds a threshold value, a rather severe failure event will, according to the theory, induce a corresponding feeling in the opponent of considerable lack or loss of control. This in turn will instigate a fairly strong need to assert or reassert control. Finally, the stronger this need to assert or reassert control, the more severe, on average, will presumably be the reproach or any corresponding behaviour during the reproach phase. In a case of severe violation of a normative expectation held by the opponent the unmistakable attribution of blame to the actor is likely to be an efficient way of restoring subjective feelings of control since this attribution helps to preserve or re-establish the image of a basically just and orderly world (Lerner 1980).

There may be two other routes mediating the assumed influence of severity of failure on severity of reproach. The first one is a variant of the theoretical linkage just described. One might introduce one more component into the network by distinguishing between need for control as a general disposition and a situation-specific control need as a momentary experience which depends for its strength only in part upon the general control need and partly, if not more importantly, upon the total situational context of the account episode in question. Such a conceptualization might be preferable if it should turn out that much variance among the reproach phase reactions remains unaccounted for when severity of the failure event as well as the general need for control and its antecedent factors are held constant.

A second alternative route of influence from failure event to reproach phase that seems possible could be represented in figure 2 by an arrow leading directly from severity of failure event to severity of reproach. Widely spread, well-ingrained normative expectations for the effortless (if not 'mindless') regulation of behaviour do not only operate in the service of mitigating conflict. Such expectations also exist as guidelines for harsh confrontations. This is attested to by proverbial sayings such as the German proverb 'Auf einen groben Klotz gehört ein grober Keil' (It takes a tough wedge to cope with a tough block). Thus it seems possible that an opponent may react to a severe failure event with a severe reproach in a semi-automatic or supposedly self-evident manner, regardless of his or her own general or situation-specific control needs and feelings of lack or loss of control. Such a direct line of influence and the route via lack or loss and assertion or reassertion of control do not, of course, exclude each other; they may well jointly contribute to the severity of the opponent's reactions during the reproach phase.

> *Hypothesis 1.2.* The reproach phase reactions of male opponents are likely to be more severe than the reactions of female opponents.

Figure 2 depicts three routes of influence that may mediate the relationship stated in hypothesis 1.2. The principal one runs via need for control to corresponding feelings of lack or loss of control and the need for assertion or reassertion of control, and hence to relatively severe reproaches or corresponding reactions.

There is good reason to believe that, as a rule, males in general, and 'masculine' males in particular, have higher needs for control than females do. Research on gender roles and corresponding stereotypes (e.g. Bem 1974; and Spence and Helmreich 1978) has clearly shown that attributes such as 'dominant', 'assertive' or 'independent' are widely seen as desirable masculine traits by both men and women, and that in self-descriptions these traits are also claimed by males much more often than by females. Such data patterns, originally obtained in the United States, have been replicated in several other countries. For instance, those three traits as well as other 'masculine' ones were overwhelmingly attributed to a male rather than a female figure in a choice task by children as young as eight years of age in France, Germany, Italy, the Netherlands and Norway (J.E. Williams et al. 1981). Self-descriptive preferences of males for masculine traits as measured by Spence and Helmreich's EPAQ in the United States were closely replicated in the Federal Republic of Germany with a German version of that instrument (Runge et al. 1981).

Two further routes from masculinity to severity of reproach are hypothesized as supplementary lines of influence. Considering the stronger average potential of assertiveness among males as compared to females, it seems plausible to assume that even with feelings of lack or loss of control held constant, the average male, not to mention the very masculine one, will act from a stronger need to assert or reassert control than the average female will. Finally, in the light of the comparatively high aggressiveness of males compared to females (e.g. Maccoby and Jacklin 1974) one might expect a male opponent to react more punitively, for example, with a relatively severe reproach, than a female opponent would even if the need of each to assert or reassert control happens to be equally strong.

At present we cannot empirically distinguish among these three routes of influence in order to assess their validity, let alone their respective weights. However, we do have evidence pertinent to the more general prediction of hypothesis 1.2; this will be presented in chapter 5.

A serious rival for the hypothesis just discussed is the assertion that males are more severe than females in their reproach tendencies only in certain situations and not in others, and that in some of those other situations females are rather more severe, on average, than males. The originator (Shaver 1970) and other proponents (e.g. Burger 1981) of the defensive attribution hypothesis have probably been most hospitable to this alternative assertion, and one can indeed line up empirical support for it. For instance, Kanekar, Pinto and Mazumdar (1985) reported that in a study conducted in Bombay women proved to be much more severe than men in their judgement of rapists.

However, it seems that females will be found to be markedly more severe in their reproach tendencies than males only under rather specific circumstances, whereas many more situations seem to be conducive to the reverse pattern. At any rate, we may justifiably retain hypothesis 1.2 in its present formulation, especially if we consider the probabilistic prediction about male opponents as 'likely to be more severe' not only as a statement about male reproach inclinations in general as compared to female reaction tendencies, but also, and more specifically, as a statement about the proportion of all conceivable situations in which the average male opponent may be expected to be more severe than the average female opponent.

All hypotheses, from 1.1 to 3.4, in this section are stated as predictive, that is 'within limits', of main effects. I have, of course, also envisaged right from the beginning the possibility and indeed the plausibility of various interactive effects.

> *Hypothesis 1.3.* The higher the opponent's need to maintain control over self-relevant events, and/or the higher the need for positive self-evaluation, the more severe will be his or her reproach phase reactions.

Both factors, the need for control and the need for self-esteem, are here incorporated into one hypothesis because of the postulated reciprocal relationship between them. However, by way of qualification we should consider the following specifications. The need for control and the need for self-esteem are said to be positively correlated because of the reciprocal linkage, but they are certainly not to be seen as perfectly matched in a strict one-to-one pattern. Thus, with a given level of sense of control and need for (more) control, the level of self-esteem and the corresponding need for improvement of self-esteem may vary to some extent. We may further assume that some failure events threaten primarily an opponent's sense of control and only by implication and to some extent the opponent's self-esteem as well. Other failure events, conversely, may be a direct attack on an opponent's self-esteem, but only an indirect, and hence weaker, attack on his or her sense of control. On the basis of these assumptions we may expect the following specifications of hypothesis 1.3 to hold. If the primary target of a failure event is the opponent's sense of control, then the opponent's need for control is likely to be more important than his or her need for self-esteem as a determinant of the severity of the opponent's reactions. If, on the other hand, the failure event is primarily threatening to the opponent's self-esteem, then the order of importance of the two needs – for control and for self-esteem – as determinants of the severity of reaction should be reversed.

Hypotheses on reactions of the actor during the account phase

> *Hypothesis 2.1.* The greater the severity of a reproach, the more defensive will be the actor's reaction during the account phase.

The reaction of an actor is called defensive to the extent that it tries to bolster or regain a satisfactory sense of control and/or self-esteem by means which do not, or do not sufficiently, take into consideration the opponent's needs for control and self-esteem.

The reasoning in support of this hypothesis parallels to a great extent the arguments for hypothesis 1.1 on the effects of severity of failure on severity of reproach phase reactions in the opponent. Given a certain need for control on the part of the actor, a reproach will instil in him or her a sense of lack or loss of control (and lowered self-esteem), and this feeling will increase in strength with increasing degrees of severity of the opponent's reproach phase reaction. Strong feelings of lack or loss of control instigate a strong need in the actor to assert or reassert control and this in turn is likely to induce defensive reactions in the actor during the account phase.

The defensiveness of an actor confronted with a severe reproach may take many specific forms that cannot easily be predicted apart from the concrete situation of any given account episode. More generally one may say, however, that a defensive actor can be expected to offer some sort of justification rather than an excuse, let alone an admission of guilt or responsibility, and sometimes an actor in that state and situation may even reject the opponent's claim for an account. McLaughlin, Cody and Rosenstein (1983) proposed and tested fairly successfully a very similar hypothesis.

> *Hypothesis 2.2.* The account phase reactions of male actors are likely to be more defensive than the reactions of female actors.

Figure 2 shows the influence of an actor's masculinity on his defensiveness during the account phase as mediated in the same way as the effect of an opponent's masculinity on his reproach tendencies. The principal line of influence is again seen as running through the postulated higher need for control among males, especially 'masculine' ones, and from there via comparatively strong feelings of lack or loss of control and the contingent high need to assert or reassert control towards the inclination to react rather defensively when called upon to give an account of the failure event. Again, two supplementary lines of influence are considered and depicted in figure 2. Relevant data are as yet available only for the general hypothesis 2.2, not for the three lines of influence just discussed.

> *Hypothesis 2.3.* The higher the actor's need to maintain control over self-relevant events, and/or the higher the need for positive self-evaluation, the more defensive will be his or her account phase reactions.

Similar qualifications as for hypothesis 1.3 with respect to situation-specific prevalences of need for control and need for self-esteem, respectively, should also be envisaged in this case.

Hypotheses on reactions of the opponent during the evaluation phase

> *Hypothesis 3.1.* The greater the defensiveness of an account or an account substitute offered by an actor, the more negative will be the opponent's evaluation of the actor's reaction, the failure event and the actor's personality.

Once more the mediation of the proposed causal relationship via feelings of lack or loss of control and the need to assert or reassert control is invoked in theoretical support of the hypothesis. Opponents whose sense of control and self-esteem has already suffered from the confrontation with the failure event may be especially sensitive to further threats to their needs for control and self-esteem implied by defensive account phase reactions of the actor. Among such defensive reactions which do not honour the opponent's control and self-esteem needs, refusals to give an account, especially explicit refutations of any claimed right to a challenge or reproach, are, of course, the most serious direct attacks on the opponent's sense of control and self-worth. Therefore such refusals may be expected to elicit or facilitate the most negative evaluations not only of the account phase reaction, but also of the failure event and the actor's personality. Hypothesis 3.1, alone or in conjunction with hypothesis 2.1 on the linkage between severity of reproach and defensiveness of accounts, may well turn out to be the most important part of the whole network of escalation towards an account episode's foundering.

> *Hypothesis 3.2.* The final evaluations made by male opponents are likely to be more negative than the evaluations by female opponents.

All the arguments and considerations offered in connection with hypothesis 1.2 on the linkage between masculinity and severity of reproach phase reactions of opponents also apply to hypothesis 3.2.

> *Hypothesis 3.3.* The higher the opponent's need to maintain control over self-relevant events, and/or the higher the need for positive self-evaluation, the more negative will be the opponent's final evaluation.

Again, all the qualifying considerations offered in connection with hypothesis 1.3 also apply to the present hypothesis.

> *Hypothesis 3.4.* The greater the severity of an opponent's reproach phase reaction, the more negative this opponent's final evaluation will tend to be.

At first sight this prediction may seem straightforward, but it requires some further comment. Figure 2 shows the stated relationship between severity of reproach and negativity of evaluation to be mediated by the opponent's need for cognitive consistency or consonance, which I see as partly dependent upon the opponent's general need for control. This interpretation of dissonance theory and its inclusion in the present theoretical network has a number of implications.

Paying attention to the opponent's consonance needs as partial determinants of his or her final evaluation highlights at the same time the importance and difficulty for the actor of formulating an appropriate account that will maximize the chances of a sufficiently positive evaluation by the opponent and hence the accomplishment of the account episode as a whole, for example the maintenance or restoration of the relationship between actor and opponent. If the opponent reacts to the failure event with a severe reproach, then the probability of a successful accomplishment of the account episode is particularly small for two reasons: (1) due to his or her consonance needs the opponent is already predisposed to terminate the episode with a relatively negative evaluation, regardless of the actor's account; and (2) according to hypothesis 2.1 it is not at all likely that the actor will respond to a severe reproach with an account that might make amends *despite* the opponent's predisposition towards a negative final evaluation.

The best strategy for an actor interested in a positive outcome of the episode against all odds should be an account which satisfies as far as possible the opponent's need for control. This should not only abolish or at least reduce detrimental feelings of lack or loss of control in the opponent, but also reduce or make less salient the need for cognitive consistency as a variant of secondary control feelings.

Integrative analogy and conclusion

Figure 2 presents the ten hypotheses in a network that loosely resembles a river system in which the main stream meanders from one dam reservoir to another, fed by various tributaries on its way. Sluices at the dams regulate the flow of water. Little is known about the average and potential range of the volume of water contributed by each source; and the courses of some of the tributaries, and of any divisions and combinations among them, are unknown. Nevertheless, one thing is very clear: if precipitation is high in more than one source area to the right or left of the main river, then the danger of unmanageable floods and a dam break is particularly acute. On the other hand, if precipitation is moderate or low in all areas, then the river will run smoothly without much regulative effort at the sluices.

Returning to our domain of discourse and its language, we can make some analogous predictions with similar degrees of confidence, provided that at least major parts of the theoretical network will stand up to empirical tests. For instance, in the case of a fairly severe failure event with no or only weak societal norms prescribing a settlement of the conflict, the probability that the ensuing account episode will founder will be particularly high if both actor and opponent are males with strong needs for control and self-esteem as well as other corresponding 'masculine' qualities. The opposite prediction of a high probability of the successful accomplishment of an account episode could be made for a case of a mild or moderate failure event involving socially adept and self-confident females as actor and opponent.

Our theoretical model deals not only with the interactions (*sensu primo*) between actor and opponent, but also with the contingent interactions (*sensu secundo*) between crucial events and various dispositions in the participants. Indeed, in our empirical work so far these interactions in the second sense, and therefore the assessment of various dispositions and their effects, have played a major role. This orientation was guided not only by the conviction of the general advisability of combining dispositional and situational variables (e.g. Mischel 1973) but by two more specific considerations as well. (1) Predictions that include a number of dispositional variables on the antecedent side promise fairly good progress in the present, still very early, stages of research on account episodes. Such progress is very much needed for the further development of both theory and methods. (2) Attention to the role of actors' and opponents' dispositions in the course of account episodes seems also warranted if we accept that eventually some dispositions may be suitable targets for socialization efforts with respect to beneficial account episode behaviour.

Several of our empirical studies also included other moderator variables, notably social anxiety and self-consciousness. Due to space limitations, these variables, introduced mainly with exploratory intentions, will play only a peripheral role in this monograph. Full treatment of the relevant data must be reserved for a later report.

2.3 Supplementary speculations

In the preceding section I have stated a set of hypotheses to be tested. In this section the mood and mode of reasoning will be predominantly exploratory. Even though testing and exploration cannot strictly be distinguished, it seems appropriate to set apart cases where one is willing to assign high probability to *one* of several possible outcomes from those other cases where at least two mutually exclusive alternatives appear to be almost equally plausible, or still other cases where our knowledge is so rudimentary that at present we can do no more than delimit some subareas within the whole potential domain for an initial exploratory search for further heuristic leads.

There are two issues in my view which, in the context of the escalation network just presented, merit some speculation and subsequent investigation in an exploratory vein. These two issues are (1) the effects of the failure event on the actor's account phase reactions; and (2) the meanings attached to the concept of 'responsibility' by various actors and opponents and the consequences of these understandings for their conduct in account episodes.

The impact of the failure event on the actor's account phase reactions
One arrow in figure 2 is accompanied by a question mark. The arrow represents hypothesis A.

> Hypothesis A. The greater the severity of the failure event, the more defensive will be the actor's reaction during the account phase.

The question mark casts doubt upon this hypothesis because one can easily imagine that in many situations the opposite hypothesis holds:

> Hypothesis A^1. The greater the severity of the failure event, the more willing the actor will be to make concessions with respect to the failure event and his or her own involvement in it.

The following considerations speak in favour of hypothesis A. Clearly, a person *wrongly* denounced as actor is likely to protest more vigorously if he or she is accused of a severe failure rather than a minor mishap. A person actively involved in a severe failure event may well also react in a markedly defensive manner. A defensive strategy could serve several purposes for the actor in such a case. The actor may believe that by a staunch stand, that is a strongly justificatory account, a denial, or a refutation of the right to question or reproach him, he can ward off further more deeply penetrating questions and accusations. A defensive account or account substitute with the actor's own ego as the hidden primary addressee may also be self-serving in a more direct manner by bolstering at least temporarily the actor's self-esteem and sense of control, shaken by the realization of the failure event. Finally, strongly defensive reactions of a more cold-blooded nature may be expected from an actor who has carefully planned and executed a serious offence, perhaps in the very service of enhancing his range or degree of control.

On the other hand, in favour of the competing hypothesis A^1, one may plausibly assume that many actors involved in severe failure events try to obtain lenient judgements in a non-defensive way by various concessions such as admission of guilt, expressions of regret, or offers of compensation, or else by excuses of a kind which put them at the mercy of any judge, excuses which explicitly relinquish some measure of control and certainly do not bolster self-esteem in any direct way.

To know under which conditions, if at all, this or that hypothesis, A or A^1, is likely to prove viable would be extremely important, considering the escalation predictions of the preceding section. If indeed a severe failure event has instigated a severe reproach, and if this reproach in turn is now likely to elicit a defensive reaction from the actor, then the prospects for an accomplishment of this account episode are dim indeed if the actor is already predisposed towards a defensive account phase reaction by the very severity of the failure event. If, on the other hand, a concessive mood of the actor subsequent to the failure event prevails, despite a rather harsh reproach from the opponent, then the actor's account may turn the tide.

As we currently know almost nothing about the distinguishing conditions for the success of hypotheses A and A^1, the best research strategy is probably a systematic search for constellations of situational and moderator variables envisaged by escalation theory, which in conjunction with severe, as opposed to mild, failure events 'produce' markedly defensive or markedly concessive account phase reactions in the actor. Any such findings may then serve as a base for the development of further heuristic leads.

The meaning of 'responsibility' and its impact on account episodes

'Responsibility' is an elusive concept. At different times and places it has carried widely different meanings and implications for various kinds of people. Many authors from different fields have discussed this state of affairs, for example Fauconnet (1928), Heider (1958), Hart (1968), Fincham and Jaspars (1980), Shultz and Schleifer (1983), Lloyd-Bostock (1983) and Shaver (1985).

Kelly Shaver (1985), in his incisive treatment of causality, responsibility and blameworthiness, suggested this working definition of responsibility: 'The unmodified term, "responsibility", will be defined as a judgment made about the moral accountability of a person of normal capacities, which judgment usually but not always involves a causal connection between the person being judged and some morally disapproved action or event!' (ibid., p. 66). However, after a thorough discussion of the various implications of this definition, Shaver concluded that a concise definition of responsibility (or rather, responsibility judgement) cannot be offered: 'What can be offered instead are the *dimensions* that together can be used to ascertain the responsibility of an individual for a single morally reprehensible act' (ibid., p. 85).

The dimensions listed by Shaver are (1) the causal involvement of the person under judgement, that is local versus remote participation, (2) the degree of volition, that is coerced versus voluntary participation, (3) the degree of awareness of the consequences of the act or event in question, (4) the degree of intentionality with respect to the act and its consequences, and finally (5) the extent of the capacity to appreciate the moral implications of the action. Obviously, people may differ widely in their conscious or subconscious use of any or all of these five dimensions and in their assigning weights to them in the context of a responsibility judgement. Shaw and Sulzer (1964), for instance, in an early empirical test of Heider's levels in responsibility attributions, found clear population differences between adults and children in responsibility attributions both as main effects and as components of interactions with action outcomes and with levels of actor's involvement. Furthermore, one and the same person may shift between various conceptions of 'responsibility' according to situational pressures, as Steininger and Colsher (1980) demonstrated in their pilot study on beliefs about freedom and responsibility.

Shaver and his co-workers Null and Huff (1982; see Shaver 1985, pp. 143–54), in a rare systematic study directly addressed to the meanings of responsibility, also reported many substantial differences in the semantic networks around the core term 'responsible' between attribution research experts, on the one hand, and college undergraduates, on the other; furthermore, there were also differences within this latter sample between three groups prepared for the semantic judgement task with different instructions.

All these considerations and results suggested two related inferences for our own domain of discourse: (1) the variability of the meanings attached to the concept of 'responsibility' among different (groups of) persons, as well as within a given person from one situational context to another, is likely to increase the danger of misperceptions and failing communication between actor and opponent and thus constitutes an additional countervailing force against the successful accomplishment of an account episode; and (2) in the light of this sobering thought we should to some extent at least explore the nature as well as the causes and consequences of that conceptual variability of responsibility within our account episode context.[9]

There was little guidance for such an exploration except for the following lead. Brickman et al. (1982) emphasized a distinction between attributions of responsibility for the genesis of a problem and attributions of responsibility for the solution of a problem. This distinction and the four general models of helping and coping derived by Brickman et al. reinforced my tentative thinking that men and women, on average, might differ in their emphasis on the causal aspect and on the solution aspect of responsibility. Gilligan (1977), in her important paper on women's conceptions of self and of morality, had already pointed out that 'the moral imperative that emerges repeatedly in the women's interviews is an injunction to care, a responsibility to discern and alleviate the "real and recognizable trouble" of this world. For the men Kohlberg studied, the moral imperative appeared rather as an injunction to respect the rights of others and thus to protect from interference the right to life and self-fulfilment' (ibid., p. 511). A similar conclusion could be derived from the arguments offered in support of my hypotheses 1.2 and 2.2 on the severity of male and female reproach phase reactions and on male and female defensiveness during an account phase.

If the average man does indeed have a higher need for dominance and corresponding controls than the average woman, then we may assume that he is more sensitive than she is to the causal aspects of any infringement of these needs and less prone to consider the solution of a problem separately from the genesis of the problem. Such differential emphasis may well lead to conceptions of responsibility among average males that are more cause-oriented than the responsibility conceptions of average females with respect to both the genesis and the solution of a problem, an account episode in our case. This, then, has been my tentative hypothesis to be tested and further explored with the intention of seeing if corroborating results would aid us in explaining any results obtained with respect to our main investigation of the escalation network.

Some supportive evidence can be inferred from studies in various contexts that have been reported in the meantime by other researchers (De Man, Simpson-Housley and Curtis 1985; Ford and Lowery 1986; Schmalt 1986; Mitchell 1987). I shall return to their findings in connection with our own pertinent results (on p. 114). For the moment I should add that, given a corroboration of the hypotheses, I would envisage a reciprocal relationship as likely between dominance-oriented account episode behaviour and a cause-oriented conception of responsibility. I would assume that the fundamental needs for dominance and corresponding control behaviours play an important role in the development of a cause-oriented concept of responsibility, but I would also assume that a cause-oriented responsibility concept facilitates and enhances in turn dominance- and control-oriented behaviours, that is severe reactions of opponents and defensive reactions of actors.

Effects of age and social status
For some of our studies on opponent reactions we were able to recruit respondents from various age groups and different educational strata. I expected that severe reactions during the reproach phase and negative evaluations after receiving an account would be more prevalent among older than among younger respondents, and more prevalent also among respondents with basic education than among those with higher education. The following line of reasoning led to these expectations. In previous studies on negative attitudes towards ethnic outgroups (Schönbach et al. 1981; Wagner and Schönbach 1984) we had found the older respondents more negatively disposed towards workers from abroad than younger respondents, and persons in the lowest educational category more negatively disposed than the respondents with higher educational levels. In one study by Heinemann and Schönbach some data constellations suggested, although there was no direct measurement of control feelings, that the attitudes of the older respondents towards the workers from abroad were partly mediated by a sense of weakness and vulnerability among the older respondents (see

Supplementary speculations

Schönbach et al. 1981, pp. 80–2). This led to the inference that those with negative attitudinal dispositions towards some outgroup (e.g. a considerable number of older people) may also be expected to react severely and negatively towards an individual antagonist encountered in an account episode, and especially so if they suffer from feelings of lack of control.

Essentially the same argument applies to the prediction concerning the severity and negativity of persons of low educational status. There is ample evidence (partly summarized in Schönbach et al. 1981, pp. 161–4) that low self-esteem coupled with lack of competence and achievement is widespread in the lower educational strata, and Wagner found in a study of attitudes towards Turks among German adolescents (see Wagner and Schönbach 1984, p. 43) that sensitizing the respondents to make self-evaluations instigated significantly more negative attitudinal reactions among low-education respondents, in comparison to non-sensitized control groups.

3 Study designs and procedures

Ten studies furnished the empirical base for the assessment of the escalation theory. Three of these studies were directed at the reactions of opponents during the reproach phase. These three reproach phase studies will henceforth be labelled RPS I, RPS II and RPS III. Four studies (APS I to APS IV) were concerned with the reactions of actors during the account phase, and three studies (EPS I, II and III) with opponent reactions during the evaluation phase.

I shall first describe the design features which these ten studies have in common, and then present their specific structures. A brief description of two supplementary studies (MRS I and MRS II) on the meanings attached to 'responsibility' will close this chapter.

3.1 Common design features

The studies were designed as surveys, but the designs also included some quasi-experimental components in each case.

Respondents were recruited in various urban regions of the Ruhr area. Each respondent was interviewed singly by a co-worker from the Social Psychology section at the Faculty of Psychology of the Ruhr-Universität Bochum, or by an advanced student participating in a diploma thesis project or a high-level research seminar.

Each respondent received, with some supplementary oral instructions, a questionnaire to be read and answered in writing and/or by the marking of scales by the respondent himself or herself. In two studies, RPS I and APS I, the first reactions requested had to be given orally; they were tape-recorded and later transcribed for the analysis.

The central part of each interview consisted of a role imagination task in which the respondent had to identify either with the actor or the opponent after a specific failure event which was presented in a vignette. All the vignettes used will be described in the following section. In three studies, RPS I, RPS III and APS I, two more vignettes were presented with corresponding role-playing requests after the first vignette task had been completed.

Each questionnaire also contained a number of Likert scale items that represented various moderator variables. Both the programme of testing the hypotheses of the escalation network theory and the supplementary exploratory strategy required several first- and higher-order interactions of manipulated and/or selected independent variables and moderator variables to be analysed with respect to their effects on actor or opponent reactions. For that reason most of the studies were conducted with fairly large samples that allowed for the necessary subdivisions.

3.2 Vignettes of failure events

Altogether ten different failure events are included in one or more of our ten main studies. Four vignettes describe sins of commission, namely the vignettes labelled Breach of Trust, Dubious Self-Defence, Stolen Motorbike Lamp and Assault and Robbery. Six vignettes describe sins of omission. These six vignettes consist of three pairs of failure events. Each pair comprises two versions of the same core event, one version coupled with a mild, and the other version with a severe, violation of a normative expectation. The core events are labelled Neglected Supervision, Neglected Oil Puddle and Dog off Leash. No such label was presented to the respondents. These designations are only used here for convenient reference.

Six vignettes were presented only to opponents, and one, the Stolen Motorbike Lamp, only to actors. The remaining three vignettes, Breach of Trust, Dubious Self-Defence and the basic or mild version of Neglected Supervision were used for both role-playing actors and – in different studies – role-playing opponents. These three vignettes will here be presented in the version for actors, with an indication of the slight changes necessary to make them suitable cues for opponents.

Neglected Supervision – basic or mild version

> A couple you know has asked you one evening to babysit with their three-year-old son for a few hours, and you agree. The parents put the child to bed and leave. You settle down in the living room in front of the television. Unnoticed by you, the child gets out of bed, goes to the kitchen and drinks from a bottle of cleaning fluid. Upon the child's screaming you rush into the kitchen and, realizing what has happened, you call the emergency ambulance. They take the child to the hospital where his stomach is pumped out. The parents return, hear about the incident on the staircase from a neighbour and call you to account. What do you have to say about your conduct in this situation?[10]

This vignette was used in the account phase studies APS I, II and III. Corresponding versions were employed in RPS I, II and III, and EPS II, addressed to respondents in an opponent's role. These respondents were asked to imagine being either the father or the mother, or a friend of the parents who has asked a friend to babysit with the child. Further explanations follow in section 3.3.

Neglected Supervision – severe version

> You have asked a friend to babysit with your three-year-old son for a few hours, and she has agreed. You put the child to bed and leave. Your friend settles down in the living room and writes a letter. About an hour later she leaves the house in order to post the letter in a night letter-box. After 20 minutes she returns and hears the child screaming in the kitchen. She rushes into the kitchen and notices that the child has apparently drunk from a bottle of cleaning fluid and calls the emergency doctor. He gets the child to the hospital, where his stomach is pumped out. You return, hear about the incident on the staircase from a neighbour and ask your friend to give an account.

This version was used in RPS II, alternating with a variant in which the respondent had to role-play a friend of the negligent babysitter whom the respondent had supposedly asked to substitute for him or her as a babysitter. The same failure event was also used in RPS III, but here the respondent was asked to role-play a friend of the parents and to render various judgements on the incident. Further details will be given in section 3.3.

Breach of Trust

> In the company in which you work a new employee has been hired. You have known this man since school and you also know that he has been in jail for burglary. This man comes to you and asks you not to tell anybody in the firm about his previous conviction; only the personnel manager is to know about it. You agree, and you keep your promise for a while. But during an outing of the company, when in a jolly mood and a bit merry, you confidentially tell two colleagues about it. As a result the story travels round the firm, and the ex-convict gets into trouble. He is teased by some and others treat him with distrust and hostility. He consequently complains to you. What do you have to say about your conduct in this situation?

In this form the vignette was used in APS I. In RPS I the respondents had to imagine the same failure event from the perspective of a friend of the ex-convict. The instruction in this case was: 'You then talk with your friend's colleague. What will you say to him?'

Dubious Self-Defence

> It is already dark. You are on your way home from the shops. In a side alley a well-built man staggers towards you, obviously drunk. He bars your way, grabs your arm and mumbles: 'You swine, I'll kill you.' With some effort you

Vignettes of failure events

> tear yourself loose and run a few steps away. You turn around and see that the man is trying to follow you, reeling. Thereupon you grab a beer bottle from your shopping bag, throw it at the man's head, and then run on. There is a witness to the incident, and you are called in for questioning. The beer bottle has caused a fracture of the drunken man's skull; you are quite likely to be charged with assault. What do you have to say about your conduct in this situation?

This version of the vignette was employed in APS I. In EPS I the same incident was presented with Herr Müller, a 35-year-old employee, as the actor accosted by the drunkard. The respondents' tasks as opponents are described in section 3.5.

Stolen Motorbike Lamp

This vignette was specifically designed and pretested as being suitable for 15–16-year-old *Gymnasium* students as respondents in APS IV. It read as follows in one of eight variants:

> Twice a week Michael rides his motorbike 10 km to an indoor swimming-pool for training. There he meets Christian, a classmate, with whom he trains. One evening Michael has to return home quickly and therefore leaves early. Outside he notices that the bulb of his motorbike lamp is broken. Quickly he exchanges it for the bulb from Christian's motorbike, which happens to be standing close by. He leaves without saying anything to Christian. The latter now has to make his way home on a motorbike without lights. On the dark country road a car driver sees the motorbike too late and forces it into the ditch. Christian gets off with a fright and a bruised knee, but the front wheel of his motorbike is badly bent. Next morning at school he talks about his accident, and another classmate tells him that he had seen Michael unscrewing Christian's bulb. The day before, he had thought that Christian would know about this. Christian turns to Michael, who is standing next to him in silence, and asks him: 'Why did you do that?'

The respondent was then confronted with the question: 'What would you say in Michael's place?'

In another version of the vignette Christian's reproach was more severe: 'I would not have expected this from you, I am very disappointed! Why did you do it?' In two more versions, with the same mild and severe reproach, respectively, Christian was replaced by Herr Seibt, the class teacher, in the opponent's role. The four versions just mentioned were used with boys as respondents. For girls four corresponding versions were used with Michaela and Christiane as female classmates; the class teacher, however, remained Herr Seibt for the female respondents. More details follow in section 3.4.

Four core vignettes and their variants were employed only in RPS III. Here, by way of example, is one variant for each vignette:

Neglected Oil Puddle – mild version

> Herr Lautler works as a car mechanic in the shop in which the son of a friend of yours gets his occupational training. One Thursday he gets the assignment to change the oil in a customer's car. Herr Lautler drives the car into the workshop and does this routine job, with the used oil being collected in a special drip basin. After finishing the oil change he pulls the basin from under the car and carries it to the storage tank. At this point some of the oil spills over and forms a puddle on the workshop floor. Before he can remove the oil puddle a customer who is in a hurry asks him to drive his car out of the workshop, and Herr Lautler complies with this request. During his absence the son of your friend slips on the puddle. As he complains about considerable pain in his right arm he is taken to the doctor, who diagnoses a simple fracture of the forearm.

Neglected Oil Puddle – severe version

The same core event is described as in the preceding version. However, instead of being asked by a customer to drive his car out of the workshop, the car mechanic is asked by a colleague to join him for lunch and the car mechanic goes along.

Dog off Leash – mild version

A good acquaintance of yours gets involved in a car accident in the following way:

> Herr Dahl takes his dachshund for a walk. As he lives in a street with a lot of traffic he firmly puts him on his leash as usual. At a shop window Herr Dahl stops and looks with interest at the display. At this moment the dog discovers a cat on the other side of the street. He violently tugs at the leash, the collar comes loose and – suddenly freed – the dog races across the traffic lanes. At the same time, an acquaintance of yours draws near in his car. He tries to avoid the dog, but he loses control over the vehicle and hits a streetlamp. This results in considerable damage.

Dog off Leash – severe version

The preceding event of the dog causing the accident is coupled with the following variant of the dog owner's behaviour:

> Herr Dahms takes his dachshund for a walk. As he lives in a street with a lot of traffic the dog is used to the traffic. Today Herr Dahms does not bother to put him on his leash. At a shop window Herr Dahms stops, looks with interest at the display and enters the shop. At this moment the dog discovers a cat on the other side of the street . . .

The last four vignettes, that is the mild and severe versions of the Neglected Oil Puddle and the Dog off Leash, were also used with a female car mechanic and a female dog owner, respectively. The design of RPS III will be explained in section 3.3.

Assault and Robbery

> One evening you are on your way home on a not much frequented side street. An adolescent comes your way. Two steps away from you he suddenly throws a handful of sand into your face. Momentarily you are blinded and shocked – the assailant snatches your handbag with your money, keys and identity card and runs away. Fortunately, after some 20 metres he is stopped and seized by a well-built man who has just come out of his door and had witnessed the assault. You approach them, thank the man, and then you turn to the adolescent. What will you say to him?

This vignette was used in EPS III.

3.3 Reproach phase studies (RPS)

I shall now present the design and procedure of each main study, and I shall do so in a somewhat schematic manner in order to facilitate comparisons the reader might wish to make.

RPS I

Project. Diploma thesis research conducted by Gabriele Berten (1981) and Birgitta Holland (1981).

Time of fieldwork. November and December 1979.

Respondents. Male ($N=60$) and female ($N=60$) students at the Ruhr-Universität Bochum with major subjects other than psychology were recruited via the notice boards in the Departments of History, Education, Philosophy and Theology. Each respondent received 5 DM in payment for participation in the study.

Task of respondents. Role-playing an opponent by responding orally to each of three failure event vignettes. Each vignette was presented in a tape-recording, immediately followed by an identical typed version to be read. After the three role-playing responses the interview continued with the request to mark a number of judgement scales (see moderator variables below).

Vignettes. The three vignettes used were Neglected Supervision (basic version), Breach of Trust and Dubious Self-Defence. Each of the six possible permutations of order of vignettes was assigned to the male and the female respondents by a random procedure. Due to limitations of time and capacity only the data pertinent to the failure events Neglected Supervision and Breach of Trust were analysed.

Independent variables. Gender of respondents and type of failure event (Neglected Supervision vs Breach of Trust).

Dependent variables. Open oral answers tape-recorded, transcribed and coded according to various category systems (see chapter 5). Responses on scales with four to six steps, asking for judgements on the actor's attractiveness, responsibility for the failure event, punishability, and liability for restitution or compensation.

Moderator variables. Locus of control, measured by Schopler's (1973) North Carolina Internal–External Scale – Short Form, translated into German by Petra Flaßhove, Ralf Teichgräber and Hans-Joachim Schellenberg-van Holt in connection with the account phase study APS I (see below). Private self-consciousness, public self-consciousness and social anxiety, measured by the Fenigstein, Scheier and Buss (1975) scale in Wolfgang Heinemann's (1979) German translation. The moderator variable scales were presented in this order after the subject had answered all the questions pertaining to the failure events.

Purpose. This first reproach phase study was largely exploratory with respect to types of opponent reactions to various failure events in conjunction with some moderator variables. However, the study also provided a preliminary test of hypothesis 1.1 on the effects of failure severity, and a regular test of hypothesis 1.2 on gender differences between opponent reactions during the reproach phase.

RPS II

Project. Study conducted in an advanced research seminar in social psychology at the Ruhr-Universität Bochum in the winter semester 1984–5.[11]

Time of fieldwork. December 1984 and January 1985.

Respondents. A quota sample of 176 adult respondents was intended; 172 usable interviews were obtained. Each of 11 student participants in the seminar acted as interviewer and took responsibility for 16 interviews with equal quotas ($N=4$) in each of the following four cells: young men (18–35y.), old men (56y. plus), young women (18–35y.), old women (56y. plus). Students were excluded from this sample. Within each cell the respondents were assigned on a random basis to one of four experimental conditions (see below). The respondents were inhabitants of several cities in the Ruhr area.

Task of respondents. Reading one of four vignette variations of the failure event 'Neglected Supervision' and then, by using various scales, making judgements about the actor's responsibility for the event, her financial liability and her degree of guilt. In addition, each respondent had to mark the items of the Fenigstein–Scheier–Buss scale in Heinemann's (1979) translation and to answer a few questions about age, education and occupational status.

Vignettes. Four vignette variations were used in a 2×2 arrangement. The mild and the severe version of Neglected Supervision constituted one of these two factors. The other factor was the role and the relation to the actor which the respondent was asked to assume. In every case the actor was portrayed as a female friend of the respondent. But in half the cases the respondent had to imagine being the father or the mother of the boy, and in the other half the respondent had to conceive himself or herself as being a friend of the parents who had originally been asked to do the babysitting. A serious illness in the family had prevented him or her coming and sitting with the child; so upon the respondent's suggestion this other friend had been asked to step in.

Independent variables. Originally a $2 \times 2 \times 2 \times 2$ design was envisaged with the factors (1) gender of respondent, (2) age of respondent, (3) severity of failure and (4) relation to actor. Since this fourth factor did not produce any significant differences, alone or in interaction with other variables, it will be omitted from the analyses to be presented in chapter 5.

Dependent variables. The first response was elicited by the question 'How large is your friend's share of responsibility for the accident?'[12] The answer had to be given by marking a thermometer-like graphic scale ranging from 0% to 100%, with each 10% interval marked and labelled (10%, 20%, etc.). In addition, the end points were labelled 'She is not at all responsible' and 'She is fully responsible', respectively.[13]

Essentially the same scale was used for the second question, 'Suppose that the costs for the emergency doctor and the hospital are not covered by insurance. Should the friend take on part of the costs or the total costs, or should she not contribute anything to the costs?',[14] but the end points this time were 'No cost contribution at all' and 'The total costs'.[15]

The third question tried to suggest a distinction between responsibility and guilt: 'To be responsible for something and to be guilty in this respect is not always the same thing. Hence this additional question. Has your friend made herself guilty through the accident?'[16] In this case the respondent had to choose from one of four alternative answers ranging from 'No guilt at all' to 'Fully guilty'.[17]

Moderator variables. Social anxiety as measured by the corresponding Fenigstein–Scheier–Buss subscale was of particular interest in this study. Another moderator variable used was the respondents' educational status, that is either (1) most elementary schooling (*Volksschule*) including continuation school (*Hauptschule*) within a programme of occupational training, or (2) lower-grade secondary school (*Mittelschule*), technical school (*Realschule*) or equivalent training, or (3) at least leaving certificate (*Abitur*) of a *Gymnasium* or an equivalent certificate as entrance requirement for technical college or university.

Purpose. The main goal of this study was a more rigorous test than in RPS I of hypothesis 1.1 on the effects of failure severity on opponent reactions. In addition, a further investigation of gender differences among opponent reactions was intended. Additional tests of a more exploratory nature dealt with the possible influences of the respondents' age and educational status on their reactions either by way of main effects or in conjunction with other variables. Considering the comparatively punitive reactions against outgroups frequently found[18] among older as opposed to younger persons and among those with low educational status as opposed to those with higher education, I tentatively expected to obtain from the older respondents more severe judgements of the actor than from younger respondents, and likewise more severe reactions from the respondents with limited formal education than from the better-educated respondents.

RPS III

Project. Diploma thesis research conducted in a joint project by Barbara Birkendorf, Susanne Bubber and Dagmar Tonscheidt (1987).

Time of fieldwork. December 1985 and January 1986.

Respondents. A quota sample of 192 adults, interviewed by Birkendorf, Bubber and Tonscheidt in various cities of the Ruhr area. Equal quotas ($N=48$) were assigned to the following four categories: young men

(18–35y.), older men (36y. plus), young women (18–35y.), older women (36y. plus). Within each quota respondents were equally distributed by a random procedure into the cells of the experimental design (see below under the heading 'Vignettes').

Task of respondents. Reading three vignettes and making judgements on each actor's responsibility, cost liability and guilt as in RPS II. A fourth question inquired about the reliability of the actor's behaviour in the situation described by the vignette. As in RPS II, the Fenigstein–Scheier–Buss items followed the vignettes, and questions about the occupational status, age and education of the respondent completed the interview.

Vignettes. Each of the three basic failure events – Neglected Supervision, Neglected Oil Puddle and Dog off Leash – was incorporated in four vignette versions: mild failure – female actor, mild failure – male actor, severe failure – female actor, severe failure – male actor. Thus 12 vignettes altogether were employed in this study, equally distributed among the four gender-by-age quotas in the following way:

1   Each respondent read and judged one version of each basic failure event.
2   The order of vignettes was rotated across the 192 questionnaires in such a way that each of the 12 vignettes appeared in each position (1st, 2nd and 3rd place) equally often, namely 16 times.
3   Severe and mild failure versions alternated from position to position. Thus two severity orders were employed: mild–severe–mild and severe–mild–severe.
4   The actor's gender was also rotated and balanced in such a way as to ensure that in each position every vignette version was connected an equal number of times with a male and with a female actor.

Independent variables. The basic design has a $2 \times 2 \times 2 \times 3 \times 2$ format with the factors (1) age of respondent (18–35y., 36y. plus), (2) gender of respondent, (3) gender of actor, (4) gender typicality of actor's role (typically male = car mechanic; typically female = baby sitter; gender-neutral = dog owner), and (5) severity of failure (mild vs severe). In some analyses with repeated measurement designs, the respondents' judgements of all three vignettes were included. Other analyses concentrated on the responses to the first vignettes read and judged by the respondents. Further details will be explained in connection with the results.

Dependent variables. Scale responses were as in RPS II on the actor's share of responsibility for the failure event, share of cost liability and degree of guilt. In addition, scale responses ranging from 0% (completely unreliable) to

100% (completely reliable)[19] were obtained with respect to each actor presented in a vignette.

Moderator variables. Social anxiety, educational status and occupational status. The groupings employed with these variables will be described in connection with the results.

Purpose. The data constellation obtained in the preceding study, RPS II, lent itself to two divergent interpretations: (1) partial support for hypothesis 1.2's predicting male reproach phase reactions to be more severe by and large than female reactions in this phase; and (2) situation-specific defensive attributions (see Shaver 1970) of female respondents. The pertinent data will be presented and discussed in the chapter on results. The main reason for the inferential uncertainty just mentioned is due to the fact that in RPS II only the vignette Neglected Supervision with the typically female babysitter role, and only with a woman portrayed in this role, was employed. Therefore we decided to conduct a further study, RPS III, with an orthogonal variation of all three relevant variables – gender of respondent, gender of actor and gender typicality of the situation and of the actor's role in it.

3.4 Account phase studies (APS)

The first study to be described in this section was conducted in conjunction with RPS I, matching this study with respect to the failure situations employed and presented to an equivalent student sample.

APS I

Project. Diploma thesis research conducted in a joint project by Petra Flaßhove (1981), Hans-Joachim Schellenberg-van Holt (1981) and Ralf Teichgräber (1981).

Time of fieldwork. Winter 1979–80.

Respondents. Male ($N = 92$) and female ($N = 88$) students at the Ruhr-Universität Bochum and a college for social work in Düsseldorf. No psychology students were included in the sample. Volunteers were recruited via noticeboards. Each respondent received 5 DM in payment for participation.

Task of respondents. As in RPS I, listening to and reading and then responding orally to each of three failure event vignettes. However, in this

Account phase studies

case the respondents had to assume the roles of the actors involved in the failure events. The marking of the same scales on locus of control and self-consciousness as in RPS I concluded the interview.

Vignettes. Neglected Supervision (basic version), Breach of Trust and Dubious Self-Defence were also employed in this study. Each of the six possible orders of these vignettes was again randomly assigned to equal numbers of male and female respondents.

Independent variables. Gender of respondents and type of failure event. In this study the data pertaining to all three failure events were analysed.

Dependent variables. The accounts or account substitutes offered by the respondents were transcribed from tape-recordings and coded according to various category systems (see chapter 4).

Moderator variables. Internal and external locus of control, private and public self-consciousness, and social anxiety, measured by the same scales as in RPS I.

Purpose. The intention of this first account phase study was also mainly exploratory, in particular with respect to actors' reaction tendencies in offering or avoiding accounts after various failure events. In addition, this study furnished the first regular test of hypothesis 2.2 on the defensiveness of male as compared to female account phase reactions. The exploratory perspective did of course also include the moderator variables, social anxiety in particular.

APS II

Project. Diploma thesis research conducted by Petra Kleibaumhüter (1988).[20]

Time of fieldwork. October to December 1986.

Respondents. Female ($N=93$) and male ($N=92$) teachers from various types of secondary school.

Task of respondents. Each respondent first had to fill in a questionnaire of 57 Likert items with five response alternatives each, and then had to perform in a role-playing task as the actor after a failure event by writing down verbatim his or her likely reaction to an opponent's challenge (see below). Two multiple-choice questions on (1) the incident and (2) the respondent's reaction to the challenge, and a few demographic questions, concluded the interview.

Vignettes. All the respondents were confronted with the basic version of the failure event Neglected Supervision; however, three different versions of the parents' reaction, as described in the following paragraph, were attached to the description of the failure event. Thus three vignette versions were available and were included an equal number of times in the questionnaires, which were distributed within each gender group of respondents by a random procedure.

Independent variables. The basic design, excluding moderator variables, had a 2 × 3 format, with the factors gender of respondent and severity of reproach. This latter factor was represented by the following three variants:

1. Neutral question. Parents ask for an explanation.
2. Derogation of self-esteem. Parents say: 'How could that have happened to you? You seem to have been much too preoccupied with yourself.'
3. Derogation of sense of control. Parents say: 'Why couldn't you prevent this from happening? We wouldn't have thought you would lose track of events so easily!'[21]

Thus a neutral question, at most an implicit mild reproach, was contrasted with two more severe reproach versions. The reason for this choice will be explained shortly.

Dependent variables. The accounts or account substitutes furnished by the respondents in reaction to the stimulus question 'What do you reply to the parents?' constituted the core data, coded according to our revised taxonomy for account phase reactions (Schönbach 1985). These data were supplemented by the responses to the following two scale questions:

1. 'What effect do you think your answer has on the parents of the child?' The respondents could choose from among five answer levels ranging from 'My reply has put them in a very good mood' to 'My reply has made them very angry'.[22]
2. 'How justified did the parents' reproach appear to you in this situation?' Again, five answer levels were presented, ranging from 'The reproach appeared to me completely justified' to 'The reproach appeared to me completely unjustified'.[23]

Moderator variables. The questionnaire started with the 23 Fenigstein–Scheier–Buss self-consciousness items in Heinemann's (1979) translation. They provided once again the moderator variables private self-consciousness, public self-consciousness and social anxiety. Of the remaining 34 items 20 statements represented a German version[24] of the desirability of control scale by Burger and Cooper (1979). These 20 items were interspersed with 6 items on self-satisfaction adopted from the scales of Hormuth and Lalli (1986) and Bergemann and Johann (1985), and 8 dummy items on leisure activities.

A factor analysis of the 20 items of the Burger and Cooper scale of control desirability produced a meaningful two-factor solution. Factor 1 comprised nine items with loadings between .70 and .46; they furnished a subscale labelled 'Need for competence and influence'. A typical item of this subscale reads: 'I would prefer to be a leader rather than a follower.' Factor 2 comprised nine items with loadings between .65 and .35. These items furnished a subscale labelled 'Need for constancy and shielding'. A typical item of this subscale reads: 'I try to avoid situations where someone else tells me what to do.'

Purpose. The primary goal of this study was a test of all three major account phase hypotheses within the escalation network, that is tests of the effects on the defensiveness of accounts by the severity of the reproach (hypothesis 2.1), by the gender of respondents (hypothesis 2.2), and by the need for control over self-relevant events and/or the need for positive self-evaluation (hypothesis 2.3). Both main effects and interactions among these variables, and further moderator variables, were envisaged in the planning and conducting of the analyses.

Two different reproach versions, one mainly attacking self-worth and the other mainly directed at the sense of control, were included because of a supplementary tentative hypothesis that specific interactions between type of reproach and moderator variables such as degree of self-acceptance and need for control might occur. Our basic assumption of a reciprocal causal relationship between self-esteem and sense of control does not imply a perfect correlation. Hence we thought those predominantly concerned with their control competence and only more moderately with their self-worth might be more strongly affected by a direct attack on their sense of control than by a primary attack on their self-esteem, and it might be the other way around with those predominantly concerned with their self-worth. However, no general predictions as to the relative severity and strength of derogation of sense of control and derogation of self-esteem seemed justifiable. In a pretest

58   *Study designs and procedures*

with student judges the two reproach versions had been rated as nearly equally severe. Both versions were, of course, taken to be more severe than the baseline version neutral question.

APS III

Project. Diploma thesis research conducted by Joachim Studt (1988).

Time of fieldwork. November and December 1986.

Respondents. Male ($N=45$) and female ($N=45$) students at the Ruhr-Universität Bochum with fields of study other than psychology.

Purpose. In design and procedure this study was an exact replication of APS II. In addition, Studt explored the relationships between utterance length (Schönbach et al. 1979; Müller-Eckhard 1974) and various indices of defensiveness during an account phase.

APS IV

Project. Joint diploma thesis research conducted by Delia Nixdorf and Ilona Prystav (1988).

Time of fieldwork. October 1986.

Respondents. Female ($N=87$) and male ($N=84$) *Gymnasium* students in year 10 (15–16y.) in various schools in a city in the Ruhr area and a town in the Rhineland. The interviews took place in classroom settings supervised by a teacher at the school.

Task of respondents. Reading the vignette of a failure event and then role-playing the actor in this event after a challenge by an opponent. The actor's account or account substitute had to be given in writing. This free response was followed by a question about one's (i.e. the actor's) share of responsibility for the event. This question was accompanied by a thermometer-like graphic scale to be marked; it ranged from 0% ('No responsibility at all') to 100% ('Total responsibility') with each 10% interval marked by the corresponding number (10%, 20%, etc.).

The second part of the interview consisted of the 34 items that have already been mentioned in connection with APS II (and III) as measures of desirability of control and of self-satisfaction, including 8 interspersed dummy items on leisure activities. Five further items in the same format were included in the questionnaire with the exploratory intent of measuring a more general disposition to act with responsible care towards others.[25]

In contrast to the procedure in APS II and APS III the measurement of the moderator variables just mentioned did not precede, but followed, the role-playing task. This order was chosen for APS IV because pretests had indicated that this way the *Gymnasium* students' interest could be much better sustained throughout the interview.

Vignettes. The core vignette presented to all 171 respondents was the Stolen Motorbike Lamp. It was followed by one of eight variants of an opponent's challenge, as described in the following paragraphs.

Independent variables. The basic design, omitting moderator variables, had a $2 \times 2 \times 2$ format, with each of the eight cells containing 20–5 respondents. The three factors were (1) gender of respondents, (2) severity of reproach (mild vs severe) and (3) status of opponent (classmate vs teacher).

The two levels of the severity factor were created by adding the following texts to the core vignette: (1) 'Why did you do that?' (mild reproach) and (2) 'I would not have expected this of you, I am most disappointed! Why did you do it?' (severe reproach).

The two levels of the status factor were represented by the classmate victim – Christian for male respondents and Christiane for female respondents – and the class teacher – Herr Seibt for all respondents.

Examples of the incorporation of the two factors severity of reproach and status of opponent in the wordings of the vignette variants have already been given in section 3.2.

Dependent variables. The main data were again the accounts or account substitutes written down by the role-playing respondents and coded according to the revised 1985 taxonomy for account phase reactions to be described in the next chapter. These data were supplemented by the responses to the scale question on the share of responsibility the respondent would be willing to accept for the failure event.

Moderator variables. As in APS II and III various aspects of need or demand for control, as measured by different subscales of the Burger and Cooper instrument, served, along with degree of self-satisfaction, as moderator variables pertinent to the escalation theory. In addition, in a more exploratory vein, an index presumably measuring a more general attitude of responsible care for others was included as a moderator variable in some of the analyses.

Purpose. The study was planned as a modified replication of APS II and III, that is as a further test of the major account phase hypotheses 2.1, 2.2 and 2.3, and as a probe of their viability across different settings. Thus adolescent respondents were asked to take part, and a new failure event was used which, on the basis of expert opinions and pretest results, had been deemed to be particularly meaningful for this age group.

In addition, as a peculiarity of APS IV, possible effects of opponent status on account defensiveness were explored without any firm preconceived hypothesis. In all the studies of our research programme which we have completed so far, actor and opponent have been portrayed on an equal footing. The employment of an adolescent student sample provided us with the opportunity to contrast a peer and an adult authority figure in the opponent role. For the sake of the credibility of the vignettes and for practical reasons we settled for the experimental impurity of two confounding covariations in opponent status: (1) the peer opponent was also the victim of the failure event, while the adult opponent was not; and (2) in the case of the peer, the gender of opponent and actor was always identical, whereas in the case of the adult opponent, Herr Seibt, this was true only for the male respondents. In presenting the pertinent data I shall pay due attention to these facts.

Finally, as already mentioned, the functioning of a tentative index of a more general attitude or disposition of responsible care for others was explored in this fourth account phase study.

3.5 Evaluation phase studies (EPS)

Three studies in our research programme have so far been directed at the fourth account episode phase, in which the opponent may evaluate the actor's account phase response as well as the failure event and/or the actor's personality in the light of the account or account substitute.

EPS I

Project. Diploma thesis research conducted by Gunther Damerow (1982).

Time of fieldwork. Winter 1980–1.

Respondents. Male students ($N = 64$) at the Ruhr-Universität Bochum with fields of study other than psychology or law. Respondents were recruited as volunteers via noticeboards. Each respondent took part in an individual experimental session and received 5 DM in payment for participation.

Task of respondents. Reading and filling in a questionnaire consisting of three parts. The first part started with the vignette Dubious Self-Defence and the request to judge the actor's conduct on six seven-step scales ranging from

'Not at all' to 'Extremely'. These six scales were labelled: 'Correct', 'Brutal', 'Criminal', 'Understandable', 'Primitive' and 'Justified'.[26] The respondent then received a card with one of four 'explanations' for his conduct, supposedly offered by the actor during his interrogation. In response to this cue further judgements were requested with respect to the actor's account, his conduct as described by the vignette and his personality. Six- to nine-adjective scales of the same seven-step format as before were attached to these questions. Further judgements, again to be rendered by marking seven-step scales, were obtained with respect to the actor's responsibility for his conduct, the extent of guilt he incurred, and his liability for sanctions. Part 1 of the questionnaire ended with a simultaneous presentation of four cards with all four versions of 'What Herr Müller might have said during the interrogation'. After comparing these four versions – the one which the respondent had already received and judged earlier and three new ones – the respondent had to evaluate each one on a seven-step scale as to the degree of its acceptability.

Part 2 of the questionnaire consisted of the 24 items of Levenson's (1974) IPC scale for measuring locus of control convictions, in a German translation by Schönbach and Damerow.[27] The Fenigstein–Scheier–Buss (1975) self-consciousness scale in Heinemann's (1979) translation formed part 3 of the questionnaire.

Vignettes. The core vignette Dubious Self-Defence was presented to all 64 respondents. However, four different continuations, that is four different accounts of the actor, had been constructed and each one was assigned by a random procedure to 16 respondents.

Independent variables. The four account versions resulted from a 2 × 2 design with the factors type of account (excuse vs. justification) and locus of account (internal vs. external). They read as follows:

> Internal excuse: 'I am sorry, but I felt threatened, and I did not know how to help myself otherwise. If one is frightened like that one acts in a way instinctively. The beer bottle was the only thing at hand at that moment.'
>
> External excuse: 'I am sorry, but I was threatened and I did not know how to help myself otherwise. I just saw that man in front of me, bigger and stronger than me, and dangerously drunk. Thus I somehow automatically grabbed the beer bottle.'
>
> Internal justification: 'I felt threatened, and therefore I defended myself. I was entitled (es war mein gutes Recht) to protect my health and possibly even my life. The beer bottle was the only usable thing at hand at that moment.'

External justification: 'I was threatened, and therefore I defended myself. I was entitled to do that; the man was bigger and stronger than me, and dangerously drunk. The beer bottle was the only usable thing at hand at that moment.'

Dependent variables. Scores for single items as well as summary scores for groups of items of judgements on the accounts, the actor's conduct, his personality and his liability for various sanctions, as described in the paragraph on the respondents' initial tasks.

Moderator variables. Indices derived from the subscales internality, power and chances of the Levenson (1974) instrument for measuring locus of control convictions, and indices of private self-consciousness, public self-consciousness and social anxiety derived from the Fenigstein–Scheier–Buss scale.

Purpose. Similar to RPS I and APS I, this first evaluation phase study was also a predominantly exploratory venture with respect to the effects of different accounts on the tendency, positive or negative, of opponents' evaluations. There was not yet any firm hypothesis to be tested. Some guidance was provided by the tentative hunch that in general, or in conjunction with some moderator variable, reactions to justifications might show greater variance between the extremes of decidedly positive and decidedly negative evaluations than reactions to excuses. This hunch rested on the speculation that those with a particularly strong need for believing in a just (and hence controllable) world might be more eager to accept a credible, non-threatening justification than a meek and possibly somewhat lame excuse, but that this order of evaluations would be sharply reversed if the justification sounded even slightly inappropriate or carried a threatening message for the opponent.

EPS II
This study and the next one (EPS III) focus on the evaluation phase just as EPS I does. However, they also contain reproach phase components.

Project. Study conducted in an advanced research seminar in social psychology at the Ruhr-Universität Bochum in the winter semester 1987–8.[28]

Time of fieldwork. November 1987 to January 1988.

Respondents. Male ($N=96$) and female ($N=97$) students at the Ruhr-Universität Bochum with fields other than psychology. Approached individually by the interviewers, each respondent was promised and paid 5 DM for participation.

Task of respondents. Each respondent received a questionnaire with the description of the failure event Neglected Supervision (basic version), with some additional information, and the request to write down verbatim what the respondent would reply in the parents' stead. Subsequently the respondents had to check the answer scales of the 34 items described in connection with APS II as indices of various aspects of the need for control and of the degree of self-satisfaction; these were interspersed with dummy items on leisure activities.

Vignettes. The basic version of the failure event Neglected Supervision constituted the common core of the vignette, but in half the cases the babysitter was described as a male neighbour and in the other half as a female neighbour. The description of the failure event was either followed by one of the accounts rendered by the babysitter (evaluation phase conditions), or by the instruction to call on the babysitter to account for the event (reproach phase condition).

Independent variables. The basic design, again excluding moderator variables, had a 2 × 2 × 3 format with the factors gender of respondent, gender of actor and phase condition. These 12 cells were filled with roughly equal numbers of respondents. The account versions of the two evaluation phase conditions read as follows:[29]

> Low defensiveness: 'I am terribly sorry, I don't know how this could have happened – but of course it is my fault, I should have been prepared for something like that. I am just glad that I caught on at once and called the emergency doctor. Thank heavens, for once it turned out all right. But if there is still something I can do for you and the child – anytime – just tell me, please.'
>
> High defensiveness: 'Take it easy. I am of course sorry, but how could I have prevented it? This could have happened to you just as well. You did not expect me to sit at his bedside all the time and keep watch, or did you? Besides, rather careless of you to leave cleaning fluid standing there within easy reach. Be thankful that I caught on at once and called the emergency doctor. That way a real disaster was prevented.'

In the reproach phase condition the following instruction was given to the respondents: ' . . . The parents return, they learn on the staircase from other people what has happened and call upon the neighbour [i.e. the babysitter] to give an account. Put yourself in the parents' place. What would you say to the neighbour?'

Dependent variables. The free responses to vignette and account were coded according to the taxonomy for opponent reactions to be described in the following chapter. Both frequency counts for single relevant categories, as well as summary indices of the negativity of evaluations, were employed during the analyses. Further details will be given in the next chapter and in connection with the results.

Moderator variables. Again, various aspects of need or demand for control and degree of self-satisfaction served as moderator variables envisaged by the escalation theory.

Purpose. Three major evaluation phase hypotheses, 3.1, 3.2 and 3.3, were tested in this study, that is separate as well as joint effects of (1) defensiveness of account, (2) gender of opponent, (3) opponent's need for control and (4) opponent's degree of self-satisfaction on the evaluations of account, failure event and actor's personality were investigated. As a possibly differentiating factor the actor's gender was also introduced into the analysis.

EPS III

Project. Study conducted in an advanced research seminar in social psychology at the Ruhr-Universität Bochum in the summer semester 1988.

Time of fieldwork. June to September 1988.

Respondents. Male ($N=56$) and female ($N=67$) adult citizens of various urban communities in the Ruhr area. Roughly equal quotas from three age groups, 20–35y., 36–50y. and 51y. plus, were envisaged and obtained for each gender.

Task of respondents. Each respondent received a questionnaire which, after some introductory instructions, started with the vignette of the failure event Assault and Robbery and the request to take the victim's role and write down verbatim one's immediate reaction to the captured adolescent assailant. After that, the questionnaire continued with an account offered by the adolescent and the further request to the respondent to write down his or her reply to this account. The remainder of the questionnaire contained three multiple-choice questions, the need for control and the self-satisfaction measures used in APS II and EPS II, and a few demographic questions. The multiple-choice questions with ordinally arranged answer alternatives elicited judgements of the account, of the attack and of appropriate consequences for the assailant.

Vignettes. The description of the Assault and Robbery and the respondents' reproach phase reaction was followed either by a concessive-excusatory account with low defensiveness or a highly defensive refutational-justificative account.

> Concessive account: 'I am sorry for what I have done – frightened you and all that. I know it's bad, but I didn't know what else to do. I had no more dope, and I needed the next shot. Those guys won't give you anything if you haven't got any dough!'

> Refutational account: 'I don't give a shit what you say or think. Nobody hands it to you, so I had to see about getting hold of it myself. I had no more dope, and I needed the next shot. Those guys won't give you anything if you haven't got any dough. So I chanced my arm with you. Tough!'

Independent variables. The basic design, not counting moderator variables, had a 2×2 format with the factors gender of respondent and defensiveness of account. In some of the $2 \times 2 \times 2$ design extensions during the analysis severity of reproach served as a third quasi-independent variable.

Dependent variables. The free responses during both phases – reproach and evaluation – were coded and treated in the same manner as the responses in EPS II. These main dependent variables were supplemented by the three multiple-choice questions mentioned above.

Moderator variables. The same measures of need or demand for control and of self-satisfaction as in APS II and EPS II were included as moderators in some of the analyses. Indices of age, education and occupational status were also used as moderator variables.

Purpose. Hypotheses 3.1, 3.2 and 3.3 were tested in connection with a much more severe failure event than those employed in EPS I and II. This was the first test of hypothesis 3.4 on the relationship between severity of reproach and negativity of evaluation with respect to main effects as well as partial effects in interaction contexts.

3.6 Studies on the meaning of responsibility (MRS)

Two pilot studies were directed at ordinary understandings of the word 'responsibility' (Verantwortung). These studies are labelled MRS I and MRS II.

Purpose. As already indicated in section 2.3, much variance and uncertainty can be noted with respect to the meanings attached to 'responsibility'. Furthermore, there are reasons to believe that systematic differences might exist between the preponderant aspects of responsibility among men and among women, and that these differences might influence the reactions of male and female respondents in our main studies.

It was not feasible to incorporate such a semantic factor as yet another variable, or set of variables, in our main research programme. Thus for the time being we settled for a preliminary, exploratory assessment of the meanings attached to 'responsibility' in order, hopefully, to provide at least some basis for future, more systematic considerations of the semantics of the concept of 'responsibility' in account episode research.

MRS I

Project. This study was conducted in my research seminar in the winter of 1984–5, which has already been mentioned in connection with RPS II. The same participants conducted the interviews for MRS I and took part in the analysis.

Time of fieldwork. October and November 1984.

Respondents. A quota sample of 71 adult inhabitants of the Ruhr area, excluding students. The sample plan had a 2 × 3 format, that is gender by age group (18–35y., 36–55y., 56y. plus). Roughly equal numbers of respondents (11–13) were indeed obtained for each of these six cells.

Task of respondents. Responding orally to the following question posed by the interviewer: (1) 'How do you understand the concept of "responsibility"? What does it mean to say that a person is "responsible"?' Two supplementary questions were available to the interviewer for optional probing: (1.1) 'Is there something else that is required for one to be able to say that a person is responsible?'; and (1.2) 'Are there any other cases or situations in which one would say that a person is responsible?'[30]

Analysis. The answers of the respondents, written down by the interviewers, were coded according to a category system that was partly preconceived and partly guided by the data, but with the information on the respondents' gender deleted. Further details will be explained in connection with the results.

MRS II

Project. A study conducted by Anne Heynen as co-worker in our social psychology unit.

Time of fieldwork. Summer semester 1985.

Respondents. Male ($N=43$) and female ($N=40$) adults (19–36y.), all with an educational status of at least *Gymnasium* level, most of them psychology students.

Task of respondents. Reading and responding in writing to three questions. The second question existed in two versions, equally distributed among the questionnaires, and thus among the respondents, on a random basis. The questions read as follows:[31]

1   What does 'responsibility' mean to you?
2.1   What does it mean if a person is 'responsible for something'?
or, stressing the causal aspect of responsibility:
2.2   What does it mean if a person 'is responsible for something that has happened'?
3   Please write down five concepts that come to mind in connection with 'responsibility'.

Five lines, numbered 1 to 5, were provided for the answers to the third question.

Analysis. The answers to the first and the second question were coded according to the category system developed in connection with MRS I. The answers to the third question were grouped under superordinate headings that were partly derived from the category system for the preceding questions. Further details will again be given in connection with the results.

4 Category systems and codings

In the first section of this chapter I shall discuss the reasons for developing category systems to be applied to the statements of actors and opponents, some basic problems encountered in this endeavour, and strategies chosen to cope with these problems. Two further sections will present and explain the structures of two category systems, one for the reactions of actors during account phases and the other for the reactions of opponents during phases of reproach and evaluation. For the sake of brevity I shall henceforth label these two category systems Actor Taxonomy and Opponent Taxonomy. The taxonomies with all their categories are listed in appendices A and B.

4.1 Reasons, problems and strategies of category constructions

Quite early, during my first exploratory moves into the problems of account episodes, it became clear to me that it would not do to rely solely on preconceived scales for measuring attributions of responsibility, guilt, liability or any other sanctions during phases of reproach or evaluation by an opponent, nor on scales for measuring degrees of admission or denial of responsibility and/or liability by the actor. Although such scales are very useful, almost indispensable in large-scale studies with complex designs and a limited time available for interviewing the respondents, a measurement strategy which relies exclusively on pre-structured scales suffers in our domain of discourse from two serious limitations. (1) It does not encompass the richness of the reactions that may be encountered in both actors and opponents. Statements about responsibility, guilt or liability are often qualified on several dimensions. (2) In role-imagination tasks, instructions which limit the reaction potential to the marking of scales may detract from the vividness of the situation one wants to engender through a realistic vignette and the plea to empathize with the actor or the opponent. I suspect that this may have a dampening and levelling effect on the respondents' reactions.

To avoid these limitations, one should encourage the respondents, at least in some studies within one's research programme, to offer their immediate reactions verbatim. Obviously, the content analyses that are subsequently necessary will require much work, both in constructing a set of appropriate categories beforehand and in applying them during the coding stage. Furthermore, with this strategy one will encounter at least two basic difficulties which have to be resolved one way or another.

These difficulties may be stated in the form of two related dilemmas. (1) The set of categories to be formulated and assembled for each taxonomy should be comprehensive and universally applicable within each domain – the account episode reactions of either actors or opponents. Otherwise the taxonomy could not fulfil its exploratory mission very well. On the other hand, the categories, or at least a major proportion of them, should be sufficiently specific to match the theoretical guidelines that already exist. (2) The categories should also be sufficiently specific in a second sense. They should enable the coder who employs the taxonomy to go beyond a crude classification of each relevant statement and to represent its important individual features and their complexity. On the other hand, such efforts must not degenerate into mere descriptions of single cases. In order to avoid such idiographic extremes and provide a crucial condition for a nomothetic success potential the categories must be sufficiently broad to cover subsumable and hence countable instances. A second look reveals that the two dilemmas are close to forming a quadrilemma, because the specificity demand of the second dilemma also collides with the comprehensiveness demand of the first dilemma, and the theoretical specificity demand of this dilemma may only poorly be served by the countability demand of the other dilemma. In trying to achieve a viable compromise among these four conflicting demands I decided upon the following principles to guide the development of each taxonomy and its application.

Deductive and inductive category formation

A taxonomy of some scope and complexity cannot be conceived at a stroke. After an initial set of categories of whatever origin has been collected, one would be well advised to run this set through several cycles of testing it with new material, adding categories that had been lacking, or revising, and possibly regrouping, existing categories, and to tap as many sources as possible in this recurrent process.

Specifically with our taxonomies we shuttled back and forth between (1) the escalation theory with its major concepts as sources that would deliver 'top down' categories, as it were, or frames from which categories could be deduced, and (2) several fairly sizable pilot studies with various vignettes of failure events and role-playing instructions to 'actors' and 'opponents' which furnished a wide range of statements pertinent to the three account episode phases subsequent to the failure event. From this rich raw material many categories could be induced, 'bottom up' so to speak, which preserved the specificities of particular situations, yet also gained an encouraging degree of generality, and together, as a set, seemed to cover a near exhaustive scope of relevant statements to be expected in account, reproach or evaluation phases. Top-down intentions and bottom-up suggestions were, of course, not pursued independently of each other. In many instances they could be amalgamated to form categories which promised to preserve theoretical relevance within the semantics of mundane realism.

Analytic versus synthetic categorization

In constructing a category system one always has to aim for some balance between synthetic comprehensiveness and analytic particularity of the category domains. Synthetic comprehensiveness means that all relevant aspects of a given statement are covered by one specific category. A case in point would be an excusatory category 'Claim of impairment of volition due to provocation by the victim'. This category comprises four aspects: (1) the effect of the event impinging upon the speaker (impairment rather than facilitation), (2) the target of the event (volition rather than mental or physical capacity), (3) the nature of the event (provocation rather than threat or physical force), and (4) the source of the event (the victim of the failure event rather than some other agent).

A move in the direction of analytic particularity could, for instance, be the separation of two sets of categories, one set devoted exclusively to the nature of the event claimed by the actor as part of his or her excuse (e.g. participation, provocation, coercion, etc. by some agent), and a second set devoted exclusively to the type of agent claimed to be responsible for the excusatory event. Any specific constellation of event X and agent Y could then be represented by selecting and coding two categories, that is the appropriate one from each set. Carried to its extreme a strategy of analytic categorization would employ nothing but categories strictly limited to one aspect of any complex statement, and would rely on multiple codings for representing the complexity of the statement.

Neither extreme is feasible. To push for synthetic comprehensiveness all the way would be self-defeating for three reasons. (1) It would be impossible to foresee all potential data constellations to such a degree that adequately accommodating categories could be constructed in advance. Constant additions and revisions would be necessary, fatally hampering the coding process. (2) The number of categories required would be too large for any halfway efficient handling during the coding stage and the subsequent analyses. (3) Such a large category system could hardly retain any explanatory power. Each single category would necessarily be so specific as to apply only to very few cases, if not just to one instance. Thus the researcher's explanatory intent would amount to no more than a host of summarizing descriptions at best. The other extreme of pure analytic particularity is also not a desirable goal because, with the requirement of extensive category combinations, both coding task and subsequent analyses would become unbearably cumbersome, if possible at all.

So neither extreme is attainable or desirable; but there is considerable leeway in both directions, and one has to choose. Guided by the rule of thumb that it is easier to lump together than to prise apart, I tried in the construction of the taxonomies to find a point of optimal balance with a slight preponderance of analytic over synthetic features. This choice can be substantiated by the following arguments, partly gained from our work experiences with the taxonomies. In many cases the theoretical interest focuses on just one dimension, for instance explicit versus implicit admission of responsibility, or no admission of responsibility for a failure event in any circumstances. Clearly, in such cases a quasi unidimensional set of categories, for example categories representing various levels of admission of responsibility or guilt, is most appropriate and much more economical than the accumulation procedure one would have to perform with synthetic categories, each of which would have to incorporate a number of different aspects in addition to referring to one and the same level of responsibility admission. The same advantage of analytically oriented category sets does, of course, also hold in those other frequent cases in which theoretical interest has to be limited to just one dimension of the relevant statements because the frequency of these statements is not high enough to permit further subdivisions *and* subsequent meaningful and testable comparisons. Finally, if the popularity of a certain complex statement is sufficiently high to allow its multidimensional aspects to be taken into consideration during the analysis, then the combination of the appropriate quasi unidimensional categories assigned to such statements in the coding phase can be efficiently performed by a computer.

Clusters and hierarchies
The reader will notice in the following sections (4.2 and 4.3) that – discounting peripheral exceptions – each of our two taxonomies consists of a triple-layered hierarchy of categories. There is a basic level of categories which, as a rule, are used for the primary coding of the statements furnished by the respondents. These categories are grouped according to various similarities; each such similarity is represented by a superordinate category at the next higher level, and these superordinate categories in turn are grouped and subsumed under cardinal categories at the highest level.

Such hierarchical structures of category clusters serve a number of useful functions.

1 They ease the tension between synthetic and analytic intentions,

because a set of basic categories together with its superordinate category allows for variations in both directions. To move from the superordinate to the basic layer is a step towards synthetic comprehensiveness. To move from the specificities of the basic categories to their superordinate category, which preserves their similarity yet necessarily neglects their specificities, is a step in the analytic direction.

2 If certain types of statement turn out to occur infrequently during a first informal survey of the data, or if the sample of respondents is small in the first place, one may have to dispense with the analysis of multi-aspect constellations and will then be thankful for the routes of retreat to the superordinate level provided by the taxonomy. Such a retreat may be realized in two ways. One may either have the computer constitute the categories of the superordinate (or the cardinal) level by appropriate combinations of the basic categories, or one may decide right at the beginning to restrict the primary coding to categories of the superordinate level.

3 Both taxonomies are sizable and complex. We have found that the hierarchical structure of category clusters has been of great help both for the newcomer, who has to get acquainted with one of the taxonomies, as well as for the old hand, who has to apply it as coder.

4 Last but not least, the hierarchical structures of the taxonomies are quite useful as heuristic matrices. They encourage and facilitate the division of basic categories into subordinate categories without interfering with other parts of the taxonomy when such subdivisions are justified by theoretical reasoning and actual or potential data density. The taxonomy structures also stimulate the formation of new superordinate categories by selecting and combining some basic categories across the existing clusters. Finally, new theoretical vistas may require entirely new categories. The taxonomies serving as heuristic matrices are likely to be helpful in pinpointing and filling such lacunae.

Primary and secondary codings

The term 'primary coding' refers to the direct matching of the respondents' statements with categories of the appropriate taxonomy, regardless of the level, basic or superordinate, from which the categories are selected. By 'secondary coding' I mean (1) processes by which, in addition to primary codings, categorized statements are assigned to further categories, but also (2) processes by which, independently from primary codings and often beforehand, categories of the taxonomy are coded according to some supplementary criteria. Five types of secondary coding may be distinguished:

1   *Superordinate codings of categorized utterances.* This type of secondary coding has already been mentioned in the preceding subsection on

clusters and hierarchies. Statements or statement parts categorized during primary coding may either be assembled under the superordinate heading of the cluster to which the assigned categories belong, or they may be assembled across different clusters and recorded under a new superordinate category which marks a secondary similarity of categories not represented by one of the basic clusters of the taxonomy.

2   *Résumé codings of categorized statements.* Taking into consideration all primary categories coded with respect to the complete statement of a respondent, one may wish to evaluate this statement in a comprehensive way and code it accordingly. For instance, our Opponent Taxonomy provides a set of secondary categories which may be used to indicate if an opponent's reproach phase reaction is uniformly negative in judging the actor and his account episode behaviour, or ambivalent, or moving from a harsh verdict at the beginning towards a more moderate view, etc.

3   *Dimensional codings of primary categories.* This type of secondary coding merits special attention in discussing principles of category constructions. The dilemma between the demand for comprehensiveness and universal applicability of our taxonomies, on the one hand, and the demand for their theoretical relevance, on the other, may be mitigated by a theoretically guided secondary coding superimposed upon some or all of the primary categories. For instance, all primary categories of our Opponent Taxonomy received two superimposed codings according to an evaluation as to whether the average (partial) statement falling into a given category could be considered supportive, destructive, ambivalent or neutral for (1) the actor's sense of having control and (2) his or her self-esteem. These evaluations were based in part on pretest experience, but they were made before the primary codings of our main studies. Similar superimposed codings with respect to self-addressed reassuring messages on control potential and self-worth were also performed on relevant categories of the Actor Taxonomy. Further details will be given later (see p. 90).

4   *Transfer codings for computer storage.* Obviously, any study which uses a computer for the data analysis requires the categories used with the statement material from the study to be relabelled in order to fit these categories into the computer memory.

5   *Matching taxonomies.* Comparisons of results across studies by different authors who have used partially similar category systems require a careful matching, and hence secondary coding, of the categories from the two systems.

Coding unit, interpretive context and coder reliability

The term 'coding unit' refers to any part of an actor's or an opponent's statement which contains enough information to be assignable to one or more categories of the relevant taxonomy. Sometimes a speaker reiterates a certain point several times, or returns to it after he or she has said something else in between. For such cases one has two options, occurrence coding and frequency coding. 'Occurrence coding' refers to that procedure which assigns a relevant category to a complete statement just once, regardless of the number of reiterations of the point covered by the category. With 'frequency coding' a category is marked just as often as a pertinent point is made and repeated in the complete statement. Within the scope of our studies, with repetitious statements being relatively rare, we have found that frequency codings did not noticeably add to the insights gained by occurrence coding, our standard procedure. However, this should not be understood as a prescription. There may be research problems where the repetition of an argument is a crucially important criterion.

For coding of an account episode statement to be successfully performed requires, among other things, a range of knowledge and a set of presuppositions tacitly shared by the coder and the actor or opponent who made the statement. Everything the coder knows about the speaker and the failure event, including the situation in which it occurred, and also about the prevalent norms for judging failures of this kind may be helpful, if not essential, for selecting the appropriate categories in coding the account. One may use the term 'interpretive context' in a broad sense to denote this wide range of knowledge on the part of a coder. Here I shall use the term 'interpretive context' in a narrower sense, referring to a subset of the coder's relevant knowledge, namely his or her information about all the actor or opponent said or did during the account episode.

Reliance on such a minimal interpretive context in choosing the appropriate category for a coding unit is often indispensable. As making a reproach or rendering an account after a failure event is usually at least mildly (if not painfully) embarrassing for both opponent and actor, he or she may be inclined to speak in hints and adumbrations rather than be very explicit. The context of a specific unclear utterance may then help to disambiguate its implicit meaning.

There are, of course, unmistakably explicit statements. Take, for instance, the sentence: 'I am sorry to have caused so much trouble for you!' This sentence is self-explanatory with respect to its inclusion in category c 133 of the Actor Taxonomy (see appendix A) and does not require any wider interpretive frame for its proper assignment. There are also cases in which reliance on an interpretive context is undesirable. For instance, it is

A taxonomy for reactions of actors

important to distinguish between explicit accusations and attributions of guilt or responsibility for a failure event, on the one hand, and an implicit opinion about the actor's guilt or responsibility which may clearly be inferred from an opponent's total statement even though he does not directly voice this opinion, on the other. For the sake of such a distinction the categories F 551 and F 552 of the Opponent Taxonomy (see appendix B) are marked, and bound in their application, by an explicitness rule. That is, these categories must not be coded unless the opponent has explicitly attributed *partial* (F 551), or *full or preponderant* (F 552), guilt or responsibility for the occurrence of the failure event to the actor. Several other categories are also bound by such an explicitness rule.

All these explicit cases notwithstanding, the interpretive context has to play a central role in the coding procedure. This fact does, of course, open the way for subjective coder perspectives, and hence discordance among coders. It has been encouraging to see that despite this hazard, and despite the size and complexity of the two taxonomies, they are quite manageable and can, after some training, be applied with satisfactory degrees of reliability. Concordance levels between .70 and .85, according to Holsti's (in North et al. 1963, p. 49) formula, were easily achieved by pairs of student coders after about a semester-long participation in a research seminar devoted to one or the other taxonomy.

In coding the data from our main studies we have observed the following procedure. Each statement offered by an actor or an opponent was coded by two coders working independently of each other. After completing their individual assignments they compared their codings and tried to resolve discrepancies by discussion. Cases of remaining disagreement were referred to a supervising coder, who also checked a sample of codings on which the coder pair had agreed. I am confident that with this procedure we have been able to keep coding errors within tolerable limits.

4.2 A taxonomy for reactions of actors during account phases

Development and acknowledgements

The Actor Taxonomy came first. The initial version was developed in the late 1970s, partly guided by the accounts given by some 120 student respondents in two pilot studies, with vignettes of various failure events and the instruction to role-play the actor in each situation as stimulus material. This first version of the Actor Taxonomy appeared in the *European Journal of Social Psychology* (Schönbach 1980).

A second, thoroughly revised and extended version emerged from an intensive analysis of the accounts collected in APS I. This second version was presented in a mimeographed report (Schönbach 1985; see also Schönbach and Kleibaumhüter 1989). The taxonomy listed in appendix A is identical with the 1985 version, except for some editing and a few minor additions.

The first general-purpose taxonomy for accounts was published by Scott and Lyman (1968). Their work provided the basis, as well as a major impetus, for my own initial taxonomy. The revision also benefited from relevant discussions in the literature. I want to mention especially Kelley's (e.g. 1979) and his co-workers' studies, the extensive comparisons and comments by Semin and Manstead (1983), including the taxonomy proposed by Tedeschi and Reiss (1981), the studies done and reported by Jaspars, Fincham and Hewstone (e.g. 1983) and their colleagues on the attribution of responsibility, the book *Excuses* by Snyder, Higgins and Stucky (1983), Schlenker's monograph on impression management (1980), as well as the chapter by Jones and Pittman (1982) on that topic, and, last but not least, the encouragement and enlightenment received from the article on the management of failure events by McLaughlin, Cody and O'Hair (1983).

Aspects and themes

Scott and Lyman (1968) subsumed their categories under two superordinate headings – excuses and justifications. They defined 'excuses' as accounts which admit that a norm has been violated by the act in question, but deny the full responsibility of the actor. In contrast, 'justifications' in their view accept the causal responsibility of the actor, but assert that the act in question was legitimate or at least permissible under the prevailing circumstances.

This distinction between an excusing and a justifying type of account has remained very influential and at the centre of discussion (e.g. Tedeschi and Reiss 1981; and Semin and Manstead 1983), even though other forms of reconciliatory responses on the part of the actor, such as anticipatory disclaimers (Hewitt and Stokes 1975) or apologies after the fact (e.g. Goffman 1971), were noticed and discussed by the authors just mentioned and others (e.g. Schlenker 1980; and Synder, Higgins and Stucky 1983). I also consider the basic distinction between excuses and justifications to be very important. However, influenced by my own informal experiences with accounts and by the data from our pilot studies conducted in 1978, I have felt the need to extend and modify the category system proposed by Scott and Lyman (1968), mainly in two respects (Schönbach 1980).

The data thus gathered clearly suggested (1) that on an equal footing with excuses and justifications two further superordinate categories with various basic categories, namely concessions and refusals, should be included in a taxonomy for responses offered during an account phase; and (2) that the other main inference from informal experience and exploratory data was that several account themes cannot neatly be subsumed under just one superordinate heading. For instance, 'appeal to loyalty', presented by Scott and Lyman

Table 1. Aspects and themes of the taxonomy

	Cardinal aspects			
	Concessions	Excuses	Justifications	Refusals
Intracardinal themes				
Peripheral concessions	C 111–13			
Admission of guilt, shame, responsibility	C 121–4			
Expressions of regret	C 131–4			
Impairment of capacity or volition due to ...				
... unspecified source		E 110		
... physiological factors		E 120–40		
... mental or affective factors		E 150–80		
Denial of failure event or own involvement in it				R 111–17
Unrestricted attribution of responsibility to other agents				R 121–3
Evasions and mystifications				R 131–9
Cross-cardinal themes				
Situational constraints		E 210	J 210	R 210
Appeal to loyalties		E 220–40	J 220–40	R 220–40
Influence of powerful agents		E 310	J 310	R 310
Provocations by various agents		E 411–13	J 411–13	R 411–13
Participation of various agents in the failure event		E 421–3	J 421–3	R 421–3
Limitations, negative traits, misdeeds of various agents		E 431–3	J 431–3	R 431–3
Actor's self, past and present		E 511–13	J 511–14	R 511–14
Actor's role concerning the failure event	C 524	E 521–5	J 521–4	R 521–4
Characteristics of the failure event		E 611–14	J 611–14	R 611–14
Apology and pardon	C 710	E 710–11		

(1968) as a justification category, can also be used with a primarily excusatory intent, or else sometimes even as an argument for refusing any further account.

During the revision of the initial taxonomy of 1980 I retained the major divisions into concessions, excuses, justifications and refusals. Henceforth I shall call these four superordinate categories of the highest level 'cardinal categories', or alternatively 'cardinal aspects', and reserve the term 'superordinate category' for intermediate levels of abstraction. The cross-cardinal relevance of many themes had to receive much more prominence during the systematizing revision of the taxonomy than it had already been given in the preliminary version of 1980.

Table 1 presents a matrix of the cardinal aspects and themes of the revised taxonomy. This matrix is supposed to fulfil two functions. (1) As a summary table it should aid the reader in finding his or her way through all the basic and superordinate categories listed in appendix A. The code numbers in the matrix cells refer to the categories in the list. (2) The matrix form should show at a glance if a given theme or theme class is of cross-cardinal relevance, and hence has to be incorporated into categories under more than one cardinal aspect, or if it can be considered as an intracardinal theme or theme class that is confined to just one of the four cardinal aspects.

Four cardinal categories or aspects

There may be cases in which a coarse distribution of accounts and account alternatives into concessions, excuses, justifications and refusals is sufficient or even the exclusive goal of the analysis. In such cases it seems appropriate to speak of four 'cardinal categories'. If, on the other hand, the raw data are sufficiently rich and complex to match a research ambition looking for exclusive versus mixed, dominant or auxiliary account phase strategies of a concessive, excusatory, justificative or refuting character, then it seems more appropriate to refer to 'cardinal aspects' in order to denote the functions of those four modes of responding.

Concessions. A concession is an admission of a violation of some normative expectations held by others, particularly the opponent in the account episode, and at the same time an explicit or implicit admission of the actor's full or partial causal responsibility for the failure event. Obviously, there is much overlap between concessions thus understood and apologies as treated by other authors (see above). But there are borderline cases subsumed under the heading 'concessions' which may not normally be considered as apologies. The acknowledgement of negative aspects of the failure event by the actor without any reference to his or her own involvement (c 111) is a case in point. Another example is the expression of regret concerning the failure event without any further specification (c 131). On the other hand, an expression of regret concerning the actor's *own role* in the failure event (c 132) is a clear example of a concession or apology in a strict sense, and so is a full admission of responsibility or guilt (c 122).

Excuses. The term 'excuse' has been used with widely differing meanings by various social psychologists. Snyder, Higgins and Stucky

(1983, p. 4) employ the most comprehensive definition: 'Excuses are explanations or actions that lessen the negative implications of an actor's performance, thereby maintaining a positive image for oneself and others' (italics omitted). Snyder et al. explicitly subsume under this definition denials, alibi statements, blaming, justifications and derogations, as well as partial concessions combined with pleas for mitigated judgements on the basis of arguments of the type 'I couldn't help it', 'I didn't mean to', or 'It wasn't really me' (ibid., p. 7). At the other extreme, the most restricted usage of the term 'excuse' refers to admissions of a failure event accompanied by denials or minimizations of responsibility for the offence, and very often also by some supportive claim of impairment of the actor's capacity of volition, or both. In accord with Austin (1961) and Scott and Lyman (1968), Semin and Manstead (1983, p. 80) summarize this most restricted conceptualization in the following succinct definition: 'Excuses deny some or any measure of responsibility for what is admittedly an offensive act. Justifications deny some or any measure of offensiveness in an act for which the individual admits responsibility.'

Originally, following Scott and Lyman (1968), I also adhered to such a restricted concept of excuses. However, in the course of revising and extending the account taxonomy, I came to prefer a definition of excuses which covers an intermediate range between the two extreme positions just described. I now call an excuse any account which admits the occurrence of a failure event and some involvement of the actor in it, but pleads for mitigation in judgement on the basis of various arguments including, but not limited to, claims of impairment and hence reduced causal responsibility.

Impairment claims, to be sure, play a major role among all excuses. The categories E 110 to E 413 illustrate this. Furthermore, impairment and diminished responsibility claims are sometimes, but not always, expressed or implied also in accounts that refer to the participation of other agents in the failure event (E 421–3), or to characteristics of others or of oneself (E 431–524). However, there are other accounts in which a mitigation plea is clearly expressed or implied, but where it does not draw upon a claim of diminished responsibility because of some impairment of volition and/or capacity. Good examples are the account strategies 'Minimization of the failure aspects of the event' (E 611). 'Denial or minimization of damage' (E 612, E 613), or 'Appeal to positive consequences or side effects of the failure event' (E 614), if used in the service of a mitigation plea. Other relevant cases are the references to the actor's self and the actor's role within the range of categories E 511 to E 513 and E 521 to E 524, for example an 'Appeal to own good record in the past, apart from the failure event, implying a plea for mitigation in judgement' (E 512) or an 'Appeal to effort and care in connection with the failure event', offered in the context of a mitigation plea (E 523). I subsumed all these categories under the cardinal heading

'Excuses', and thereby extended the scope of the excuse concept, because of their basic similarity with respect to the mitigation plea component. To place them anywhere else would have appeared rather awkward.

Justifications. The definition of this cardinal category need not be changed. In agreement with Scott and Lyman (1968) and others (see above) I still consider a justification as an account strategy by which the actor accepts causal responsibility for the event in question, but asserts that it was legitimate or at least permissible under the given circumstances. This definition is quite useful and often helps to distinguish between different types of account. Sometimes, however, it does not become clear if the actor intends a certain comment to be a justification or an excuse, or even a refutation. This point will be taken up again shortly.

Refusals. One may distinguish two kinds of refusal. (1) There are outright denials to give an account in the strict sense, that is an excuse or a justification. This type of refusal comprises, for instance, assertions that the alleged failure event had not happened at all (R 111), or clear denials of any personal involvement in the failure event (R 112) and/or attributions of full responsibility to other persons (R 121-3), as well as various sorts of evasion or mystification, such as sheer silence (R 134) or irrelevant talk (R 133). (2) Another type of refusal consists of explanatory statements, sometimes indistinguishable from an account, which are offered in support of refutations of any right to question or reproach the actor or as an explanation of a denial of any further comment or account. This second type of refusal ranges across all the categories from R 210 to R 614; they have their parallels in the columns Excuses and Justifications in table 1.

In many failure situations and subsequent account episodes refusals of the second type may not be very common; hence much coarser categories may have to be formed in combination for analytic purposes. Nevertheless, I decided to detail and list the categories from R 210 to R 614 in full correspondence to the excuse and justification categories with equivalent themes, and I did so for two reasons. First of all, it is always easier to lump together than to divide up and, more importantly, for our basic aim of discovering and investigating factors which predictably influence the fate of account episodes, whether accomplishment or foundering, accounts or account-like comments with refutational overtones are probably highly relevant. It stands to reason that any response falling into one of the categories from R 210 to R 614 will seriously enhance the chances of the account episode foundering.

Intracardinal and cross-cardinal themes

There are accounts with a core content or theme which can represent only one cardinal aspect and are therefore called intracardinal themes. For instance, an actor's admission of full causal responsibility for an offence without any hedging is a case of concession and cannot be anything else; it should always be coded as an instance of category c 122. On the other hand, there are also themes which can be invoked in the service of more than one cardinal aspect; these are labelled cross-cardinal themes.

Each category code consists of a letter to denote the cardinal aspect and a three-digit number. Three digits provide sufficient degrees of freedom for further subdivisions of this or that category when the need for such differentiation should arise, and they also allow for a convenient distinction between the intracardinal and cross-cardinal themes embodied in the categories. All intracardinal themes are marked by a 1 in the first digit of the code number, all cross-cardinal themes by a figure greater than 1 as first digit.

Now for some intracardinal and cross-cardinal examples. A clear case of a purely excusatory theme is the claim of impairment due to alcohol consumption (E 130). The bald denial of an opponent's right to question or reproach the actor (R 113) is an intracardinal refusal theme and nothing else. On the other hand, a rueful reference to a compensation already offered or delivered can either be a concession or an excuse. Here are two illustrations:

> 'Yes you are right! I have realized that myself in the meantime, and when I got the message that it was really *my* fault, and not the other driver's, I phoned him up right away and asked him to send me the bill.'
> (A case of category C 524)

> 'I am sorry that I bumped into your car. I know, it shouldn't have happened, but Betty kept talking about her mother's cancer, and so my mind was not on the road; and I'll certainly pay for it, so I hope you won't bear me any grudge.'
> (Among other things a case of category E 524)

Furthermore, a very similar reference to an already delivered compensation, made in a defiant mood and context, can either be a justification, or a refusal, or both. Here are two more examples:

> 'Everybody was paid the exact amount of money fixed for the expropriated land. We adhered strictly to the law!'
> (A case of category J 524)

> 'I paid for it, didn't I. So what else do you want? I am fed up with this!'
> (A case of category R 524)

The distinction between intracardinal and cross-cardinal themes cannot be separated from a decision about the boundary of the concept of 'theme'. Borrowing the linguistic terms 'topic' and 'comment' (e.g. Hockett 1958), we may say that in the propositions 'compensation offered' and 'compensation denied' the component 'compensation' is the topic, and 'offered' and 'denied' are both comments. To equate themes with topics would not be very informative for our purpose.[32] For example, 'compensation' would certainly be a cross-cardinal theme. But the heuristic value of such a theme, thus broadly defined, would be greatly diminished by the fact that it comprises heterogeneous and even contradictory propositions. For that reason I decided to use the concept 'theme' in the more specific sense of 'topic-and-comment'. According to this definition, 'compensation offered' is still a cross-cardinal theme, but a much more interesting and fruitful one that can carry excusatory as well as justificative and/or refutational intentions (see E 524, J 524 and R 524). 'Compensation denied', on the other hand, is a purely intracardinal theme and category (R 115).

Only two cardinal categories, excuses and refusals, include a substantial number of both intracardinal and cross-cardinal themes. Most concessive themes are limited to just this aspect, that is of concession; and two exceptions, categories C 524 and C 710, are borderline cases. One could forcefully argue, although I would not go quite so far, that the announcement of restitutions or compensations in acknowledgement of one's own responsibility or guilt (C 524) and the formal offer of an apology or a request for pardon or mercy, addressed to the victim or other related persons in acknowledgement of one's own causal responsibility for the failure event (C 710), always (or almost always) imply a plea for mitigation in judgement and thus really belong to the excuse categories.

At first glance it may come as a surprise that in contrast to the intracardinal character of most, if not all, concessions the taxonomy does not contain any exclusively justificative themes. Second thoughts, however, support this result of the construction and ordering of all the categories. Any justification which seems convincing to the actor may carry the seed of impatience, which is bound to say 'enough' to further queries or remonstrations. On the other hand, the distinction between justifications and excuses is less clear than the defining formula 'responsibility accepted but offence denied versus offence admitted but responsibility diminished' would make us believe. There are several reasons that often make it difficult in practice to decide whether a given account is an excuse or a justification, and these reasons may also help to explain why each justificative category has its excusatory counterpart.

1 First of all, there are cases where, for lack of information, it is not clear which cardinal aspect is implied. For instance, a car driver's account may consist of nothing but the words 'I have paid the bill', after he had been held responsible for damage to another driver's car.

2 More importantly, there are fundamental similarities between excuses

and justifications. There cannot be any justificative account unless a norm and hence also some affirming consensus exists which furnishes the legitimation that is necessary to make the account recognizable as a justification, quite apart from the judgement of its acceptability. Yet essentially the same preconditions also exist in the case of an excusatory account. An excuse can be recognized and treated as such only if some norm and corresponding consensus exists according to which the mitigation or even the complete suspension of a punitive judgement might be legitimized (or 'justified' for that matter). This common trait of warrantability in both excuses and justifications may be at the core of various uncertainties as to their distinction.

3 Furthermore, there are cases of true mixtures of cardinal aspects. Quite often some, but not all, features of an act can be warranted as clearly legitimate. Other features, however, may at best be excused on the basis of an impairment claim or some other excusatory account. A good example is the excessive intensity of an act of self-defence which, according to some opinions (see below), cannot be justified but may be excused because of an impairment of volition due to extreme affective arousal. Such cases of multiple accountability do not only present difficulties for concrete attempts at distinguishing between justifiability and excusability, but contribute more generally to uncertainties and confusion as to what is an excuse and what is a justification.

4 Finally, the consensus concerning norms for acceptable justifications versus excuses is not stable; it varies over time, and at any given time also across different groups of norm-senders (e.g. Anon. 1977). Opinions vary as to what is indubitably legitimate, or even required, and what is only permissible or just barely tolerable, and opinions also differ as to where on that continuum of degrees of acceptability (if at all!) the dividing line between justifiability and excusability should be drawn (see below). This state of affairs also adds to the uncertainty of actors and opponents in many specific cases with respect to the nature as well as to the adequacy of the available account strategies. It may even be that sometimes, in the face of such ambivalence, an actor, after learning about the opponent's reaction to the initial account, deliberately avoids making it clear whether he or she intends an excuse or a justification in order to leave room for negotiations in *both* directions during the further course of the account episode.[33]

It has been encouraging for my views on the cross-cardinal relevance of many themes (and the contingent ambivalence of many accounts) to notice a recent controversial discussion among legal experts concerning the concepts of justification and excuse and their legal implications. Fletcher (1978) proposed a strictly limited concept of justification. According to his view, as presented by Dressler (1984, pp. 63–4):

justification implies morally right, good, or proper conduct. Conduct which is 'permissible' or 'tolerable' is not 'justified'. There is no intermediate concept. Second, Fletcher says that '[it] is in the nature of justification . . . that if two people are locked in a[n incompatible] conflict, only one person can be justified'. Third, he claims that justification implies objectively right conduct. A putative justification – when an actor believes reasonably, but inaccurately, that justifying conditions exist – is not a justification, but is, at most, merely an excuse. Fourth, he believes that justifications are 'universalized'. If true, this would mean that the rights of third parties are derived inextricably from the rights of the primary party. (Note references omitted.)

In an incisive analysis, invoking various types of argument and presenting many intriguing examples, Dressler (1984) criticized this view. In the opening part of his paper (p. 64) he announced the conclusions from his analysis in the following way:

I shall argue that each claim is partly mistaken. First, there are important moral gradations that cannot be captured without intermediate categories. Fletcher's theoretical structure is too narrow, and his vocabulary is too limited. He posits a mode of analysis suited to a world of black and white ethical situations rarely present in the world in which we live. Second, it is sometimes possible, to speak coherently of incompatible justifications. Third, justifications need not always involve objectively right conduct. Sometimes mistaken conduct can be justified, not merely excused. Fourth, justifications need not always be universalized. Sometimes a third party should be justified in doing an act which the primary actor may not do, or vice versa. (Note references omitted.)

Greenawalt (1984), also critical of Fletcher's position and presenting many arguments similar to Dressler's, pursued a somewhat different goal. Firmly believing 'that the basic distinctions between justifications and excuses are important in the law' (p. 1898), Greenawalt emphasized borderline problems. He stated as the central theme of his article (p. 1898)

that Anglo-American criminal law should not attempt to distinguish between justification and excuse in a fully systematic way. I explore three possible bases for drawing the distinction: (1) a distinction between warranted and wrongful conduct; (2) a division between general and individual claims; and (3) a distinction based on the rights of others. I show why none of these bases yields a clear and simple criterion for categorization. The difficulty rests largely on the conceptual fuzziness of the terms 'justification' and 'excuse' in ordinary usage and on the uneasy quality of many of the moral judgements that underlie decisions that behavior should not be treated as criminal. Beyond these conceptual difficulties, there are features of the criminal process, notably the general verdict rendered by lay jurors in criminal trials, that would impede implementation in individual cases of any system that distinguishes fully between justification and excuse.

Clearly, both authors, Dressler and Greenawalt, although partly focusing on different aspects of the problem, argue strongly (and convincingly, I believe) against the view that all accounts can easily be assigned either to a justification or an excuse category.

I should perhaps emphasize that all this is not meant to imply that we should abolish distinctions between excuse and justification. On the contrary, in full agreement with Dressler and Greenawalt, as well as Fletcher, I would say that there are many reasons for observing and marking the distinction between excuses and justifications wherever this is feasible. For instance, from a theory of control needs and Lerner's (e.g. 1980) notions concerning the 'belief in a just world', one may develop the hypothesis that people in general, but in particular those with high social anxiety and corresponding subjective impressions of lack of control, are likely to respond more favourably to a plausible justification account than to an excuse, if put into the opponent's role, *provided* that this account does not violate the opponent's control needs any further, beyond the damage done by the failure event. The reasoning behind this hypothesis is that an acceptable justification is much better suited than is an acceptable excuse to restoring a shaken belief in a just world, including subjective feelings of having at least some sort of control. However, the hypothesis also implies the corollary that some slight changes in a justificative strategy are likely to incur quicker and more radical shifts in judgement towards a negative evaluation than similarly slight changes in an excusatory account would instigate. Coding suggestions for the treatment of accounts with singular, multiple or uncertain cardinal relevance are offered by Schönbach (1985, pp. 44–6).

Combinations and differentiations

Any user of the taxonomy should note that beyond (and sometimes crosscutting) the listed superordinate categories other higher-order groupings of basic categories can be formed and labelled either beforehand for coding purposes, or after the coding stage – preferably by a computer if the data base is large. For instance, one such grouping – to be labelled 'Negative comments on other persons involved in the failure event' – could consist of the themes 310, 410, 420 and 430 with or without a cardinal marking. Another new superordinate category might be formed and called 'Points in favour of the actor' by unifying the themes 511 to 514, 521 to 524, and possibly also 611 to 614.

All basic categories can be subsumed under one or more superordinate heading. At the same time many of the basic categories can also clearly be differentiated even further. A potentially important case in point are the impairment claims, E 110 to E 413. In the taxonomy as it stands no distinction has been made between impairments of capacities of the actor and impairments of his or her volition. In many failure situations it is quite clear which of these two aspects – capacities or volition – is meant by the actor's account; so a distinction need not be specified in the coding process. There are other cases and accounts where it is quite unclear whether the actor is referring to the impairment of a capacity, or of his or her volition, or both. Again, a specification of the categories in this respect is not called for. However, there may be cases and research problems where it is crucial to make a distinction between claims of capacity impairments and claims of volition impairments. Take, for instance, category E 310 'Claims of impairment due to powerful agents, e.g. denial of access to information or threat of punishment for disobedience'. This category can easily be subdivided, if need be, into four subcategories, related to impairment of volition (E 311), impairment of capacity (E 312), impairment of both volition and capacity (E 313), and target of impairment unspecified or uncertain (E 314).

Other candidates for subdivision might, for instance, be the evasion categories R 133 'Irrelevant talk' and R 139 'Other evasions and mystifications'. In our studies instances within these categories have been too rare to warrant any further differentiations such as those proposed by Schwitalla (1979).

4.3 A taxonomy for reactions of opponents during phases of reproach and evaluation

Development and acknowledgements

In constructing the Opponent Taxonomy we had no base to start from comparable to Scott and Lyman's category system for the development of the Actor Taxonomy. There were, of course, concepts and categories for specific domains such as Kelley's (1979, p. 19) 'classification of problems reported by heterosexual couples', or the measures for 'Account Adequacy', 'Account Credibility' and 'Moral Worth' (of the actor) proposed by Blumstein et al. (1974, pp. 555–6). But there was no matrix of categories that was both generally applicable and sufficiently detailed to enable analysis of an opponent's verbal reactions during phases of reproach and evaluation. Somewhat later McLaughlin, Cody and O'Hair (1983) and McLaughlin, Cody and Rosenstein (1983) (see also Cody and McLaughlin 1985) offered important contributions to that effect and have provided strong stimulation and encouragement for our own ongoing work on a general-purpose taxonomy for opponent reactions.

Our starting point was the first reproach phase study (RPS I) with the provisional categories conceived and used by the diploma candidates in charge of this study, Gabriele Berten (1981) and Birgitta Holland (1981). They had concentrated on various degrees and modes of guilt attribution. In a research seminar in 1982 we extended and differentiated the range of available categories, still using the RPS I material.[34] With this background I drafted a first version of the present Opponent Taxonomy in the spring of 1987, after having returned in the meantime to problems of reproach phase and evaluation phase reactions, subsequent to a period of concentration on account phase phenomena.

Two research seminars, in the summer of 1987 and the winter of 1987–8, were devoted to further work on the taxonomy, in the course of which the first version underwent three revisions. The latest version is given in appendix B. The taxonomy was tested by applying it to the material obtained in a pilot study with 133 male and female respondents from various age groups and different walks of life. The respondents had to role-play the opponents after two different failure events. Three failure event vignettes altogether were employed in this study: a case of purse snatching, a neglected washing machine which flooded the flat below, and a precious coffee-pot accidentally broken by a reckless dancer.[35]

Transphase applicability

It seemed essential to construct a category system that would cover both the reproach phase and the evaluation phase reactions of opponents. It was evident from the beginning that many categories would be applicable to both phases anyway, since evaluations are often part and parcel of reproaches or occur separately from reproaches prior to the account phase, and reproaches may well be repeated or newly formulated after the actor's account. In addition, and more importantly, hypothesis 3.4 of the escalation network provides a theoretical linkage between the two phases of opponent activity. For a test of its prediction of a positive association between the severity of an opponent's reproach phase reactions and the negativity of his or her final evaluations a common-category matrix seems highly desirable if not indispensable.

As a consequence of this coverage requirement the taxonomy does, of course, also contain categories that are applicable only, or predominantly, to one of the two phases. Obviously, all the categories (A 30–50) for various reactions to an account can be invoked only after an account or some substitute for it has been given by the actor. On the other hand, requests for information about the failure event (A 20), or a refusal to listen to an account (A60), are typical of the reproach phase. Such reactions may also occur during the evaluation phase, but if that happens one may consider it rather as part of a recycling process with a return to the reproach phase.

Table 2. Targets, themes and judgement tendencies of the Opponent Taxonomy

Targets and themes	Judgement tendencies		
	Positive	Ambivalent or neutral	Negative
Accounts			
Relief from obligation to render an account	A 11–17, 19		
Questions about causes, course, consequences of failure event		A 21, 23	A 22, 24
Reactions to an account given or offered:			
Understanding	A 31–7, 39		
Critique			A 41–4, 49
Refutation			A 51–9
Refusal to listen			A 61–7, 69
Other comments on accounts		A 99	
Failure events			
Inability, unwillingness, hesitation to comment on failure event		F 11–15, 19	
Attributions of responsibility/guilt to persons other than the actor	F 21–6		
Comments on actor's conduct during the failure event	F 31–9		F 51–9
Comments on actor's liability for the consequences of the failure event	F 41–6, 49		F 61–6, 69
Other comments concerning the failure event		F 98–9	
Actor's personality			
Comments on capabilities	P 11		P 21
Comments on moral qualities	P 12		P 22
Comments on other characteristics	P 13		P 23
Other comments		P 99	
Relationship between actor and opponent	B 11–13	B 99	B 21–3
Secondary codings of intrastatement trend and differentiation			
Reproach phase comments	SV 11	SV 13–17	SV 12
Evaluation phase comments	SW 11	SV 13–17	SV 12

Judgement tendencies, targets and themes

Table 2 presents an overview of the Opponent Taxonomy to show its hierarchical structure, and acts as an aid in finding one's way through the categories listed in appendix B. Consider first the judgement tendencies: positive, negative, ambivalent and neutral. 'Positive' means that the opponent's statement or some part of it reveals a favourable attitude towards the actor, for example enduring or momentary friendliness, understanding, compassion, support, trust. 'Negative' means an unfavourable attitude, for example hostility, relentlessness, readiness to punish, distrust. 'Ambivalent' means a mixture of positive and negative sentiments or attitudes, and 'neutral' refers to statements that do not indicate any positive or negative attitude components related to the actor.

In a certain sense one may regard the four judgement tendencies as forming the highest level of the taxonomy, equivalent to the cardinal level of the Actor Taxonomy. As yet we have not explicitly provided 'cardinal' categories such as 'positive' or 'negative' judgement tendencies, but if need be this could easily be done by combining the categories in the appropriate column in table 2. For the sake of clarity, as well as for theoretical reasons, we have used as our highest ordering principle the distinction between the four primary targets to which an opponent's statement may be addressed, that is A the account expected from, or already delivered by, the actor, F the failure event and the actor's involvement in it, P enduring characteristics of the actor's personality, and B the bond or relationship between actor and opponent.

The four targets form a rank order along a dimension of severity of threat to the relationship between actor and opponent, given some constancy with respect to the negativity of the statement content. By and large, the implications of a negative evaluation of an actor's account for his or her self-esteem are less significant than the implications of a critique of the actor's involvement in the failure event, and such a critique, referring to a temporary phenomenon, does not cut as deeply as a comparable negative remark about the actor's character. Obviously, a negative comment about the opponent's relationship to the actor is most immediately and seriously threatening for the chances of a peaceful solution of the account episode conflict and for the continuation or restoration of an amicable relationship between its two participants.

Needless to say, the comments addressed to each of the four targets may vary widely between the extremes of positivity and negativity, and any one of these comments may become decisively important for the further course of events. The themes listed in table 2 under each target refer to a second level of superordinate categories. The basic categories beneath this level are represented in table 2 by their code numbers.

Secondary codings
The targets and themes mentioned so far are the domain of the primary codings. In addition the Opponent Taxonomy contains two types of secondary categorization.

1   *Dimensional codings.* As indicated in section 4.1 all primary categories were assigned to one of six secondary categories according to their average potential for (a) the actor's self-esteem and (b) his or her sense of being in control. The six secondary categories range from 'Strongly supportive . . .' to 'Strongly detrimental for the actor's self-esteem' (or sense of control), with two categories, 'Ambivalent' and 'Neutral', in the middle of the range.

2   *Résumé coding.* In an exploratory mood I designed seven secondary categories to capture the judgement trend *within* the complete statement of an opponent during a reproach phase (sv) or an evaluation phase (sw). It seemed reasonable to assume that, for instance, a reproach phase statement with an internal transition from negative or ambivalent to positive judgement tendencies would be more likely to engender a friendly reaction in the actor than a uniformly negative statement. And a considerate account in turn may be expected to facilitate such an internal transition towards a more positive ending in an opponent's reaction during the evaluation phase.

Secondary codings of this type were performed on each opponent statement in our studies immediately after its primary coding.[36]

5 Reproach phase results

I shall present our data grouped into three chapters (5 to 7), according to the account episode phase to which they pertain, and within each chapter according to the major hypotheses and additional hunches to which they are relevant. In chapter 8 the longitudinal inferences will then be drawn with respect to the escalation theory and desirable future research.

5.1 Effects of severity of failure on severity of reproach

Data from RPS I

The two failure situations Neglected Supervision and Breach of Trust presented to the respondents of RPS I differ in several respects; thus they are not easily compared. Still, it seems safe to say that on moral grounds the breach of the promise not to divulge the new colleague's criminal past appears to be a more serious violation of a legitimate expectation than the unintentional failure to notice and prevent the boy's excursion into the kitchen. According to hypothesis 1.1 we should therefore predict higher rates of reproach, and more severe reproaches, launched at the gossip than at the babysitter.

In their main coding procedure Berten and Holland assigned each verbatim statement in reaction to a vignette to one of the following four categories:

1 No attribution of guilt.
2 Qualified attribution of guilt.
3 Unreserved attribution of guilt in a calm manner.
4 Unreserved attribution of guilt in a sharp manner – vituperation.[37]

In later sections data differentiated according to this four-step scale will be presented. For the moment it may suffice to say that the babysitter in Neglected Supervision received unreserved guilt attributions (offered calmly or sharply) by only 27% of the respondents; the disloyal colleague in Breach of Trust received such guilt attributions by 83% of the respondents – a highly significant ($p < .0001$) difference according to a sign test.[38]

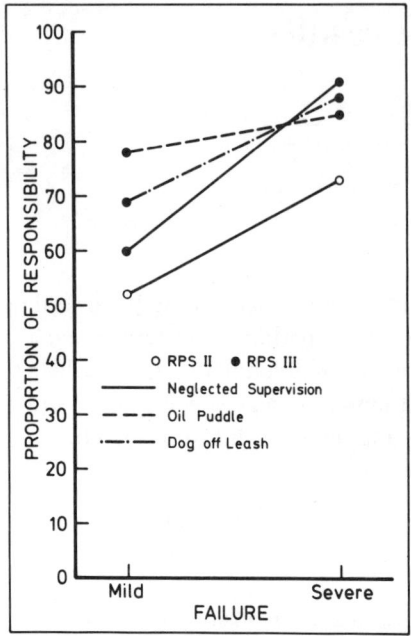

Figure 3. Average proportions of responsibility attributed in RPS II and RPS III to actors of mild and severe failures in the situations Neglected Supervision, Oil Puddle and Dog off Leash

Equivalent data patterns, each one highly significant ($p < .001$), were also obtained using the scale questions that requested judgements of the actors' responsibility, their punishability and their liability for compensation.

Data from RPS II

The second reproach phase study provided a stricter test of hypothesis 1.1, since the mild and the severe failure were embedded in the same core vignette, Neglected Supervision in this case.

The data again clearly support the hypothesis. The average share of responsibility assigned to the babysitter by the 87 respondents in the mild failure condition amounted to 52%; for the 85 respondents in the severe failure condition the corresponding value was 73% ($p < .001$). Very similar data patterns and significance levels[39] also resulted from the responses on the scales for cost liability ($p < .001$) and degree of guilt ($p < .003$) attributed to the actor. The averages are graphically represented in figures 3 to 5, together with the corresponding values from RPS III.

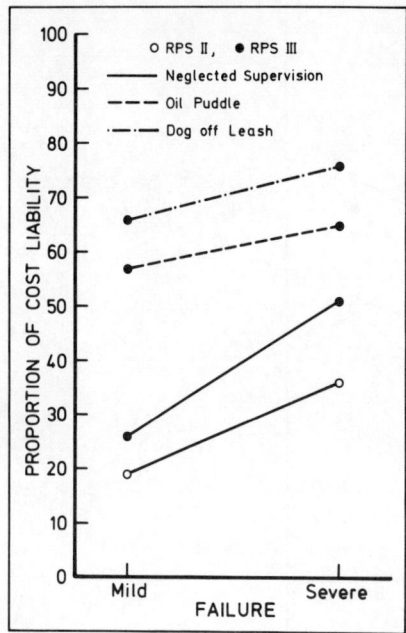

Figure 4. Average proportions of cost liability attributetd in RPS II and RPS III to actors of mild and severe failures in the situations Neglected Supervision, Oil Puddle and Dog off Leash

Data from RPS III

Further corroboration of hypothesis 1.1 came not only from the replication with the two versions of Neglected Supervision, but also from the contrasts between the mild and severe failures in the situations Oil Puddle and Dog off Leash.

The four mild–severe comparisons portrayed in each of figures 3, 4 and 5 are completely independent of each other, since these figures include only those respondents from RPS III for any of the failure events who received the corresponding vignette as their first task assignment. Each average value from RPS III in figures 3 to 5 is based on 32 respondents. The judgements on responsibility, cost liability and guilt are, of course, not independent of each other, as the reader may remember. They were requested from each respondent in that order.

Not only the three judgement comparisons from RPS II but also all nine comparisons from RPS III show a rising gradient from mild to severe failure. For Neglected Supervision all three mild–severe differences are significant (p

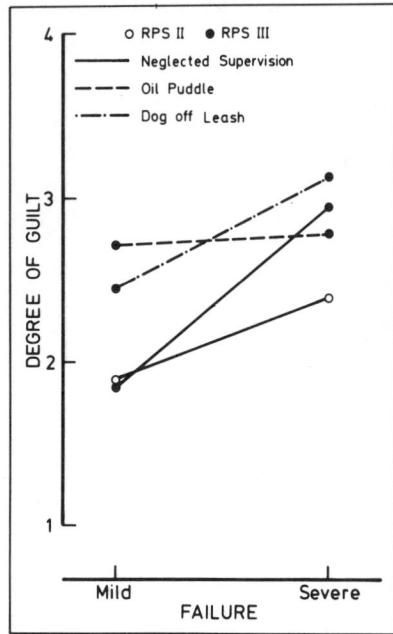

Figure 5. Average degree of guilt attributed in RPS II and RPS III to actors of mild and severe failures in the situations Neglected Supervision, Oil Puddle and Dog off Leash

between .02 and .001). For Dog off Leash the judgements of responsibility ($p<.02$) and guilt ($p<.01$) differ significantly between the mild and severe failure versions, whereas the cost liability judgements do not. For Oil Puddle none of the three measures produced a significant main effect of failure severity. This result, however, will soon have to be qualified in the light of additional factors introduced into the analyses.

Conclusion
Hypothesis 1.1 concerning the effects of severity of failure on severity of reproach received strong support from all three studies. The reader may not find this particularly surprising, and neither do I. After all, the hypothesis concurs with common-sense knowledge, and Blumstein et al. (1974) had already reported corroborating evidence. Nevertheless, I would maintain that the presentation of the data summary in the figures 3 to 5 has been appropriate for several reasons. (1) Even the obvious bears brief confirmation, because sometimes the seemingly obvious is contradicted by the facts. (2) The results carry a reassuring message as to the sensitivity of our measures. (3) The data patterns presented in this section provide a backdrop

Effects of gender

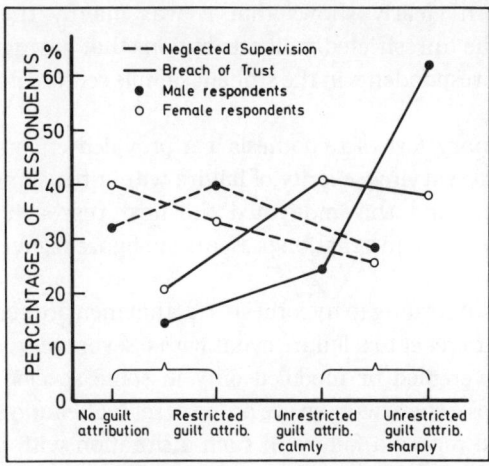

Figure 6. Distribution of male and female respondents across four guilt attribution categories according to their reactions in the situations Neglected Supervision and Breach of Trust in RPS I

for the evaluation of the differentiations that appear when additional independent factors and moderator variables are introduced, as the following sections will show.

5.2 Effects of gender on severity of reproach

Data from RPS I

Figure 6 presents the distributions of male and female respondents across the four categories of opponent reactions described in the preceding section. It emphasizes the support for hypothesis 1.1 already mentioned. Confronted with the mild failure Neglected Supervision, both gender groups produced so few reactions qualifying for one of the two severe categories that even combined they did not reach the frequencies of any of the two more lenient categories. Conversely, lenient reactions to the disloyal colleague in Breach of Trust were so rare among both male and female respondents that the frequencies in the two lenient categories combined within each gender group still did not match the weight of any of the more severe categories within that group.

Over and above this basic similarity, however, one may recognize a clear gender difference. In both failure situations more men than women tended towards the severer reactions. This trend is not significant as regards the Neglected Supervision case. But in the Breach of Trust situation the 3 × 2 contingency table of category frequencies yielded a chi^2 = 6.81, significant at

$p<.04$. The data pattern clearly shows that it was mainly the more aggressive language in the unrestricted guilt attributions that distinguished the male from the female respondents in the student sample recruited for this study.

Thus the first preliminary test of hypothesis 1.2 provided encouraging support, but a stricter test, varying severity of failure within the same basic situation, was called for, and this motivated the next reproach phase investigation, RPS II. The data constellation presented in figure 6 gave rise to the following questions:

1 Can we still assume, according to hypothesis 1.2, that men are generally more likely than women to react to a failure event with a severe reproach? Is this general tendency overruled or modified only in some specific cases, 'female situations' perhaps, where women are prone to set higher and stricter standards or are likely to regard a failure in such a situation with greater apprehension than men do? The babysitter situation may have been such a case.

2 Alternatively one may ask if the stronger reproach severity of men proposed by hypothesis 1.2 is not due to a general disposition but, rather, is restricted to cases of severe failure, or perhaps situations in which the higher levels of Heider's responsibility criteria – foreseeability or intention, for instance – are clearly met. Section 5.3 will have more to say about this issue and the responsibility notions of men and women. For the time being let me turn to the variation of failure severity within the same basic setting of Neglected Supervision.

Data from RPS II

The main data from this study are presented in figure 7. They form a tantalizing constellation from which partially affirmative answers to both questions just raised can be inferred together with a third partial explanation. I shall explain this in a moment, but let me first give some supplementary information.

Each mean value represented by a data point in figure 7 is based on 42–4 respondents. Multifactor analyses of variance yielded highly significant main effects for the severity of failure factor on all three measures: responsibility ($p<.001$), cost liability ($p<.001$) and guilt ($p<.002$). Most noteworthy are the three interactions of gender of respondent with severity of failure. They are also at least marginally significant, with responsibility at $p<.08$, cost liability at $p<.03$ and guilt at $p<.07$. On the cost liability measure a main effect of gender ($p<.004$) also turned up, but obviously it should not be interpreted apart from the interaction.

At first sight hypothesis 1.2 about the reproach severity of males fares badly, at least in its general form. Yet a defender might point out this aspect of

Effects of gender

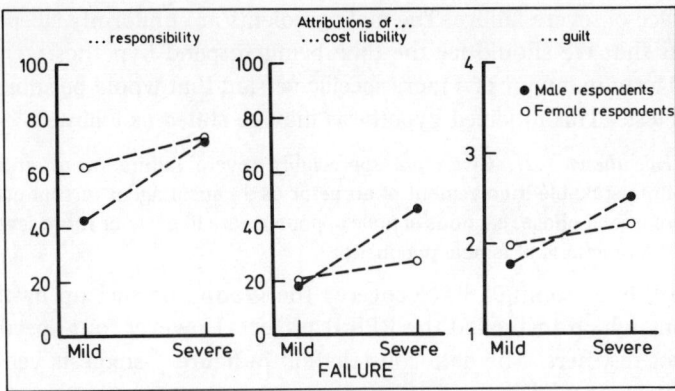

Figure 7. Average attributions to the female actors of mild and severe failures in the situation Neglected Supervision by male and female respondents in RPS II

the data: in figure 7 the measures of responsibility, cost liability and guilt attribution are offered in the order in which they were presented to the respondents. But I would maintain that their psychological order starts with the attribution of causal responsibility, moves from there to the assessment and attribution of guilt and then to the question of sanctions such as cost liability. This order seems to be reflected in the correlations between the dependent variables, that is responsibility–guilt ($r = .63$), guilt–cost liability ($r = .58$), responsibility–cost liability ($r = .46$) ($N = 175$). Shultz, Schleifer and Altman (1981) reported very similar data in support of their 'entailment model' of cause attribution leading to blame, and blame leading to punishment, which implies a comparatively weaker linkage between cause and punishment.

Whatever the status of this model,[40] it seems clear that 'moving' from responsibility assignments to blame or from guilt attributions to negative sanctions, the judgements become more serious and hence also potentially more severe. In this respect, then, in 'moving' from responsibility judgements via guilt attributions to cost liability demands, the relative gain in severity is clearly greater among the males than among the female respondents in *both* situations – mild and severe failure. This may speak for some generality in a disposition towards severity in reproach phase reactions among males. At the very least it is undeniable that, with respect to any level of responsibility assigned, the men were significantly[41] more severe in their attributions of guilt ($p < .003$) and cost liability ($p < .001$) than the women.

However, I do not wish to belabour this point any further. The most salient aspects of figure 7 are the differences between the male and the female gradients from the attributions in the mild failure situation to the attributions in the face of severe failure. The male gradients are uniformly steeper. This suggests that we should for the time being suspend hypothesis 1.2 in its general form in favour of a more specific version that would be subjected to further tests. This modified hypothesis may be stated as follows:

> *Hypothesis 1.2¹.* Given an appreciably severe failure event and/or the unmistakable involvement of an actor as a causal agent in that event, the reproach phase reactions of male opponents are likely to be more severe than the reactions of female opponents.

With this reasoning I have covered the ground opened up by the two questions which instigated the RPS II project. However, our speculations must not rest here. The data constellation in figure 7 suggests yet a third explanatory possibility.

The differences between the attribution patterns of male and female respondents in RPS II are perhaps not so much due to a steeper rise of the male gradients over and above a more 'normal' course of female attributions, as hypothesis 1.2¹ would predict, but are, rather, due to overly flat gradients between the female attributions in the mild 'television' failure and the more severe 'letter-box' failure. The babysitter situation Neglected Supervision is a typically feminine situation, and in RPS II the babysitter was also always a *female* friend of the boy's parents. According to Shaver (1970), the vignette presented was both situationally and personally relevant for the female respondents, and thus fairly likely to elicit from them defensive attributions of the blame avoidance type. If we are entitled to assume that such a defensive attribution tendency was particularly strong in the face of the severe failure, then we would have a very plausible contending explanation for the marginal and non-significant rise of the female attributions on all three measures over and above the levels in the mild failure situation. The fact that the discrepancies between the responsibility attributions, on the one hand, and the guilt and cost liability attributions, on the other, are much larger for the women than for the men could also well have resulted from defensive blame avoidance among many female respondents.

The desire to distinguish between the potential explanations just discussed motivated the planning and performance of a further study, RPS III, with the requirement that it would furnish systematic comparisons of situations that are either preponderantly relevant for females or predominantly relevant for males or neutral with respect to gender. Each such situation would be qualified by a mild or a severe failure; each of these six versions would be staffed with male and female actors; and, finally, each of the resulting 12 vignettes would be evenly distributed among male and female respondents.

Data from RPS III

The main results of this study are represented in figures 8, 9 and 10, each reserved for one of the failure situations Neglected Supervision, Neglected Oil

Effects of gender

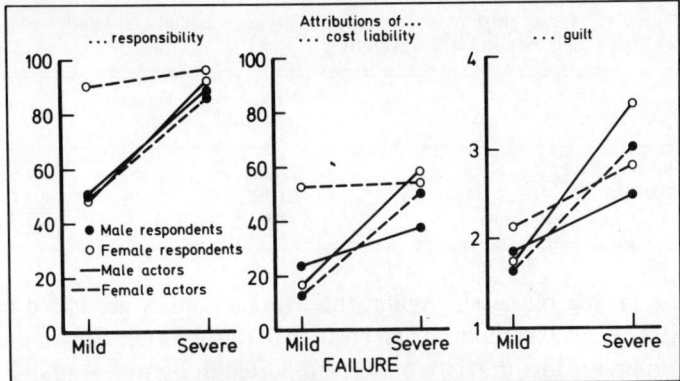

Figure 8. Average attributions to male and female actors of mild and severe failures in the situation Neglected Supervision by male and female respondents in RPS III

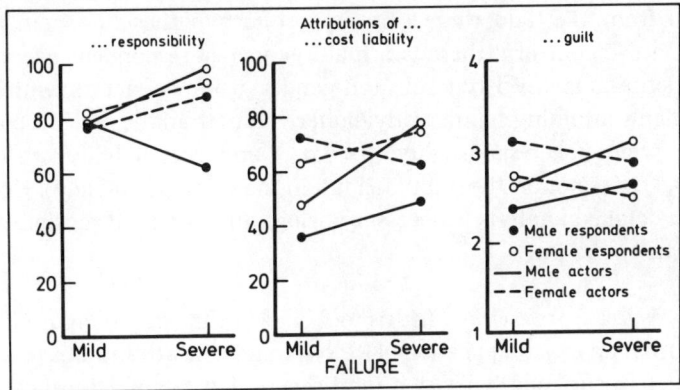

Figure 9. Average attributions to male and female actors of mild and severe failures in the situation Neglected Oil Puddle by male and female respondents in RPS III

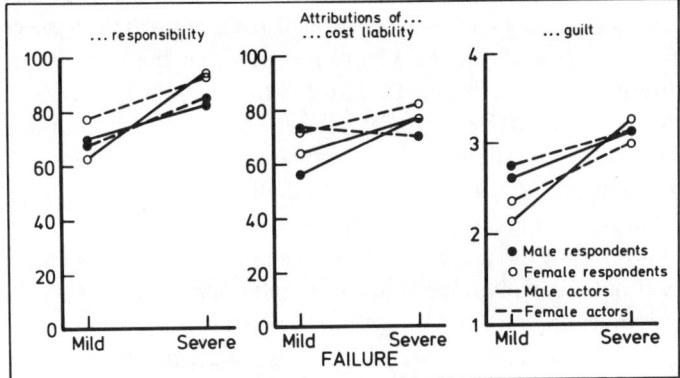

Figure 10. Average attributions to male and female actors of mild and severe failures in the situation Dog off Leash by male and female respondents in RPS III

Table 3. Average attributions of responsibility, cost liability and guilt by all males and all female respondents in RPS III

	Men (N=96)	Women (N=96)	p
Responsibility	73.50	83.40	.015
Cost liability	51.60	61.40	.051
Guilt	2.64	2.66	n.s.

Puddle, and Dog off Leash. Again, the average values are based only on responses to a given vignette in first position in the ordering of vignettes in the questionnaires. Thus the data patterns reported in figures 8, 9 and 10 are independent of each other. Each data point in these figures represents a mean based on eight cases.

A first survey of all three figures clearly leads to the same basic inference as the data from RPS II do: there is no support for hypothesis 1.2 in its general form. On the contrary, there is a main gender-of-respondent effect across failure situations, severity levels and gender groups of actors, with female respondents attaining significantly higher values than the male respondents on the scales for responsibility ($p < .015$) and cost liability attributions ($p < .051$), but not on the guilt attribution measure (see table 3). However, again a detailed analysis is necessary before any further defensible conclusions can be drawn.

Neglected Supervision. Let us look first at that part of figure 8 which results from an exact replication of RPS II, that is the attributions to a female babysitter in the mild 'television' and severe 'letter-box' failure condition, represented by the dashed-line gradients. These data patterns are strikingly similar to the corresponding data from RPS II in figure 7 in almost every respect. Again, the gradients between mild and severe failure attributions by male respondents are clearly steeper on all three measures than the gradients of the female respondents. Once more it seems that the men discriminated much more sharply between the two failure levels, whereas the women apparently did not differentiate at all between the two situations. They attributed to the female babysitter captivated by the television screen just about as much responsibility and cost liability as to her counterpart who went out to post her letter. The interaction of a corresponding 2 × 2 ANOVA is not significant; but *t*-tests, which seem permissible on the predictive basis of the RPS II data, corroborated that in the mild failure situation the women reacted significantly more severely than the men in attributing responsibility ($p < .030$) and cost liability ($p < .024$). By the way, the comparatively high values of the female respondents on the cost liability scale constitute the one

Effects of gender

notable difference between the strictly matchable data from RPS II and RPS III, and I shall return to this point shortly.

All in all, then, the high degree of similarity between the data from the original study RPS II and its replication within the frame of RPS III encourage us to turn now to the other half of the data, the attributions to the male babysitter, for enlightenment with respect to the tentative explanations offered for the data constellations of the preceding study.

Do we get support for the hunch that a tendency towards defensive blame avoidance was sensitized in female respondents by the severe failure situation? The answer suggested by the responsibility and cost liability diagrams in figure 8 is a clear No. There is no indication that the women judged the man in the babysitter role any more severely in these two respects than they judged the female babysitter. In fact, in the mild failure situations they attributed to the male babysitter significantly less responsibility ($p < .019$) and cost liability ($p < .039$).[42]

The most plausible interpretation of these data patterns to my mind is this: women expect other women to be knowledgeable about the vicissitudes of dealing with small children and to be wary of potential dangers in seemingly harmless situations. Thus they tend to set strict standards, which are reflected in harm avoidance attributions to female babysitters whatever the situation that facilitated a failure. Judging a man in a babysitter role, women do not expect him to foresee all possible mishaps in a seemingly quiet situation; hence they are relatively lenient in their responsibility and liability attributions to him in such situations and become severe only if he blatantly violates his supervisory obligation, as in leaving the child alone for some errand.

In short, then, contrary to the tentative hunch, and in contrast also to Shaver's (1970) defensive attribution theory, in the 'feminine' babysitter situation with a personally similar female babysitter, female respondents do not tend towards blame avoidance in their responsibility and cost liability judgements but rather to harm avoidance attributions. However, this inference has to be qualified in the light of the guilt attribution data.

The guilt attribution diagram in figure 8 reveals an intriguing pattern. In the mild failure condition the four guilt judgements on male and female actors by men and women form a comparatively dense cluster; in the severe failure condition the guilt judgements diverge due to differentially steep gradients and four telling cross-overs among these gradients between mild and severe failure judgements.

First of all, as in the RPS II data, there is a cross-over of the two gradients for male and female respondents attributing guilt to a female babysitter. Again, the male gradient is the steeper one; in the severe failure condition the men's guilt attributions surpass, albeit slightly, those of the women. But now it also becomes clear that the obverse holds for the attributions of guilt to the male babysitter. In this case the women's judgements are far more severe than the men's judgements in the severe failure condition. Furthermore, it is also true that in this condition women judging a woman were more lenient than in judging a man and, conversely, men judging a man were more lenient than in judging a woman. The second-order interaction of severity of failure, gender of actor and gender of respondent is significant at $p < .032$.

The data constellation just described suggests that in the case of guilt attributions, both men and women tend towards defensive blame avoidance in judging an actor of their own gender, given a sufficiently clear and severe failure event. Thus different conclusions emerged from the responsibility and cost liability data, on the one hand, and the guilt judgements, on the other, with respect to the attribution tendencies of female opponents. This may be taken as a first indication that women do perhaps make a comparatively sharp distinction between responsibility and guilt. This will be discussed in more detail in section 5.3. At this juncture it is worth pointing out that other researchers, for example Wilson and Jonah (1988), also reported that responsibility attributions and blame or penalty assignments are not always closely associated.

What about the men, and what about the second tentative explanation offered for the data patterns from RPS II? Can we support the proposition that even though hypothesis 1.2 does not seem to hold, a special version of it, namely hypothesis 1.2^1, is compatible with the data? Once more the answer must be No, at least for the time being. There is no indication whatsoever in figure 8 that, at least in the face of severe violations of normative expectations, male judgements would surpass female judgements on any severity dimension.

The most notable aspect of the male attributions is the cross-over of the gradients of judgements about male and female babysitters on both the more consequential dimensions – guilt and cost liability attributions. For cost liability the corresponding interaction between severity of failure and gender of actor is significant at $p < .05$. It seems that male respondents in the opponent role tended towards defensive blame-avoiding attributions to actors of their own gender even more strongly than female actors did, although the babysitter situation presumably was less situationally relevant for them than for the women. Let us now see how male and female opponents reacted to failure events in the 'masculine' environment of a car repair shop.

Neglected Oil Puddle. Two things can be quickly inferred from figure 9: (1) there is again no support for hypothesis 1.2; and (2) several aspects of the data constellations point to a strong blame avoidance tendency of male respondents in judging the male car mechanic who neglected the oil puddle.

On the responsibility measure there is actually an amazing drop in the judgements of the male actor by the male respondents in the severe failure condition as compared to the corresponding attributions in the mild failure condition, whereas the other three gradients rise in agreement with the general prediction of hypothesis 1.1. The second-order interaction of severity of failure, gender of actor and gender of respondent does not reach a conventional significance level ($p < .11$), but the difference between male and female responsibility attributions to the male car mechanic in the severe failure condition is significant at $p < .01$.[43]

Defensive blame avoidance patterns for males judging males are also visible with the other two measures, and most clearly with the most consequential, and hence serious, cost liability attributions. In this case the male-on-male judgements were lowest in both severity conditions. Mainly this leniency constituted a marginally significant ($p < .07$) main effect of the factor actor's gender in a multifactorial ANOVA.

The data on the attributions made by women show very interesting parallels to their attribution patterns elicited by the Neglected Supervision vignettes. Again, there are no signs of blame avoidance on the responsibility and cost liability dimensions. In these two respects their judgements of the negligent car mechanic, whether male or female, are rather stern, especially in the severe failure condition. In this very condition, however, there is some indication for defensive blame avoidance among females with respect to guilt attributions to the female car mechanic, in contrast to their guilt attributions to the male car mechanic.

Dog off Leash. The story of this third independent segment of the study is quickly told. Figure 10 shows that the mean attribution values within the two severity conditions cluster much more closely than in the other two failure situations just discussed. Beyond the clear severity effects already pointed out in section 5.1 no other main effects or interactions appeared. Neither women nor men produced any indications of blame-avoiding attributions in this gender-neutral situation. Furthermore, for the third time within the scope of RPS III, no support at all can be mustered for hypothesis 1.2 that men are generally more severe in their reproach behaviour than women, nor for the more specific variant, hypothesis 1.2^1, that such differential severity of reproaches would manifest itself in cases of unmistakably serious failures.

It should be noted in passing that, again, females judging females were rather severe in attributing responsibility and cost liability, but comparatively lenient (or reticent?) in assigning guilt.

Supplementary effects of age and education

The two samples of respondents in RPS II and RPS III were drawn from the general population according to quota assignments, with age being one of

Table 4: Average attributions of responsibility, cost liability and guilt by young, middle-aged and old respondents in RPS II and RPS III

	Age groups			
	18–35y.	36–55y.	56y. plus	p
Responsibility				
RPS II	60.00		64.30	n.s.
RPS III	73.80	84.10		.022
Cost liability				
RPS II	27.70		27.30	n.s.
RPS III	52.30	59.20		n.s.
Guilt				
RPS II	2.06		2.20	n.s.
RPS III	2.50	2.80		.049

the quota dimensions. The samples also proved to be sufficiently heterogeneous with respect to the respondents' degree of education to allow for contrastive comparisons on this dimension too. Let us then see if we can get any further enlightenment on the gender differences so far presented by looking for any connections they might have with the respondents' age and educational status.

Age effects in RPS II and III. In RPS II the respondents were recruited from a young (18–35y.) and an old (56y. plus) age group. In RPS III the quota split was between 18–35 years and 36 years and older. The number of respondents within this latter group who were older than 55 years was comparatively small ($N=20$); therefore we decided to restrict the age comparisons for the RPS III data to the young group (again 18–35y.) and the middle-aged group (36–55y.).

Age emerged from multifactorial ANOVAs on all three attribution dimensions as a main effect not involved in any notable interactions with severity of failure, gender of actor or gender of respondents. One exception to this will be reported shortly. Thus table 4 is confined to overall age comparisons. The mean values in table 4 are based on the following numbers of respondents: RPS II, 18–35y. – $N=85$, 56 plus – $N=87$; RPS III, 18–35y. – $N=96$, 36–55y. – $N=76$. The data from both studies are included in one table in order to save space. No direct comparisons between them are intended since most of the judgement situations from which the RPS III means were derived differ in several respects from those of RPS II.

Table 4 shows that the young respondents were generally less severe than the older ones in their attributions of responsibility and guilt; but with respect to cost liability attributions the two age groups did not differ appreciably. Since this pattern holds for men and women alike the main age data do not

Effects of gender

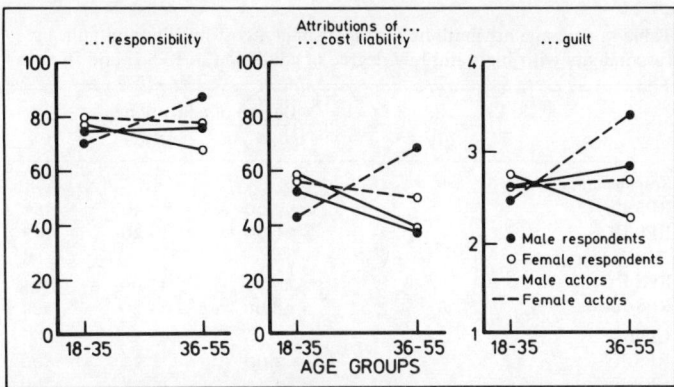

Figure 11. Average attributions to male and female actors in the Oil Puddle failure situations by young and middle-aged male and female respondents in RPS III

provide any further insight into the viability of hypothesis 1.2 nor into the defensive attribution dispositions so far discovered. However, there is that one exception just mentioned. It is presented in figure 11.[44]

In the case of a failure, whether mild or severe, by a female in the typically 'masculine' role of a car mechanic the older men are particularly severe in their attributions. This is noticeable as a non-significant tendency in the responsibility attributions, and it becomes clear with the more serious attributions of guilt and cost liability.

Multiple ANOVAs revealed that with respect to guilt attributions age interacted significantly with both gender of respondents ($p < .02$) and gender of actors ($p < .04$), and with respect to cost liability attributions significantly only with gender of actors ($p < 0.1$); but it is obvious from figure 11 that this latter interaction was also mainly sustained by the men's severe attributions to the female car mechanic. Here, then, for the first time within the data set of RPS III we encounter clear, if rather isolated, support for a specific version of hypothesis 1.2.

Furthermore, the male car mechanic received an intriguingly lenient treatment by older men and women alike, particularly in the cost liability judgements. It seems that in the older age groups both genders looked with scepticism upon the female intruder into the masculine world of the car repair shop, and thus were quick to judge her failure severely – the male respondents even more so than the women – whereas the male car mechanic was apparently accorded a fair amount of understanding by the older respondents for his mishap, and hence was judged less severely.

Education effects in RPS II and III. The short label 'Age effects on attributions' does not, of course, imply that chronological age in and of itself

Table 5. Average attributions of responsibility, cost liability and guilt by respondents with high and low degree of education in RPS II and III

	Degree of education		
	High	Low	p
Responsibility			
RPS II	59.60	67.30	n.s.
RPS III	71.60	86.20	.030
Cost liability			
RPS II	29.20	32.60	n.s.
RPS III	48.60	63.20	n.s.
Guilt			
RPS II	2.00	2.53	.003
RPS III	2.42	2.78	.061

has those effects. The label refers to certain experiences and dispositions that are associated with this or that age group for that matter. The term 'education effects' should likewise be understood to cover a range of potential factors associated with type and years of schooling that are truly instrumental in guiding attributions regarding a failure event. I am alerted to make this cautionary remark against possible misunderstandings in the present context because in our studies on the relationship of education and intergroup attitudes (Schönbach et al. 1981) we had to consider a number of possible factors correlated with educational status that could contribute to the comparatively high degree of prejudice towards outgroups among persons of low educational status.

Table 5 contrasts the two opposite groups on the educational dimension, the 'low group', which comprises all respondents with elementary schooling including instruction received in a continuation school within a programme of occupational training, but no formal education beyond this level, and the 'high group', confined to those respondents who have at least obtained the *Abitur* or an equivalent certificate as entrance requirement for technical college or university. The middle group, with lower-grade secondary school, technical school or an equivalent training, is not included in table 5. Its attributions are close to, and certainly not significantly different from, the attributions of the high-education group. The four cell frequencies for the low- and high-education groups in RPS II and RPS III range from 53 to 69. Evidently, respondents with a low degree of education were more severe in their responsibility and guilt attributions than the high-education group. This leads first of all to the following consideration.

Educational status could not be included in the quota assignments for the recruitment of respondents in RPS II and RPS III. In both samples more men than women fell into the high-education group and, conversely, more women than men into the low-education group. These are the figures: RPS II, low education – 23 men and 30 women, high education – 39 men and 20 women (chi^2 = 5.82, $p<.02$); RPS III, low education – 26 men and 43 women, high education – 35 men and 20 women (chi^2 = 8.25, $p<.005$). This may raise the question of whether the relatively lenient attributions of males in RPS II and III are perhaps mediated to a large extent by their 'education'. However, controlling for the education factor does not appreciably alter the data patterns of male and female attributions, and the inferences drawn so far with respect to hypothesis 1.2 and the defensive attribution tendencies discovered need not be altered.

The breakdown of the data according to the respondents' degree of education shows a number of remarkable similarities to the partitioning according to age. The low-education group produced comparatively severe attributions on all three dimensions, just as the old respondents did, and in both cases this tendency manifested itself in significant differences only with responsibility and guilt judgements, not with respect to cost liability attributions. Furthermore, both factors, age and education, engendered clear main effects, but did not enter into any appreciable or significant interactions with gender of respondent, gender of actor or severity of failure. Nor do age and education interact; the two main effects coexist side by side.

This pattern similarity suggests that older age and lower educational status are conducive to similar, if not identical, mediating processes that lead to relatively severe attributions of responsibility and guilt to an actor involved in a failure event. I have no evidence as to what these processes might be, but I am willing to speculate: many people with a low degree of education, as well as those advanced in age with accumulated experiences of lack or loss of control over their environment, perhaps feel a comparatively strong need for a controllable world that is easily made salient and augmented by any failure event. That, perhaps, is why they tend to react to a failure with severe attributions of responsibility and guilt: they are seeking to restore, directly or vicariously, an orderly world.

Data from EPS II

This study's main focus is the evaluation phase, to be treated in chapter 7, but it does include a reproach phase condition, and hence data relevant for the present section.

The vignette used in EPS II again described the babysitter situation Neglected Supervision. For the reproach phase condition the design and the instructions were quite similar to the corresponding part of RPS III. Male and female respondents, non-psychology students, were asked to imagine being a returning parent who reacts to the neighbour-babysitter. For 17 women and 15 men the neighbour was presented as a female, for 15 women and 16 men as a male. The procedure differed from RPS III with respect to the dependent variables. No attribution scales were introduced; the respondents were asked instead to call upon the babysitter to account for the failure event and to write down verbatim what they would say in this situation. These free answers were later coded according to the Taxonomy for Opponent Reactions.

It is obvious from many indices that the feminist movement has gained momentum during the last eight or nine years since our first studies on account episodes. It is my informal impression, though I have very few data (see APS III in section 6.3) to support it, that this has led to an approximation of male and female responses to questionnaire studies in university quarters. Furthermore, compared to other failure situations, the vignette Neglected Supervision had produced relatively weak male–female differences. So I hesitated to expect any signs of greater leniency among the female student respondents as predicted by hypothesis 1.2. Still, some such signs did appear in the coded reactions.

Significantly ($p < .01$) more women (50%) than men (19%) asked the babysitter about the causes or the course of the failure event *without* a reproachful innuendo or comment (category A 21). Non-significantly more women (25%) than men (10%) admitted their own partial guilt or responsibility for the occurrence of the failure event (F 21). Non-significantly more men (32%) than women (16%) accused the babysitter of carelessness or negligence.

In a secondary coding procedure[45] weights ranging from $+3$ to -3 were assigned to each category of the Taxonomy for Opponent Reactions in order to indicate the average degree of favourability or unfavourability for the actor of statements falling into this category. These secondary codings allow for the construction of a comprehensive evaluation index COMPREVAL for each respondent which includes any evaluative reaction to the account expected or received, to the failure event, to the actor's personality, and to the relationship between actor and opponent. The COMPREVAL score for any opponent is computed by adding the weights of all the categories coded for that opponent's statement and by subtracting this sum from a constant of 10. Negative numbers are avoided thereby, and the direction of scoring corresponds to our other indices employed so far: the higher the score, the more negative or severe the comprehensive reaction.

The difference between the average COMPREVAL scores for males (9.06) and females (8.72) in the reproach phase condition of EPS II also corresponds to hypothesis 1.2, but it is far from being significant. However, a further, intriguing, male–female difference on the COMPREVAL dimension in connection with the moderator variable desire for competence will be presented in section 5.4.

Data from EPS III

This study employed the vignette Assault and Robbery, a much more serious failure event than Neglected Supervision in EPS II. This choice was guided by the wish to see if a specified version of hypothesis 1.2, limiting its claim of males surpassing females in their reproach severity to situations of severe attacks on the opponent's control needs, would fare better than the original general version of the hypothesis. Furthermore, considering the possibility mentioned above that in recent years male and female university students may have converged in their attitudes and response tendencies in our domain of discourse more than men and women in the population at large, we decided to recruit once more a quota sample from the adult population, excluding students.

It will come as no surprise that the Assault and Robbery event elicited much more severe and negative reproach phase reactions than the Neglected Supervision one in RPS II. A comparison of the two overall COMPREVAL scores from the two studies illustrates this. As mentioned above, the COMPREVAL index was constructed in such a way that a value of 10 represents an exact balance between positively and negatively weighted categorizations of a given reproach phase (or evaluation phase) statement. Any value greater than 10 represents a preponderance of negative categorizations, any value below 10 a preponderance of positive categorizations. The overall COMPREVAL mean for the respondents confronted with the Neglected Supervision event in the reproach phase condition of RPS II amounted to 8.89. The corresponding value for the RPS III respondents confronted with the Assault and Robbery event was 14.36. The difference between these two means is significant far beyond the .0001 level.

A comparison of male and female respondents on various indices of their reproach phase reactions did indeed yield encouraging data constellations. The statements in this phase covered a wide range of themes, which had to be coded into 35 categories of the Opponent Taxonomy. With such a wide spread many categories received too few cases to allow for meaningful male–female comparisons at the level of single categories.

The few popular categories with a sufficiently large number of cases for meaningful comparison provide good support for the hypothesis of higher reproach phase severity among males than among females. Physical violence against the adolescent robber (categories F 67 and F 68) was mentioned by significantly ($p < .04$) more men (30%) than women (15%). Women (28%), on the other hand, were more concerned ($p < .07$) than men (11%) with the violation of norms by the failure event (F 541). A further, non-significant, difference points in the same direction: more women (32%) than men (25%)

offered negative evaluations of the actor's moral qualities (P 22) during their reproach phase reactions.

The summation index COMPREVAL yielded a non-significant difference between the means for males (14.02) and females (14.69), which is not in accord with hypothesis 1.2. This difference is partly due to the fact that the women produced longer statements (2.57 codings on the average) than the men (2.20). This difference is marginally significant at $p < .08$. Turning the summation index COMPREVAL into an averaging index MEANEVAL, that is dividing the raw COMPREVAL scores by the number of codings applied to a given statement, again with a constant of 10 added, shows the males now to be slightly, but not significantly, more severe (11.92) than the females (11.83).

At present we do not know anything about the relative validity of the averaging index as compared to the summation index. It remains for future research to establish whether, and if so under what conditions, a long string of negative comments should be marked as more influential with respect to its adverse effects on the recipient than a brief but very negative statement.

Clear support again for hypothesis 1.2 emerged from the comprehensive secondary codings according to categories sv 11–17. With coders still blind as to the respondents' gender, 82% of all male, but only 62% of all female reproach phase statements ($p < .02$), were categorized as 'uniformly negative' (sv 12). Conversely, only 9% of the male statements, yet 28% of the female statements ($p < .01$), were coded as ambivalent or as lacking any evaluative judgement tendencies (sv 15, 16, 17).

Discussion

Male severity. What does a synopsis of the results from the five studies RPS I, II, III and EPS II, III suggest as to the future of hypothesis 1.2 about males being more severe than women in their reproach phase reactions towards an actor involved in a failure event? In its general, unqualified form the hypothesis fares badly. Two studies (RPS II, III) flatly contradict it, the first study (RPS I) would provide support only on the unlikely assumption that in the situation Neglected Supervision a bottom effect depressed the difference between male and female guilt attributions to non-significance, and the last two studies (EPS II, III) also provide at best scant support.

A clearly better survival chance may be accorded to some specific version of the hypothesis which stipulates a number of limiting conditions for the predicted effect – males surpassing females in the severity of their reproaches – to occur. The data from RPS I are in good agreement with a specific hypothesis of this nature which invokes as necessary conditions (1) a clear causal, and perhaps also the intentional, involvement of the actor in the failure event and (2) the passing of some threshold value of severity of the failure event. This hypothesis could also accommodate some of the data from RPS II, namely the guilt judgements and particularly the cost liability attributions, and it is in good accord with the results from EPS III. However, in order to glean some support from RPS III as well, that is the severe guilt and cost liability attributions of older men in the masculine situation Neglected Oil Puddle, further rather restrictive conditions have to be introduced, for example specific, situation-based needs for control.

Such an accumulation of limiting conditions may be seen as rather embarrassing for the hypothesis, but it should also be noted that further support for it comes from other quarters. Penfold (1985), in a study on parents' perceived responsibility for children's problems, found that female parents were much more likely to attribute all or some responsibility to themselves whereas male parents were much more likely to blame the child's female parent. One may also point to a number of studies, for example Thornton, Robbins and Johnson (1981), that demonstrate stronger male than female tendencies in cases of rape to blame the rape victim. However, the issues are particularly complex in this domain, and caution in making inferences is advisable, as Krahé (1985) has convincingly argued. De Man, Simpson-Housley and Curtis (1985), in an exploratory study on the assignment of responsibility after a flood disaster in Louisiana, found that for men, but not for women, a reliable connection existed between their attribution of responsibility to an engineer in charge and their confidence in assuming that the engineer had or had not fulfilled his duty in inspecting the dams. This result is in good accord with my previous assumption that men are more prone than women to consider and ascribe responsibility under causal aspects. Women in the flood hazard study were more strongly influenced in their responsibility judgements by the severity of the flood consequences. Ford and Lowery (1986), in their study on gender differences in moral reasoning, reported (p. 777) that their 'female subjects were more consistent in their use of a care orientation, and that male subjects were more consistent in their use of a justice orientation'. This finding also supports the assumption that the violation of a normative expectation is particularly salient for men and hence has a comparatively strong influence on their responsibility and guilt attributions as well as on related judgements. Higher degrees of judgement severity among males than among females can also be inferred from the studies of Kleinke (1977) on marital conflict scenarios.

Male and female blame avoidance. Two previous studies on defensive attribution tendencies in men and women have furnished incompatible evidence. Whitehead and Hall (1984), in a study on sex differences in the assignment of responsibility for an accident, concluded in favour of Shaver's

(1970) defensive attribution theory that females judged the behaviour of an accident perpetrator in a feminine occupation more positively than did males, and males in turn judged the behaviour of an accident perpetrator in a masculine occupation more positively than did females. Howard (1984, p. 504), on the other hand, in a study on blame attributions to assault victims, did not find instances 'in which men blamed female victims more or women blamed male victims more ... Men did blame the behavior of other men substantially more than they blamed the behavior of women.'

Our own results from RPS III present yet a third pattern. Three aspects of the data should be remembered. (1) In the masculine situation Neglected Oil Puddle there are strong indications of defensive blame avoidance on the part of male respondents confronted with a male actor across all judgement dimensions. This is in good accord with Shaver's theory. (2) In the feminine situation Neglected Supervision no comparable pattern emerged for the female respondents. On the contrary, the women were very severe in attributing responsibility and cost liability to the female babysitter. Only on the guilt attribution aspect were there signs of female blame avoidance with respect to the female babysitter. (3) As might be expected from Shaver's theory, no indications of male or female blame avoidance emerged in the gender-neutral situation Dog off Leash. Surprisingly, however, each of the defensive attribution tendencies just recapitulated – weak and restricted among females, strong and more general among males – did not only appear in the one situation particularly relevant for the respondents' own gender, but also in the opposite gender-specific situation. The guilt attribution patterns in figures 8 and 9 show this most clearly; and for the male respondents, the cost liability judgements do likewise. This third aspect of the results merits further discussion.

At first sight it may seem baffling to be able to observe whatever male and female defensive attribution tendencies there are in *both* gender-specific situations. Shaver would not have predicted this, and we did not expect it. On closer inspection, however, this data pattern starts to make sense. Perhaps we should not talk about two gender-specific situations, but call them both gender-sensitive for men and women alike, for good if different reasons. Men are not normally expected to babysit. For that very reason they may tend to be self-conscious in this role and defensive in a case of mishap, and this may, in line with Shaver's reasoning, carry over to men's attribution tendencies when they have to act as opponents. Women are still not normally expected to work as mechanics in a car repair shop. Yet in the fight for equal rights and employment opportunities many of them may lay claim to such a job and therefore be defensive if a female car mechanic is charged with failure.

Women are relatively lenient and even defensive with attributions of guilt, yet they are severe with men and women alike in assigning responsibility and cost liability. This discrepancy between guilt attributions, on the one hand,

and responsibility and cost liability attributions, on the other, will be taken up again soon. For the severe female attributions of responsibility and cost liability to the female babysitter I have already offered an explanation (see p. 101). I want now to consider why the female respondents are also severe in their attributions of responsibility and cost liability to the female car mechanic. It seems possible that two antagonistic intentions have joined forces to produce this result. Some women with traditional views may have reacted harshly because they think it odd or inappropriate for a woman to work as a car mechanic, and they feel themselves reinforced in this view by the female car mechanic's negligent conduct. Other women, prone to assert equal rights and opportunities for women and men, may have reacted harshly because they were angry with the female car mechanic, who by her negligence was likely to revive old prejudices against women at work and thereby impede the fight for equal rights. At present we have no evidence for or against this speculation; it needs a specific investigation.

Finally, what message should we deduce from the men's reticence and defensiveness in making their attributions? The most immediate inference is an encouragement for hypothesis 2.2, which predicts that men will react more defensively to a severe challenge or reproach than women will. Relevant data will be presented in chapter 6 on the account phase reactions of various actors.

5.3 The meaning of responsibility for men and women – an excursus

In my supplementary speculations in section 2.3 I tentatively considered the hypothesis that men more than women are oriented towards the causal aspects, and women more than men towards the solution aspects, in their conceptions of responsibility. In the preceding section 5.2 I had reason to mention several times that in RPS III women surpassed men in their attributions of responsibility and cost liability, but not in their guilt attributions. This fact already suggests that for women the causal aspect, guilt, was less closely associated with responsibility and the solution aspect, cost liability, than it was for men, and correlational analyses support this hunch.

Table 6 presents correlations among the three main dependent variables in RPS III for each of six subgroups formed by dividing the sample according to gender and educational status. Cell frequencies range from 20 to 43. Owing to the small number of cases, male–female comparisons do not yield significant differences. However, on each educational level the correlations between guilt, on the one hand, and responsibility and cost liability, on the other, were lower for the females than for the males. This consistency has a chance probability of $p < .02$.

Table 6. Correlations among attributions of responsibility, guilt and cost liability in male and female subsamples from RPS III with low, medium and high educational status

	Educational status					
	Low		Medium		High	
	Male	Female	Male	Female	Male	Female
Correlations between						
Responsibility and guilt	.57	.30	.69	.50	.69	.56
Guilt and cost liability	.64	.50	.73	.42	.50	.20
Responsibility and cost liability	.41	.50	.47	.32	.58	.55

Similar data were also obtained in RPS II. For example, within the mild failure condition, the correlations between guilt and responsibility were $r = .65$ for men and $r = .55$ for women; within the severe failure conditions the corresponding correlations were $r = .62$ for men and $r = .57$ for women.

The correlations just presented strengthen the impression that women may be quite willing to hold actors of failure events liable to provide restitution or compensation for any damage incurred by that event. However, they are not necessarily inclined to associate such responsibility-for-solution attributions with guilt judgements and blaming, at least not as frequently or strongly as men apparently do.

Some support, albeit oblique, may also be inferred from other sources. I have already quoted from Gilligan's (1977) important paper, and referred (see p. 111) to the studies by De Man, Simpson-Housley and Curtis (1985) and by Ford and Lowery (1986).

Schmalt (1986), in a German study on power motivation and responsibility attribution, found that men and women did not differ in their causal attributions concerning an event but that women assumed more liability responsibility than men did, regardless of their power motivation level.

Mitchell (1987), in a study on the relationship of femininity, masculinity and gender to attributions of responsibility, tested the inclinations of the respondents towards the four help models proposed by Brickman et al. (1982). The data form complex patterns, but some of the findings, unexpected by Mitchell, are also in line with our reasoning. For instance, respondents with high scores on one of the femininity measures showed significantly stronger endorsement than the low scorers of the compensatory help model according to which responsibility for the solution of a problem is assumed and attributed regardless of one's causal involvement in the problem.

These examples may suffice. Considering such findings, and considering also the widespread awareness of the complexity of the responsibility concept, it is surprising that hardly any investigator had ever tried to assess directly the meaning of 'responsibility' for different groups of people. The study by Shaver, Null and Huff (1982) already mentioned (see p. 41) is a rare exception. Unfortunately for our purpose this study did not address possible male–female differences. Furthermore, the reaction potentials of the respondents were limited by prestructured answers to be chosen or rejected, and Shaver himself (1985, p. 153) offers the cautious conclusion: 'Researchers must be careful to avoid *imposing* any conceptual structure on the attributions made by the perceivers.'

Many studies have employed scales for responsibility attributions with the silent assumption that a common understanding of the term 'responsibility' would prevail among all respondents. For instance, despite Hamilton's (1978) admonitions as to the multidimensional complexity of the concept of responsibility, Sanders and Hamilton (1987), in their intriguing study on national (American–Japanese) differences in responsibility attribution, proceeded with that assumption. They reported few gender differences within each national culture. Yet the possibility remains that the overt finding of 'No difference' hides qualitative discrepancies between the responsibility assessments of men and women in Japan, in America, or in both cultures.

Within the framework of our research programme we found neither time nor occasion for a systematic full-scale investigation of the meaning of responsibility for men and women. But we did conduct two pilot studies (MRS I and II, see pp. 66–7) on that issue.

Data from MRS I

The taxonomy which we developed for the 'free answers' to the question on the understanding of the term 'responsibility' contained, among others, two major categories: (1) attention to the genesis of a problem and (2) attention to the solution of a problem.

No significant male–female difference emerged with respect to the first category. Genesis aspects were mentioned by 13% of the men and 18% of the women. However, solution aspects were mentioned significantly ($p<.05$) more frequently by women (74%) than by men (50%).

Another group of categories was provided for answers in which responsibility was associated with a societal role or position, or with power, status or prestige in general. Significantly ($p<.03$) more men (42%) than women (18%) gave answers that fell into one or more of these categories.

The category 'Care for others' gathered significantly ($p<.02$) more female (85%) than male (61%) responses.

The data just presented are based on the categorizations of two coders who, working independently, achieved a concordance level of .80 according to Holsti's (in North et al. 1963, p. 49) formula. Discrepancies between their codings were resolved in discussions with a third check coder.

Data from MRS II

That part of MRS II which provided a replication of MRS I yielded similar results. Again, significantly ($p<.04$) more women (55%) than men (24%) addressed solution aspects of responsibility, and significantly ($p<.02$) more women (68%) than men (42%) mentioned care for others as a vital part of responsibility.

Large discrepancies in the same direction between male and female responses were also elicited by the new third question in MRS II, which asked the respondents: 'Please write down 5 concepts that come to your mind in connection with "responsibility".' Anne Heynen, who conducted this study, constructed the following six categories for the classification of the responses:

Category	Examples
Maturity	Empathy, Reason, Courage, to be in accord with
Care	Protection, Help, Love, Care, Family, Fellow-man
Burden	Annoyance, Dependence, Anxiety, Stress, Irritation
Liability	Causation, Guilt, Consequences, Punishment
Control	Autonomy, Independence, Position, Self-esteem
Values	Freedom, Morality, Fidelity, Justice, Commitment, Nature

For each of these six categories Anne Heynen calculated the percentages of men and of women who gave at least one response falling into that category. The profiles of these percentages across the six categories are represented in figure 12.

Once more, the concept of responsibility was associated by the female group with much more care-orientation than it was by the male respondents. The men in turn were clearly more power- and control-oriented than the women, and there were other large male–female differences with respect to the categories of maturity and values.

It should be kept in mind that our two pilot studies were exploratory investigations. The categories associated with 'responsibility' were derived from, and applied to, the same set of data from MRS II, though without knowledge of the respondents' gender in both procedures; cross-validations

Control needs and severity of reproach

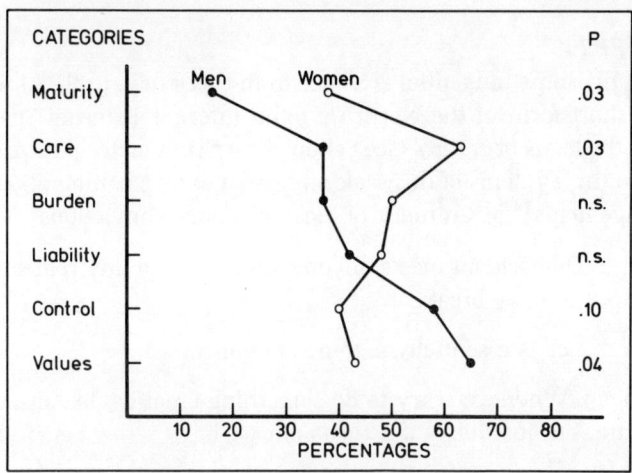

Figure 12. Categories of associations to 'responsibility' and percentages of male and female respondents with at least one response in a given category

are therefore called for. Nevertheless, the concordance of different types of data from four studies seems quite encouraging for our initial reasoning about male and female conceptions of responsibility.

Inference

The inference to be drawn from all this cannot be any firm conclusion, but this cautionary consideration. Even though we may hope that the context in which we present our responsibility measures to various groups of respondents will help to disambiguate the meaning which we attach, and expect our respondents to attach, to the term 'responsibility', we cannot be sure of this. Similar positions of two or more groups on a responsibility attribution scale may hide different connotations of such attributions (see also McGraw 1987, p. 254). Different positions, on the other hand, may suggest a discrepancy with respect to judgement severity that does not exist. The high responsibility attributions by the female respondents in RPS II and III with respect to the situation Neglected Supervision might have been such a case had we not included measures of guilt and cost liability attributions as well, with results which alerted me to the problem discussed in this section.

5.4 Control needs and severity of reproach

This section will be brief, for hypothesis 1.3 on the effects of an opponent's needs for control and self-esteem on the severity of his or her reproach phase reactions is less well researched so far than hypothesis 1.2 on gender effects.

Data from RPS I

I can offer only some tangential evidence from this study. In RPS I we used Schopler's short form of the North Carolina Internal–External Scale as a measure of the locus of control (see Schopler 1973). A factor analysis of the responses to the 25 items of this scale suggested to us a combination of the following five items[46] as an index of luck or chance convictions:

> Item 2. One seldom meets anyone who has had any real success without a lucky break.
>
> Item 7. Life is essentially a game of chance.
>
> Item 15. Whenever I try to do something creative, like drawing a picture, I'm just lucky if it turns out well.
>
> Item 17. Some of the best things that have happened in my life were due to luck.
>
> Item 18. Many events that influence the life of a person are beyond his control.

Responses had to be marked on a five-point scale ranging from complete disagreement (1) to complete agreement (5). The comparison to be presented shortly contains group means of individual scores summed across the five chance conviction items.

Obviously, a measure of chance convictions is not necessarily also a measure of need or desire for control. At times one may be quite content to let luck or chance reign, and in such a mood one may wholeheartedly agree with item 17. The other four items are less optimistic, though, and I would think that in general the belief that chance plays a dominant role in our lives creates uneasiness. Support for this proposition may be inferred from the positive correlation ($r = .21$, $p < .02$) between chance convictions and social anxiety in the respondents in RPS I. Interestingly, this correlation is much stronger, and nearly significantly so ($p < .07$), among the 60 male respondents ($r = .43$, $p < .001$) than among the 60 female respondents ($r = .12$, n.s.).

Uneasiness connected with the belief in chance playing a dominant role seems to be close enough to the desire for more control over one's life to warrant the following inference: in line with hypothesis 1.3 we may expect a positive association between the extent of chance convictions and the degree of guilt attributions. The respondents ($N = 41$) who did not attribute any guilt to the negligent babysitter had a mean chance conviction score of 12.7. The corresponding score for the respondents ($N = 73$) with restricted or unrestricted guilt attributions was 14.1. The difference between these two means is significant at $p < .05$. A similar, but non-significant ($p < .11$) difference

(13.2 vs 14.3) appeared when respondents ($N=58$) who in the Breach of Trust case made guilt attributions in a calm manner were contrasted with those respondents ($N=58$) who attributed unrestricted guilt in a sharp manner.

Studies from other quarters, summarized by Krampen (1982, p. 168), also provide some encouragement. Most relevant among them is the experiment by Goodstadt and Hjelle (1973). They state (p. 190) that 'internally and externally controlled subjects [Rotter's Locus of Control Scale, 1966] were given a range of powers with which to supervise three fictitious workers, one of whom presented a supervisory problem. It was found that in dealing with the problem worker, externally controlled subjects (high powerless) used significantly more coercive power (e.g. threat of deduction of points, threat of firing) than did internally controlled subjects (low powerless).' Higher degrees of aggressiveness and hostility among persons with external control convictions than among internally oriented persons were also reported by C.B. Williams and Vantress (1969) and by Becker and Lesiak (1977). In a study on wives' attributions for conflict in marriage in relation to feelings of control and marital satisfaction, Madden and Janoff-Bulman (1981) found that 'the most satisfied wives are those who do not blame their husbands for marital conflict and who feel they have control over the resolution of conflicts which arise' (p. 670). This finding is also quite in line with hypothesis 1.3.

Data from EPS II

This was the first study on opponent reactions in which we used the Burger and Cooper (1979) scale of control desirability and the items on self-satisfaction referred to in section 3.4. In the present context only some relevant data from the reproach phase condition of EPS II will be reported. More extensive discussions of those moderator variables, their interrelations and their effects on postaccount evaluations will follow in sections 6.3 and 7.3.

The clearest reproach phase effects emerged in connection with the control subscale desire for competence. Two data patterns deserve attention.

The Taxonomy for Opponent Reactions includes a set of secondary categories (sv) for overall assessments of the tendency and differentiation of opponent comments during the reproach phase. One of these categories is sv 12: 'Uniformly negative judgement tendencies'. Significantly ($p<.02$) more respondents with a high desire for competence (41%) than respondents with a low desire for competence (15%) offered statements that fell into category sv 12. This result accords well with hypothesis 1.3.

A similar conclusion may be inferred from an analysis made with the comprehensive category index COMPREVAL as dependent variable. Figure 13 presents the results of a comparison of male and female respondents with

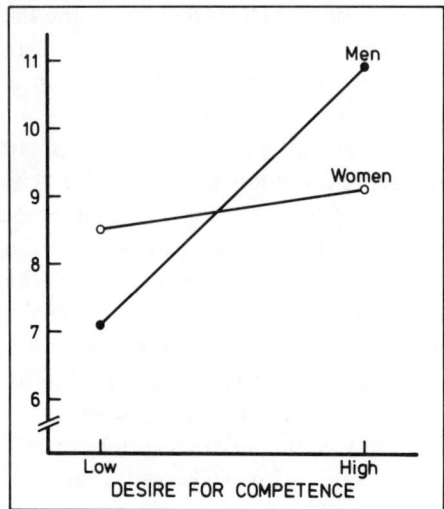

Figure 13. Mean COMPREVAL scores of male and female respondents with high and low desire for competence in the reproach phase condition of EPS II

high and low desire for competence. Cell frequencies range from 13 to 19 cases.

In agreement with our theoretical expectations respondents with a high desire for competence produced, on average, higher COMPREVAL scores than the respondents with a low competence desire. This is particularly true for males ($p < .05$); the difference within the female group is not significant, but the interaction of gender and desire for competence is also not significant. The main effect of the competence factor is marginally significant at $p < .10$. Still, it is noteworthy that once more one can observe a stronger effect, a higher degree of 'reactivity', so to speak, among males than among females.

Data from EPS III

No noteworthy differences appeared when either the index of desire for control or that of self-esteem was introduced as a moderator variable. Since marked moderator effects in accord with theoretical expectations occurred in the evaluation phase of this study (see section 7.3), it seems plausible to assume that a prolonged occupation with the failure event and its consequences was necessary to instigate, or raise above some threshold, the opponents' control needs. I shall return to this point in due course.

Taken together, the results from RPS I, EPS II and EPS III provide only partial support for hypothesis 1.3.

6 Account phase results

The focus now changes to the reactions of actors who were challenged because they seemingly had been involved in a failure event. Severity of reproach is no longer regarded as a dependent variable. In this chapter it is treated as a (quasi) independent variable.

6.1 Effects of severity of reproach on defensiveness of accounts

In the first account phase study (APS I) the reactions of the 'actors' to all three failure situations were elicited by uniformly neutral requests to explain. Thus APS I does not provide a test of hypothesis 2.1. In the subsequent studies, APS II, III and IV, comparable neutral requests served as a control condition for one or more other conditions in which the request for an account was coupled with a disparaging reproach (see chapter 3 for the details).

Data from APS II

The vignette in APS II presented the basic version of the failure event Neglected Supervision. This fact obviously had a strong effect on the general popularity of some feasible accounts. The most prominent theme for the 185 teachers interviewed was the claim of impairment due to situational constraints, for example the unforeseeability of events. The situational constraint argument was offered by 37% of all respondents in an excusatory manner (E 210) and by 18% with a justificative intention (J 210). Unspecified expressions of regret (C 131) were offered by 26%, expressions of regret concerning the actor's own role in the failure event (C 132) or regret concerning the consequences for the victim (C 133) by 20%, and expressions of concern with respect to the failure event, coupled with a plea for pardon (E 711), by 17% of all respondents. All the categories just mentioned occurred about equally often in all three conditions of the study, that is in neutral question (henceforth NQ), derogation of self-esteem (DS) and derogation of sense of control (DC).

Other account themes, however, were strongly dependent upon the type of challenge the actor had to face. Willingness to report on the event in question without excuse, justification or refutational comment was shown by 35% of the respondents in NQ, but only by 5% in DS and DC combined ($p<.001$). The two derogation conditions, DC in particular, elicited far more refutational comments than the neutral question did. A refusal to concede guilt or responsibility for the occurrence of the failure event (R 114) was stated in DC by 33%, in DS by 17%, and in NQ by 3% of the respondents. All three percentages differ significantly (at least $p<.01$) from each other. Comments falling into category R 421, 'Denial of the right to question or reproach in view of the participation of the accuser as co-actor in the failure event', were offered by 5% in NQ and by 15% in DC and DS combined ($p<.04$).

The four cardinal categories can be ordered according to the average defensiveness of their content. Refusals are most defensive, followed as a rule by justifications of one's own behaviour. Excuses which admit some fault or failure but try to minimize one's own involvement in the affair seem to be less defensive than justifications, and concessions of one's own responsibility or guilt, including expressions of regret, are obviously least defensive of all. McLaughlin, Cody and O'Hair (1983) order these four categories in the same way on a mitigation–aggravation continuum (see also Hupka, Jung and Silverthorn (1987)). We may, then, expect a weakening of concession tendencies and possibly also of excuse tendencies in all conditions which instigate or foster an actor's defensiveness. Correspondingly we may expect a strengthening of any refusal tendencies and possibly also of some, or all, justification tendencies under those conditions.

Figure 14 shows, according to expectation, that in the two derogation conditions fewer respondents offered one or more concessionary statements than did so after a neutral question. It turned out that a derogation of the actor's sense of control had a stronger overall effect than a derogation of his or her self-esteem, but the difference between these two conditions is not significant ($chi^2 = 2.32$). The difference between the conditions NQ and DS is significant at $p<.05$ and the difference between NQ and DC at $p<.001$. The data on excuse frequencies in figure 14 show a similar but less pronounced pattern. None of the differences between the three conditions, NQ, DS and DC, is significant.

On the other hand, greater proportions of respondents in the two derogation conditions, DS and DC, offered justifications or refusals (or both) than did so in the NQ condition. The following significance values corroborate the message of the figure. For justifications: DS vs NQ – $p<.03$; DC vs NQ – $p<.002$. For refusals: DS vs NQ – $p<.001$; DC vs NQ – $p<.001$. Again, no significant differences emerged between DS and DC. However, this last statement will have to be qualified in section 6.2 on gender effects.

It should be noted that the four percentages in each condition add up to more than 100%. Many respondents combined, in their accounts, themes with different cardinal aspects. Concessions and excuses in particular figured

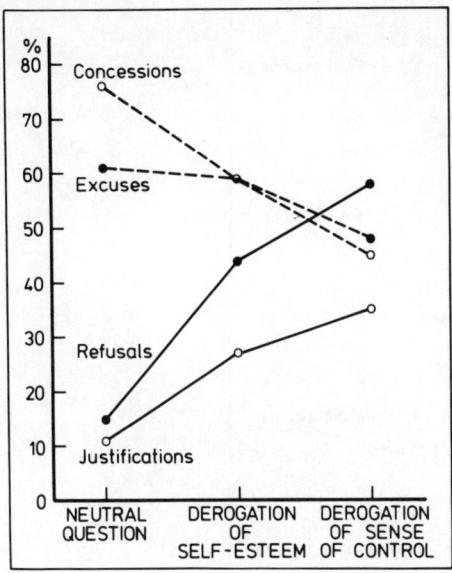

Figure 14. Percentages of respondents within each of three reproach conditions of APS II who offered at least one concession, excuse, justification or refusal

prominently in the accounts even in the two derogation conditions. Nevertheless it is clear that the results of APS II strongly support hypothesis 2.1 on the effects of severity of reproach on defensiveness of accounts.

Data from APS III

This study was an exact replication of the APS II design with a sample of 90 students with fields other than psychology. Hence the results presented in figure 15 are directly comparable to the data pattern in figure 14.

A number of striking similarities are immediately apparent. (1) In the neutral question condition just as many respondents as in APS II made at least one concessionary remark; again, many respondents also offered one or more excuses. On the other hand, refutational or justificative defences were not at all popular in this condition. Moving to the other two conditions, DS and DC, one may once more notice (2) not much change with respect to the frequency of excuses, (3) a slight (but now not significant) rise in the popularity of justifications, and (4) a marked increase in refutations, corroborated by the following chi^2-tests: NQ vs DS – $p<.03$; NQ vs DC – $p<.001$. The rise of refutations in DC beyond the DS level is again not significant.

Besides these striking similarities two differences between the data patterns from APS II and III should be noted. In the derogation of control condition

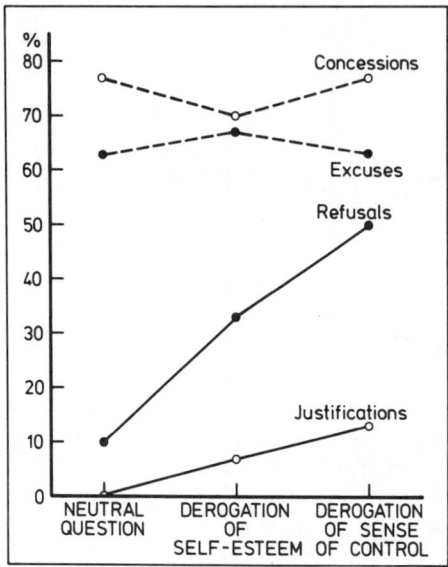

Figure 15. Percentages of respondents within each of three reproach conditions of APS III who offered at least one concession, excuse, justification or refusal

many more students in APS III than teachers in APS II offered at least one concessionary comment ($p < .005$), and in both derogation conditions fewer students than teachers employed a justificative defence ($p < .04$) in each condition.

However, a closer look at the concessions offered in the three conditions of APS III reveals an interesting difference that is again quite in line with hypothesis 2.1: the same number of students in the two conditions NQ and DC – 77% in each group – made some concessionary remark, but the two groups preferred different types of concession (see table 7).

We have grouped the basic category c 111 'Willingness to report on the event in question without excuse, justification or refutational comment' with the categories of c 120 'Admission of responsibility, guilt, mistake, shame, embarrassment' to form a new superordinate category 'Readiness to own up' and to set it apart from 'Expressions of regret' (c 130). In voicing regret concerning the failure event, especially if the focus of regret remains unspecified or uncertain (c 131), one is clearly less outspoken in admitting one's involvement in the failure event than with a statement falling into the range of categories c 111 and c 121 to c 124.

Table 7 shows that many more respondents in the neutral question condition than in either of the two derogation conditions were 'ready to own up'. The latter two groups in DS and DC preferred expressions of regret instead, and did so to a much greater extent than the NQ respondents.

Table 7. Percentages of respondents within each condition of APS III with at least one response falling into the superordinate categories 'Readiness to own up' and 'Expressions of regret'

	NQ	DS	DC
Readiness to own up	63	33	27
Expressions of regret	30	60	67
Number of respondents	30	30	30

Note: Significance levels – $p<.05$: —, $p<.005$: =.

All in all, then, it seems safe to say that the results of APS III also clearly support hypothesis 2.1, even though the student sample in this study appeared to be less defensive under threat of derogation than the teachers in APS II. At present we cannot say if this is a genuine difference in defensiveness or possibly a social desirability effect on the part of the student participants in APS III.

In passing I may mention that in both studies the two cardinal categories, concessions and refusals, which I added to Scott and Lyman's (1968) excuses and justifications, proved to be especially sensitive and useful.

Data from APS IV

The failure event in this study with *Gymnasium* students as respondents was the Stolen Motorbike Lamp. Both degrees of reproach used in APS IV appear to be relatively lenient compared to the derogations directed at the 'actors' of a much less serious norm violation in APS II and III. The 'mild' version consisted of the demand 'Why did you do that?'. The 'severe' version started with an expression of disappointment and ended with the same demand: 'I would not have expected this of you, I am most disappointed! Why did you do it?'

However, this judgement on the relative leniency of the reproaches in APS IV is in need of a qualification. It seems reasonable to assume that, spoken by a teacher, each reproach version – and the severe one in particular – would pose a more serious threat to the student respondents than if it had been spoken by a peer.

The unmistakable violation of a clear norm and the comparative leniency of the reproaches, with the possible exception of the teacher's severe reproach, probably contributed much to the deviations of the data pattern in figure 16 from the constellations in figures 14 and 15.

The high rate of concessions and excuses and the low level of refusals across all four conditions clearly show that, on average, the young

126 Account phase results

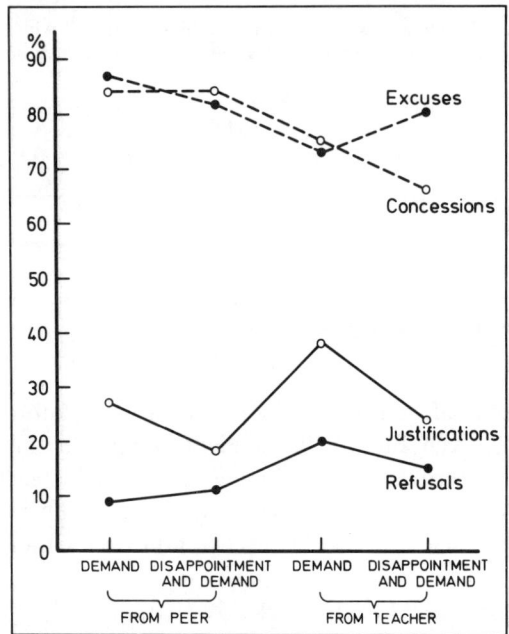

Figure 16. Percentages of respondents within each of four reproach conditions of APS IV who offered at least one concession, excuse, justification or refusal

respondents in APS IV were less defensive in their accounts than the respondents in APS II and III. Ceiling and bottom effects may have contributed to the fact that few significant differences emerged between the experimental conditions. Some weak signs in support of hypothesis 2.1 can nevertheless be recognized. Significantly fewer ($p<.03$) respondents faced with a teacher's reproach than respondents confronted by a peer offered a concession. This inequality remains significant ($p<.05$) if one restricts one's attention to the severe reproaches in the 'disappointment and demand' conditions of teachers and peers. The only other significant ($p<.05$) difference in figure 16 is the higher proportion of justifications in the 'demand by teacher' than in the 'disappointment and demand by peer' condition.

One further part of the data constellation, although not significant, deserves attention. The drop in the proportion of 'concessionary' respondents between the condition with the teacher's simple demand for an explanation and the condition with the teacher's expression of disappointment plus demand is compatible with hypothesis 2.1. The concomitant rise in excuses, more defensive than concessions, might be a partial replacement of a concessionary account strategy. However, the parallel decline in justifications and refusals goes counter to the expectation one would derive from hypothesis 2.1. This decline suggests the possibility of a curvilinear relationship between the severity of threat from a reproach and the defensiveness of an account phase reaction, at least under certain circumstances. Some of the *Gymnasium* students may have considered it unwise to risk antagonizing further an already disappointed and critical teacher. The reader is asked to reserve judgement on this point until further data have been presented in the following section. It will become apparent that the boys in APS IV showed the expected rise in defensiveness with increasing severity of reproach, whereas the girls did not; they, rather, showed the opposite trend.

Provisional conclusions
All three studies lend support to hypothesis 2.1 concerning the effects of severity of reproach on defensiveness of accounts, albeit to different degrees and with more or less prominent qualifications. Support also comes from other quarters. The studies closest to our own were conducted by McLaughlin, Cody and their co-workers. They report that 'the results of these studies indicate that aggravating forms of reproaches lead to aggravating accounts and that aggravating reproach forms rarely lead to mitigating accounts' (Cody and McLaughlin 1985, p. 66).

6.2 Effects of gender on defensiveness of accounts

All four account phase studies were planned to allow for male–female comparisons. Preferences of male and female respondents for certain cardinal categories after various failure situations will be documented first in a synopsis of data from APS I to APS IV. Supplementary evidence on the popularity of superordinate and basic categories among male and female respondents respectively will then be presented. Finally, a further index of defensiveness in rendering accounts will be introduced and applied to some of the data.

Cardinal inclinations of male and female respondents in APS I–IV
With respect to the analysis of nominal data such as the frequencies of various account categories, the division of each sample into male and female respondents precludes (or would at least render very awkward) further subdivision according to various experimental conditions. Table 8 presents an overview of the number of male and female respondents in each account phase study.

Table 9 offers a synopsis of male and female cardinal preferences after four failure events: Dubious Self-Defence and Breach of Trust in APS I, Neglected Supervision in APS I, II and III, and the Stolen Motorbike Lamp in APS IV. In

Table 8. Number of male and female respondents in four account phase studies

	Male respondents	Female respondents
APS I	92	88
APS II	92	93
APS III	45	45
APS IV	84	87

Table 9. Percentages of male and female respondents who offered at least one concession, excuse, justification or refusal in the failure event situations of APS I–IV

	Concessions		Excuses		Justifications		Refusals	
	Male	Female	Male	Female	Male	Female	Male	Female
APS I								
Dubious Self-Defence	35	34	58 ≪ 75		49	48	39 > 17	
Breach of Trust	86 < 97		73	70	0	2	15 ≫ 2	
Neglected Supervision	64 <: 77		60	58	13	17	33	24
APS II								
Neglected Supervision	60	60	49 < 63		27	22	45 :> 33	
APS III								
Neglected Supervision	82	67	67	62	9	4	31	31
APS IV								
Stolen Motorbike Lamp	75 <: 80		76 <: 85		33 > 20		11	16

Note: Indication of significance levels at .005 marked by ≪, at .05 by <. See text for differences marked by <:.

a sense, one is looking for a main effect of gender in this table, an effect that is strong enough to manifest itself over and above the variance created by the different reproach conditions in APS II, III and IV, and by the different types of respondent – students in APS I and III, teachers in APS II, and adolescents in APS IV.

First of all, among the inferences to be drawn from table 9 there are fairly strong signs in favour of hypothesis 2.2 that on average males are more defensive than females when challenged to render an account for a failure event. However, these signs do not form a monolithic picture; they vary, rather, from situation to situation, and understandably so.

Table 9 contains six male–female comparisons in which the proportion of female respondents with at least one instance of the cardinal category in question was significantly higher (or almost significantly so, by conventional standards) than the proportion of males. All six cases belong to the less defensive range of account phase reactions – the categories of concessions and excuses. Four other comparisons show significantly or almost significantly higher male than female proportions, and they are all in the range of the more defensive categories of justifications and refusals.

To be sure, these ten cases do not constitute ten independent corroborations of hypothesis 2.2. Moreover, the proportions across the four cardinal categories are not independent of each other, although in theory every combination of cardinal aspects within an account is possible, nor are the responses to the three failure situations in APS I based on independent measurements. It is intriguing to see, though, that no strong carry-over effects from one situation to the other in APS I seem to have occurred. The least justifiable failure event was clearly the Breach of Trust towards the ex-convict. This case drew the highest proportion of concessions within each gender column, yet the female students still excelled their male colleagues in this respect. The most justifiable case was the Dubious Self-Defence with the legally relevant self-defence argument readily available. Almost one half of the sample, men and women alike, made use of it, and this probably diminished their inclination to offer outright concessions. Nevertheless, the women still proved to be less defensive than the men, but now by a much more widespread tendency towards excuses, while more than twice as many males than females made at least one refutational comment.

Indications in favour of hypothesis 2.2 are weakest in the data pertaining to the situation Neglected Supervision. I have already discussed this gender-sensitive situation in connection with the reproach phase data from RPS III in section 5.2. Although the women in this study were clearly less defensive than the men in making responsibility, guilt and cost liability attributions to the negligent babysitter, they did show some defensiveness in the two gender-sensitive failure situations Neglected Supervision and Neglected Oil Puddle, especially with respect to guilt attributions. Thus it seems reasonable to assume for the time being that in the most 'feminine' situation of the four failure events employed in our account phase studies, that is the negligence of the babysitter, the female respondents in the actor's role tended to react somewhat defensively too. Such a response disposition probably contributed much to the diminution, or elimination as in APS III, of the otherwise prevailing inequalities of male and female cardinal preferences. Some reliable differences in the expected direction do nevertheless exist even in the Neglected Supervision condition, as parts of the following supplementary data will corroborate.

Supplementary information from APS I
The difference between the percentage of female students (77%) and the percentage of male students (64%) who offered at least one concessionary comment in the Neglected Supervision situation does not reach a conventional level of significance, but at $p < .07$ it is not far from it. Furthermore, a closer look at the types of concession made confirms the difference just presented. Significantly ($p < .05$) more women (66%) than men (49%) offered outright admissions of their responsibility, guilt or shame in the

imagined babysitter situation or expressed their regret concerning the accident in general or more specifically with respect to their own role in it and/or the consequences for the victim (C 112, C 122-4, C 131-3).

Another difference between men and women became apparent with the cross-cardinal theme 'Effort and care' (E, J, R 523). In Neglected Supervision this theme was mainly offered in an excusatory vein (16% of all women and 9% of all men). However, some respondents invoked this theme also with a justificative intent (8% of the women and 5% of the men), and some others even with refutational overtones (7% of the women and 2% of the men). Counting one male respondent with multiple cardinal reference (EJ 523) just once and adding these percentages within each gender group, we arrive at another clearly significant ($p < .02$) difference between men (15%) and women (31%). More women than men are eager to refer to their appropriate conduct before or right after the failure event. Correspondingly, in the Breach of Trust situation, with the possibility of making amends in the future, many more women (61%) than men (40%) showed some willingness to help (C 524) in the form of support, restitution or compensation. This difference is significant at $p < .005$. Obviously, more women than men were concerned with showing good conduct in connection with these two failure events.

With regard to the situation Dubious Self-Defence two data patterns deserve additional attention.

1 Not only did far more women than men offer at least one excuse for the self-defensive act (see table 9), but women also invoked on average significantly ($p < .005$)[47] more excusatory themes ($x = 2.10$) than men did ($x = 1.14$).

2 One of the most prominent excusatory themes was the reference to the actor's affective state (E 150) during the encounter with the drunkard. Of all men 49%, and of all women 65% ($p < .04$), said something falling into this category. The most prominent justificative category was the claim of situational constraints as fully or partly legitimizing the actor's conduct during the encounter (J 210). Within each gender group 11% employed this argument. Some respondents combined the two themes just mentioned, but the males did so significantly more often than the women. In the female group the association between the two categories E 150 and J 210 is quite low (phi $= -.11$) and not significant. In the male group the association between E 150 and J 210 is clearly positive and significant (phi $= +.36$, $p < .001$). This discrepancy between the female and the male response patterns is significant at $p < .003$ according to a log-linear analysis. The women restricted their references to the affective state mainly to its function as an excusatory impairment claim. The men tended more strongly towards connecting their affective impairment claims with a justification due to the situational constraints in the encounter with the drunkard. This may be

taken as yet another sign of the proposed higher defensiveness of males in rendering an account.

Supplementary information from APS II

The difference between excusatory inclinations of female and male teachers in this study was most pronounced among the respondents confronted with the neutral question. In this condition 74% of the females, yet only 48% of the males, offered at least one excuse ($p<.04$). Male tendencies towards refusals, on the other hand, diverged most clearly from the corresponding female response level in the severest reproach condition, derogation of sense of control. In this condition 73% of the males and only 43% of the females made at least one refutational remark ($p<.02$).

Besides R 114 (Refusal to concede guilt or responsibility), the two most popular refutational themes in the two derogation conditions DS and DC were the following:

> R 421. Denial of the right to question or reproach in view of the participation of the accuser as co-actor in the failure event.

> R 431. Denial of the right to question or reproach in view of the limitations, negative traits or misdeeds of the accuser.

Comments falling into these two categories were offered by 15% and 13% of all respondents in DS and DC, and men and women differed very little in this respect. After all, it sounds fair enough to say in this situation that the parents should have kept the cleaning fluid in a safe place or that exactly the same event, the boy sneaking into the kitchen while they were watching television, might have happened to the parents. It is, of course, a different matter to discern whether such arguments are put forward as a refutation of the opponent's challenge or reproach, or whether they are offered with an excusatory intention. In this latter respect the male and female respondents did again differ markedly. Of the female respondents 26% fell into one or both of the two excuse categories E 421 and E 431, but only 7% of the males in the reproach conditions DS and DC did so ($p<.005$). Women fairly frequently made the tentative allusion to the opponent's actual or potential role in the failure event Neglected Supervision, but it seems that, as a group, they preferred to do so in the less aggressively defensive manner of an excuse. The male group, on the contrary, showed few qualms in using such allusions as part of a refutational account strategy.

Additional information from APS IV

There is no need to present any further data from APS III in the present context. At the level of the basic categories, again no significant differences between male and female respondents could be detected in this study.

In APS IV the slight preponderance of females among the respondents with concessions, as well as among those with excuses (see table 9), becomes more pronounced with partitions nearest the median. Two or more concessionary themes were offered by 57% of the girls and by 44% of the boys ($p<.09$). Two or more excusatory themes were offered by 71% of the girls, but only by 48% of the boys ($p<.002$).

On the basic category level the biggest difference between male and female respondents appeared in the domain of the category E 522 'Appeal to good intentions or lack of bad intentions . . .' and E 525 'Appeal to own learning experience in connection with the failure event and/or promise of avoidance of similar failures in the future . . .'. Remarks falling into one or both of these categories were made by 41% of the girls and by 18% of the boys ($p<.001$). This data pattern is strongly reminiscent of the results from APS I, which pointed to greater efforts among females than among males to show good conduct in connection with the failure event.

Many (and significantly, $p<.001$) more females (51%) than males (31%) also drew upon one or more of the excusatory claims of impairment – those due to situational constraints (E 210), time pressure (E 220), loyalties to higher-order norms (E 230) or to specific other persons (E 240), or pressures from powerful agents (E 310).

Perhaps the most interesting finding that emerged from the analysis reported so far with respect to the APS IV data was a three-way interaction of gender of respondents, severity of reproach from the adult opponent and tendency to respond with multiple concessions. Even though this interaction does not reach significance (chi^2 = 1.36) according to a log-linear analysis, it deserves attention. Two or more concessionary themes were offered by 60% of the boys to the teacher with the mild reproach, but only by 30% of the boys confronted by the teacher with the severe reproach. With the girls it was the other way round. To the teacher with the mild reproach only 40% of the girls offered two or more concessions, to the teacher with the severe reproach 52% of the girls reacted in this way.

As I have already mentioned in section 6.1, such data patterns suggest the possibility that under specific circumstances a further increase of severity and the threat of a reproach does not lead to a concomitant further rise of defensiveness in an actor's accounting but rather to a reversal and a move towards a concessionary mood. But it is awkward to pursue such analysis at the nominal scale level. The percentages just presented are based on totals not larger than 20 or 21. Furthermore, much available information is neglected or inadequately represented in such multidimensional analysis at the nominal level. It is time to introduce another measure of account phase defensiveness.

Table 10. Mean CARDACOM values of male and female respondents in the failure event conditions of APS I–IV

	Male respondents		Female respondents
APS I			
Dubious Self-Defence	9.62	:>	8.78
Breach of Trust	5.92	≫	4.45
Neglected Supervision	8.60		8.38
APS II			
Neglected Supervision	9.43	:>	8.40
APS III			
Neglected Supervision	7.18		7.69
APS IV			
Stolen Motorbike Lamp	6.39	≫	4.55

Note: Indication of significance levels at .005 marked by ≫, at .10 by :>.

CARDACOM: *a comprehensive index of defensiveness in account phases*

Refusals, justifications, excuses and concessions form a rank order of decreasing average defensiveness of the themes subsumed under these four cardinal categories. This suggested to me the following summation index, which quickly proved to be sensitive and useful. I dubbed the index with the acronym CARDACOM because it represents a *Card*inal *A*spect *Com*bination. CARDACOM equals twice the number of refutational themes (r) in an actor's account, plus the number of justificative themes (j), minus the number of excusatory themes (e), minus twice the number of concessionary themes (c), plus a constant of ten in order to avoid negative numbers. For short then:

$$\text{CARDACOM:} = 2\Sigma r + \Sigma j - \Sigma e - 2\Sigma c + 10.$$

I am happy to report that in our account phase studies the CARDACOM values formed nicely bell-shaped distributions with fairly stable within-cell variances. Thus the way was open for multifactor analyses of variance.

Average CARDACOM *scores of male and female respondents*

Considering the data presented so far and the construction principle of CARDACOM, it is not surprising that table 10 mirrors the generally higher defensiveness of males shown in table 9. The CARDACOM values of male and female respondents in the various failure situations are mainly presented for purposes of comparison. What really counts is that we are now able to look for first-order and second-order interactions of several independent and moderator variables.

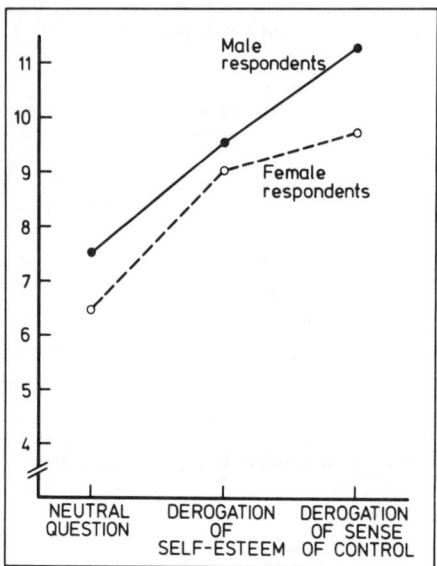

Figure 17. Mean CARDACOM values of male and female respondents within the three reproach conditions of APS II

Figure 17, with the CARDACOM values from APS II, illustrates a pure case of two main effects with no interaction. The factor version of reproach produced a highly significant ($p < .001$) effect; the factor gender is marginally significant ($p < .10$). A posteriori tests following Newman-Keuls proved these contrasts to be significant at $p < .05$: for female respondents – NQ vs DS, NQ vs DC; for male respondents – NQ vs DC.

Figure 18, with corresponding CARDACOM values from APS IV, presents an intriguing pattern of three factors: gender of respondents, status of opponents and severity of reproach. At first sight one might expect a significant three-way interaction of these factors but this expectation is not confirmed. There is a significant ($p < .04$) two-way interaction between gender and severity of reproach. Among the boys, defensiveness as measured by CARDACOM increased, as expected according to hypothesis 2.1, with increasing severity of reproach. No such increase occurred with the girls; there was, rather, a sharp drop between the two groups of girls confronted by a teacher's reproach. Newman-Keuls a posteriori tests reproduce only the main effect of gender among the four groups confronted with a peer reproach.

Even though the three-way interaction was clearly not significant, it seems obvious that the four respondent groups confronted by a teacher contributed most to the significant two-way interaction, and it also seems clear that the

Effects of gender

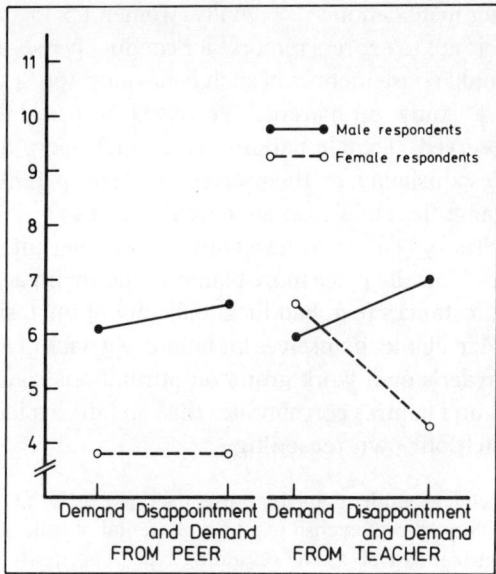

Figure 18. Mean CARDACOM values of male and female respondents within the four reproach conditions of APS IV

discrepancy between the psychological meaning of a male teacher's reproach and a reproach from a same-gender classmate was much greater for the girls than for the boys. At present we can only surmise that perhaps the teacher's reproach, even the mild version, appeared to the girls subjectively much more severe than it did to the boys. One possible inference from such a state of affairs would be the hypothesis that under certain conditions the relationship between increasing severity of reproach and defensiveness of accounts may become curvilinear, hill-shaped, to be precise.

Whatever the explanation of the reversal phenomenon in figure 18 turns out to be, it must be taken as a warning that both hypotheses, 2.1 and 2.2, well supported as they seem at present, may be in need of some limiting qualifications.

Related evidence
Manifold support for hypothesis 2.2 and some qualification has been proposed. I shall conclude this section with a look at relevant studies from other institutes.

Rothman and Gandossy (1982), in a study of accounts of convicted white-collar offenders, reported that 'women admit guilt much more often than men. They also acknowledge personal responsibility more readily, and more frequently provide strong justifications . . . Finally, women apologize more often; they are, moreover, apt to express remorse for conduct per se, and not merely refer to the personal consequences of such behaviour' (pp. 459–60).

Penfold (1985), in a study on parents' perceived responsibility for children's problems, observed: 'Female parents were much more likely to attribute all or some responsibility to themselves . . . Male parents were much more likely to blame the child's female parents' (p. 257).

Snyder, Higgins and Stucky (1983), in reviewing several relevant studies, state (p. 180) that 'males typically place more blame for failure [in academic areas] on external circumstances (e.g. bad luck, difficulty of the task) than females do. Females tend to blame themselves for failure (e.g. lack of ability).' A recent study from Snyder's own work group on attributions concerning academic achievements and failures corroborates this, and the explanations offered very closely match our own reasoning:

> Perhaps the male college students in the present sample view the apparent responsibility type of excuse (e.g., simple denial of believability of getting a poor grade) as well as the reframing type of excuse (e.g., saying the grade wasn't important, and minimizing how badly they did) as working best for them. That is, such strategies may help them preserve personal esteem, or may even work to maintain one's image with college peers. Given a choice of differing types of excuses, the present college males may have invoked the somewhat 'macho' plays of 'I didn't do it' and 'It's not so bad.' . . . the female college students in our study were less likely to employ the apparent and reframing excuses relative to males, but were more likely to utilize transformed responsibility excuses. (Snyder, Ford and Hunt 1985, pp. 13–14)

Cupach, Metts and Hazleton (1986) performed two studies on coping with embarrassing predicaments. In one study they investigated reported use and found that 'males and females do not differ in any meaningful way when describing what they would do in an embarrassing predicament' (p. 197). They duly note, though, as every researcher in our domain of discourse should, that 'the findings discussed above must be qualified given the limitations of using researcher-constructed scenarios' (p. 198). The authors note that the two predicaments used, that is spilling gravy over one's shirt and realizing at the check-out counter of a grocery store that one has forgotten the chequebook, are rather generic situations for which 'males and females [may] have internalized comparable social expectations or scripts' (p. 197).

In the other study, Cupach, Metts and Hazleton (1986) tested and corroborated the hypothesis that females would be 'significantly more likely to rate excuses as appropriate for remediating embarrassment than were males. Likewise females also demonstrated a preference for apologies when compared to males, although this trend was not statistically significant [$p < .07$]. These findings replicate those of Petronio (1984) and suggest that women are more likely than men to accept responsibility for their untoward actions' (p. 189). Males, on the other hand, 'perceived avoidance as more effective than females, although they did not indicate that it was more appropriate' (ibid).

Hupka, Jung and Silverthorn (1987), in a study on the perceived acceptability of apologies, excuses and justifications in jealousy predicaments, did not find any main effect for gender. But 'an Intent × Account × Gender interaction, ($p < .03$), revealed that males and females agreed in their preference for apologies, excuses, and justifications when the intent was to maintain the relationship with the infidelious mate ... The sequence differed when the intent was to end it. Females still preferred apologies above justifications and excuses ... whereas the first choice for the males was justifications, followed by apologies and excuses' (p. 310).

Also relevant in a wider frame is a study by Calicchia and Pardine (1984) on attributional style depending upon degree of depression, respondent's sex, and nature of the attributional event. They report (pp. 171–2):

> When the clinical depressive diagnostic classifications were collapsed and responses to the attributional events [e.g. unsuccessful job hunting] viewed in terms of respondents' sex, females, in contrast to males, were found to assume more personal responsibility for life's bad outcomes than for good ones, $F(1,306) = 7.88$. They were also considerably more evenhanded (less biased) than males whose responses were quite lopsided, $F(1,306) = 10.45$. The reverse was demonstrated for good outcomes: males reported more responsibility than females for their successes than failure, $F(1,306) = 6.32$.

All in all, then, the prediction of a main effect of gender on defensiveness during phases of account seems to be well supported. However, it remains as a task for the future to establish its limitations.

6.3 Sense of control, self-esteem and defensiveness of accounts

In this section I shall present data on the 'effects' of four moderator variables on the degree of defensiveness in the accounts offered by the respondents in APS II, III and IV. These moderator variables are (1) desire for control, as measured by the 20 items of our German version of the Burger and Cooper (1979) scale, (2) need for competence and influence and (3) need for constancy and shielding, as measured by our two subscales derived from the Burger and Cooper scale (see p. 57) and (4) self-dissatisfaction, as measured by the items adopted from the scales of Hormuth and Lalli (1986) and Bergemann and Johann (1985) (see p. 57 and note 24).

Table 11. *Correlations between moderator variables among male and female respondents in five studies*

	Male respondents		Female respondents
Desire for control and self-dissatisfaction			
APS II	$-.45^a$		$-.54^a$
APS III	$-.21^c$		$-.38^a$
APS IV	$-.26^a$	<	$-.50^a$
EPS II	$-.20^b$		$-.33^a$
EPS III	$-.38^a$		$-.19^c$
Desire for control and social anxiety			
APS II	$-.48^a$		$-.43^a$
APS III	$-.24^c$		$-.40^a$
Self-dissatisfaction and social anxiety			
APS II	$.42^a$		$.48^a$
APS III	$.24^c$		$.52^a$
Desire for competence and desire for constancy			
APS II	$.45^a$		$.41^a$
APS III	$.31^b$		$.30^b$
APS IV	$.19^b$		$.37^a$
EPS II	$.15^c$		$.21^b$
EPS III	$.43^a$	>	$.09$

Note: All coefficients (r) marked ^{a} are significant at $p < .01$, those marked ^{b} at $p < .05$, those marked ^{c} at $p < .10$. The male–female differences marked < are significant at $p < .07$.

Associations among the moderator variables

Before talking about the modifying effects of these variables it will be necessary to discuss their interrelations. Originally I assumed, perhaps naively, that desire for control and self-dissatisfaction would covary. A closer look at the content and wording of the Burger and Cooper items might have warned me, but in the light of escalation theory it seemed reasonable to expect a positive correlation between the desire (or need?) for control, on the one hand, and the degree of self-dissatisfaction (or need for improving self-esteem?), on the other.

The data, however, proved me wrong. Table 11 shows that in all five studies in which we have so far included those measures, substantial negative coefficients of correlation between desire for control and self-dissatisfaction emerged in both male and female groups of various ages and occupations. In two studies, APS II and III, we were also able to assess the association of these two moderator variables with social anxiety, and the results, also included in table 11, support the conclusion that is to be drawn from the negative correlations between desire for control and self-dissatisfaction.

Obviously, those who desire control are *not*, as a rule, self-dissatisfied or socially anxious. It seems that they not only wish to have control, but that they also rather confidently assume that they actually have control. Inspection of the Burger and Cooper items supports this view. One example (item 8) may illustrate this: 'I enjoy making my own decisions.'

The subscores for desire for competence and desire for constancy correlate positively in all four studies, among males and females alike. However, the associations documented in table 11 are only moderately strong at best. The variances 'explained' by these six correlations form an average value of 10% of the total variances. This justifies our decision not to content ourselves with a general measure of desire for control as a predictor variable, but to search also for specific effects of needs or of claims for competence and constancy.

The meaning of self-dissatisfaction is highlighted by the fairly substantial positive correlations with social anxiety in APS II and III, as well as by the negative correlations between social anxiety and desire (i.e. claim) for control. The coefficients in table 11 point to a three-way constellation of social anxiety (SA), self-dissatisfaction (SD) and desire for control (DC):

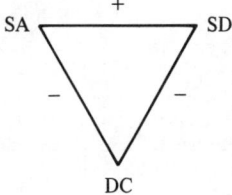

The data do not tell us anything about the causal connections in this constellation, but as a hypothesis I would propose a bidirectional vicious circle: awkward and anxious feelings of being inept in social situations are likely to engender resignation and abstention from demands for control, but this will leave the person dissatisfied with his or her self-image, and such self-dissatisfaction will nourish feelings of social embarrassment and anxiety. Or the other way round: self-dissatisfaction will detract from one's sense of having control and will lessen self-confident demands for control; this in turn will provoke social anxiety, and such anxiety is likely to increase self-dissatisfaction. Careful work will be required to test these speculations.

Male and female positions on the moderator dimensions

The first part of table 12 presents a data pattern that is quite encouraging for escalation theory. In four of the five studies male respondents produced a

Table 12. Mean male and female values on various moderator dimensions in four studies

	Males		Females
Desire for control			
APS II	3.66	>	3.53
APS III	3.62		3.63
APS IV	3.50		3.42
EPS II	3.62	>	3.49
EPS III	3.67	≫	3.39
Desire for competence			
APS II	3.47	:>	3.32
APS III	3.43		3.47
APS IV	3.12		3.14
EPS II	3.40		3.28
EPS III	3.37	≫	3.02
Desire for constancy			
APS II	3.96		3.91
APS III	3.87		3.90
APS IV	3.94		3.83
EPS II	3.90		3.83
EPS III	4.06	:>	3.88
Self-dissatisfaction			
APS II	2.58		2.72
APS III	2.51		2.40
APS IV	2.46		2.54
EPS II	2.72		2.63
EPS III	2.42	<:	2.62
Social anxiety			
APS II	2.34	≪	2.75
APS III	2.71		2.58

Note: Significant male–female differences are marked by ≪ at $p<.001$, by < at $p<.05$, and by <: at $p<.10$.

higher average value on desire for control than female respondents, and in three of these cases the differences turned out to be significant. This result is welcome because all three hypotheses (1.2, 2.2 and 3.2) concerning gender effects – on severity of reproach, defensiveness of accounts and negativity of evaluations – rest on the assumption of generally higher needs and demands for control among men than among women.

In one study, APS III, no gender differences on desire for control appeared. The female students produced a mean value on this dimension that was just as high as the corresponding mean of the male students, and significantly ($p<.04$) higher than the desire of control mean of the comparable female student respondents in EPS II. In line with this finding are the social anxiety and self-dissatisfaction means from APS III.

Contrary to all the other studies in which we assessed social anxiety and

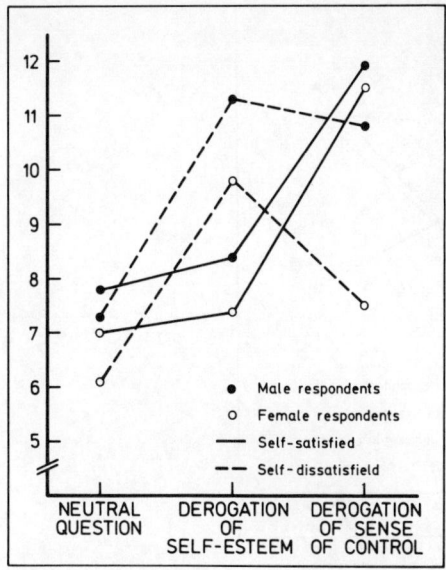

Figure 19. Mean CARDACOM values of self-satisfied and self-dissatisfied male and female respondents within the three reproach conditions of APS II

always found the females to be significantly more anxious than the males, it is the other way around, though non-significantly, in APS III. Furthermore, the females in this study obtained the lowest self-dissatisfaction value of the ten groups compared in table 12. All this suggests that the comparatively small subsample ($N = 45$) of female students in APS III contained a relatively large number of self-confident women who did not hesitate to voice their claim for control, and this composition of the female group may well have been responsible for the lack of gender differences in APS III with respect to account strategies.

With this background information we may now turn to the moderator effects on defensiveness of accounts.

Moderator effects in APS II

Many convergent data patterns could be presented, but space considerations force us to restrict ourselves to a few representative examples.

Self-dissatisfaction. Figure 19 presents the average CARDACOM values of 12 respondent groups that were formed by dividing the sample according to gender, reproach version and a median split on the self-dissatisfaction dimension. Cell frequencies range from 10 to 22 with a mean near 15 cases.

Figure 19 offers an impressively regular data constellation with two clear

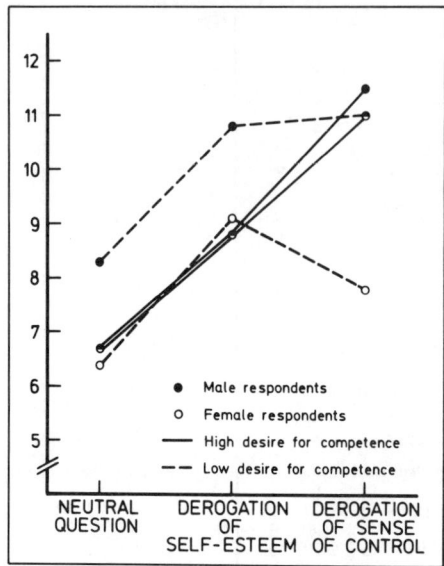

Figure 20. Mean CARDACOM values of male and female respondents with high and low desire for competence within three reproach conditions of APS II

main effects, of reproach version ($p<.001$) and gender ($p<.03$), and a highly significant ($p<.003$) interaction of reproach version with self-dissatisfaction. An actor's self-satisfaction or self-dissatisfaction did not play an important role in determining his or her account defensiveness in response to a neutral question. The reproach which contained a derogation of the actor's self left the self-satisfied respondents fairly unruffled, it would seem, but this reproach had a markedly antagonizing effect on the self-dissatisfied respondents and induced much defensiveness in the accounts from this group. Finally, the derogation of the actor's control capacity also, and most notably, awakened the defences of the self-satisfied respondents. This fact should be seen in the light of the moderating effects of high and low desire (and claim) for control.

Desire for competence. Figure 20 presents the data constellation that emerges when self-dissatisfaction is replaced by desire for competence as the moderator variable to be considered in conjunction with the factors gender and reproach version.

The parallels between figures 19 and 20 are obvious despite some noticeable differences and the fact that the interaction between reproach version and desire for competence is not significant ($p<.13$) by conventional standards. There are again two main effects, of reproach version ($p<.001$)

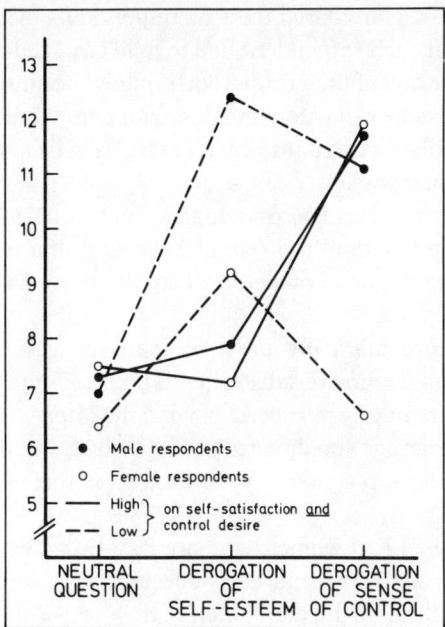

Figure 21. Mean CARDACOM values of male and female respondents high and low on both self-satisfaction and control desire within the three reproach conditions of APS II

and of gender ($p < .06$), and in addition a hint ($p < .11$) at an interaction between gender and desire for competence.

The parallels, it would seem, are largely due to the covariation between self-satisfaction and desire for control. I would venture the following interpretation. The person, man or woman, who self-confidently assumes that he or she is generally well in control is shocked to see this assumption questioned and criticized by an opponent's derogatory remark and hence reacts particularly strongly with a defensive account. The self-dissatisfied person who does not expect to have (and hence does not claim) as much control is slightly less provoked to a defensive reaction by a derogatory remark about his or her control capacities; however, such a person will be particularly sensitive to a direct attack on his or her already brittle feelings of self-worth. Men seem to be particularly vulnerable in this respect, and they also tolerate less well than women an attack on their sense of control.

Some support for this interpretation can be gained by sharpening the moderator contrast in a comparison of two groups of respondents through the following moderator *combinations*. The two groups are (1) self-satisfied people with a high desire for control and (2) self-dissatisfied people with a low desire for control. Figure 21 presents the relevant data.

The comparisons in figure 21 are based on 130 respondents in all. The attrition is due to the fact that each respondent had to fulfil two median-split criteria in order to qualify for one of the groups. Fortunately, because of the positive correlation between self-satisfaction and desire for control, sufficient cases (6 to 20 with a mean near 11) fell into each of the 12 cells to make a three-way analysis of variance possible.

The results of this analysis are clear. There is a highly significant ($p < .001$) interaction of moderator combination and reproach version and a marginally significant ($p < .09$) interaction of moderator combination and gender of respondents.

Once more, and even more markedly now, we can see very similar reactions from men and women who are satisfied with their self-images and who demand control. They are hardly disturbed, beyond the impact from the challenging question, by the derogation directed at their selves, but they are very much aroused to defensive reactions by an attack on their sense of control.

On the other hand, both men and women who are dissatisfied with their selves and do not claim much control are markedly affected by the derogation of their selves, even more so than by the derogation of their sense of control. Yet over and above this common pattern in both genders we have to note a much higher defensiveness among males than among females in the two derogation conditions. In fact, this group of self-dissatisfied males reacted to the derogation of their sense of control, despite their pronounced low desire for control, hardly less defensively than males and females with high control desire.

It may be time to entertain the possibility that marking one and the same segment on our moderator dimensions does not on average represent the same subjective meaning for male and female respondents. A man admitting to some self-dissatisfaction in response to the scale items may either be more vulnerable than a woman with the same response pattern, or in fact truly more dissatisfied than that woman. Essentially the same point will come up again shortly in connection with the results from APS IV.

Moderator variables in APS III

Neither desire for control and various subscales derived from it, nor self-dissatisfaction, contributed to any significant data constellations in this study. The result that comes closest to a conventional level of significance is a three-way interaction ($p < .08$) of reproach version, gender and self-dissatisfaction with a pattern that partly resembles, and partly diverges from, the corresponding data in APS II. Rather than try and salvage some non-significant data segments in tentative support of hypothesis 2.3, it seems best

Table 13. Mean desire for competence values of male and female respondents confronted by a peer's reproach and by a teacher's reproach in APS IV

	Male respondents	Female respndents
Peer reproach	3.21	2.99 ⎤
Teacher reproach	3.02	3.31 ⎦

Note: ⎣⎯⎯⎯⎦ indicates $p < .05$ according to the Newman–Keuls test. Cell frequencies range from 40 to 46.

to conclude that there is no corroboration from APS III for the hypothesis concerning the effects of control needs and self-esteem on defensiveness of accounts.

Moderator effects in APS IV

Pretesting had suggested that in this study with adolescents in a school setting it would be wise for motivational reasons to reverse the order of events followed in APS II and III. In APS IV the respondents first encountered the vignette of the failure event and the task of rendering an account *before* they saw and marked the scale items on desire for control and self-dissatisfaction. This arrangement allows for the possibility that the answers pertaining to the moderator dimensions are partly influenced by the experimental manipulations, and such effects did indeed occur. With respect to desire for competence a significant ($p < .002$) interaction between gender of respondent and status of opponent appeared, as can be seen in table 13.

It is apparent that the girls who had to face a male teacher's reproach reacted with much stronger claims for competence than either the boys did in this situation or the other girls did who faced the reproach from a female classmate. This is yet another indication that the teacher's reproach had rather different connotations for boys and girls – more threatening to the latter, it seems, and hence affecting not only their account behaviour but beyond that also the manifestations of their control desires.

Again, many mutually supportive data patterns for account defensiveness could be presented, but I shall restrict myself to one particularly telling case: the combined effects of the opponent's status, the severity of the reproach, the gender of the respondents and the respondents' desire for control. Two diagrams, figures 22 and 23, are required to show the relevant data constellations in a sufficiently clear form.

Besides the effects already discussed, a multifactor ANOVA produced two significant first-order interactions, namely desire for control × gender ($p < .04$) and desire for control × severity of reproach ($p < .02$), and in

146 Account phase results

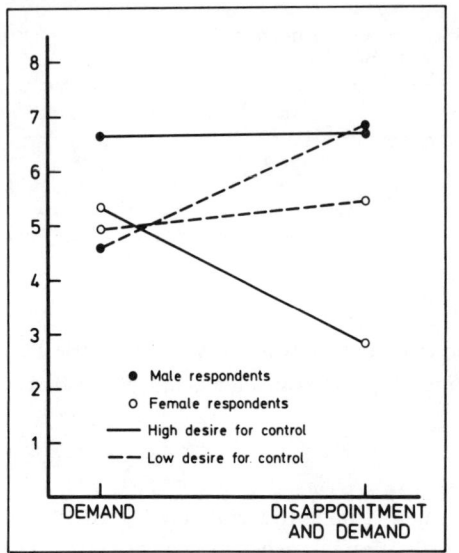

Figure 22. Mean CARDACOM values of male and female respondents with high and low desire for control, after a mild and a severe reproach in APS IV

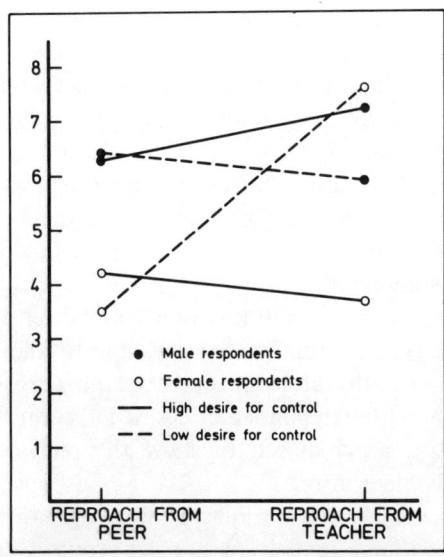

Figure 23. Mean CARDACOM values of male and female respondents with high and low desire for control, after a peer's reproach and a teacher's reproach in APS IV

addition a second-order interaction of desire for control × gender × opponent's status ($p < .002$). The two first-order interactions are depicted in figure 22, the second-order interaction in figure 23.

Consider first the interaction of control desire with reproach version. Respondents with low control desire reacted *more* defensively to the severe reproach than to the mild reproach. Respondents with high control desire (notably, though not significantly so, the girls) reacted less defensively to the severe than to the mild reproach.

The interaction of control desire with respondents' gender rests on the fact that among the boys those with high control desire reacted more defensively than those with low control desire. With the girls it was the other way round: more defensiveness was shown by the girls with low than by those with high control desire.

Figure 23 with the second-order interaction shows a partly similar pattern. Boys with high control desire reacted to the presumably more serious reproach from a teacher more defensively than the boys with low control desire did, whereas these two male groups did not differ in their reactions to the reproach from a peer. The two female groups also did not differ much in their reaction to the peer reproach. However, they markedly diverged in their reaction to the teacher reproach and in a way opposite to that of the male groups. Girls with low control desire confronted by a teacher's reproach reacted more defensively than all other groups. Girls with high control desire, on the other hand, reacted to a teacher's reproach with markedly little defensiveness compared to the other groups.

How are these complicated patterns to be explained? There are no proofs, but with the help of some further suggestive data we may speculate. Remember the associations between self-dissatisfaction and low control desire listed in table 11. In APS IV the negative correlation between self-dissatisfaction and desire for control was clearly (and near significantly at $p < .07$) stronger among the girls ($r = -.50$) than among the boys ($r = -.26$). This suggests that the gradients of the girls with low control desires in figures 22 and 23 mirror the effects of self-dissatisfaction on their reactions to lenient and serious reproaches. Table 14 corroborates this reasoning. It shows that among the self-dissatisfied respondents both males and females, but especially the girls, reacted much more strongly to a reproach from the teacher than to a classmate's reproach. The difference is significant at $p < .05$ for males and females combined. Among the self-satisfied respondents no such clear pattern emerged.

Once more, then, there is reason to believe that the male teacher's reproach, as opposed to a reproach from another girl in the class, posed a particularly serious threat to girls with low self-esteem, a threat to which they reacted rather violently. On the other hand, girls with high, and

Table 14. Mean CARDACOM values of self-dissatisfied male and female respondents confronted by a peer's reproach and a teacher's reproach in APS IV

	Male respondents	Female respondents
Peer reproach	5.55	3.92
Teacher reproach	6.67	5.86

Note: Cell frequencies range from 20 to 24.

presumably more self-assured, desire for control reacted quite differently, that is with markedly little defensiveness, to the teacher's reproach. With better control over their thoughts and feelings than their self-dissatisfied counterparts with low demands for control, many of the girls with high control desire may have considered it prudent to meet the teacher's reproach with a concessionary rather than with a defensive strategy, and to react in this manner also to a severe reproach from a classmate.

Not so the boys with high desire and claim for control! If anything, they reacted more defensively to the teacher's reproach than the boys with low control desire did; they did *not* tend to pursue a prudent concessionary strategy.

All of this leads to the following remarkable, if tentative, conclusion. Like the teacher respondents in APS II, the adolescent respondents from *Gymnasien* in APS IV were influenced in their account phase behaviour by their self-esteem and their desire for control. However, this influence did not manifest itself in any uniform way and certainly less coherently than among the teachers taking part in APS II. This latter difference is perhaps due to a less well developed stability of the self concept among the younger respondent group in APS IV as compared to the teacher sample in APS II. It may be of interest in this connection that the associations between the moderator variables presented in table 11 were stronger among the teachers in APS II than among the younger respondents from the three other studies listed.

At any rate, it seems that the psychological meaning of the situation which the respondents encountered in APS IV differed for boys and girls in at least two respects. Not only was the teacher's reproach in all probability more alien and threatening for the girls than for the boys, but the two gender groups also differed with respect to the prominent connotations which they attached to the desire and claim for control, namely self-assertiveness versus conciliatory tactics.

Let me repeat: much of this cannot be but speculation for the time being, but a speculation that casts a long shadow over any naive hope for some general hard-and-fast rules that might be inferred and recruited into service for salvaging account episodes from foundering.

Summary

As expected, the need for control and the need for self-esteem proved to be related, although – with our measures – in an unexpected yet theoretically meaningful and empirically productive way.

Neither desire for control or its components nor self-dissatisfaction produced any of the main effects, predicted by hypothesis 2.3, on actors' defensiveness in rendering accounts for failure events. However, as true moderator variables they entered into many strong interactions with other personal, that is gender-related, characteristics of the actors, and with situational context factors such as the severity of a reproach or the status of the opponent.

These reults are quite in line with the report by Whitehead and Smith (1986) that self-relevant cognitions of actors interact with situational factors (public or private settings) in partly determining which excuse strategy to choose.

Relevant also is Ellen Berscheid's summary (1985, p. 459): 'Dittes's (1959) original finding, since replicated by a host of other investigators . . . was that people who suffer from chronically low self-esteem appear to be more affected by other's appraisals of them. That is, they react more positively to favorable evaluators than do persons with high self-esteem and more negatively to negative evaluators.'

6.4 Severity of failure and defensiveness of accounts

In section 2.3 I considered two contradictory hypotheses on the impact of failure severity on the actor's account phase reactions: an increase of account defensiveness with increasing failure severity (hypothesis A) and an increase of concessionary account tendencies with increasing failure severity (hypothesis A^1). I also said that we know next to nothing about distinguishing conditions for the potential success of hypotheses A and A^1. In our own research programme we have not yet systematically addressed this problem, and evidence from other sources is scant. However, some tentative remarks are in order.

In APS I we employed three different failure events. Looking not at the consequences of these events but at the seriousness of the offence, one might say that the self-defence event, albeit perhaps exaggerated, represents the mildest case, with the inattentive (?) babysitter coming next, whereas the breach of promise and confidence event constitutes the most serious case of the three. Taken in this order, the proportion of justifications among all accounts decreases and the proportion of concessions increases markedly (see table 9), and this, of course, runs counter to hypothesis A. However, various considerations suggest that it would be too rash to discard this hypothesis right away.

The three failure situations used in APS I differ on many dimensions in various ways, and these other features, for example the severity of consequences, almost certainly influenced the accounts too, and in ways different from the degree of offence. One might argue, for instance, that hypothesis A would fare much better if we ordered the failure events according to the severity of the consequences, with the head injury in Dubious Self-Defence coming first as the most severe case, a case which also produced the highest proportion of defensive accounts. Clearly, APS I does not provide a strict test for hypothesis A versus A[1], but it was not specifically designed to do that.

In cases of extreme criminal violence, ranging from grievous bodily harm to murder, severity of offence and severity of consequences coincide. Felson and Ribner (1981), as well as Henderson and Hewstone (1984), report that in such cases justificative attempts play a very prominent role in the accounts offered by the offenders. This also furnishes support for maintaining hypothesis A for the time being.

McLaughlin, Cody and O'Hair (1983) predicted and found that severity would increase the likelihood of concessions. This is the opposite of hypothesis A. However, this result is based on self reports about very minor failures of the respondents. The respondents provided, among other things, both their response in the account phase from memory and a rating of the severity of the failure event.

In support of hypothesis A one may quote from Hupka, Jung and Silverthorn (1987). They reported from their study on jealousy predicaments (pp. 310–11):

> Apologies (M = 6.69) and excuses (M = 4.36) were perceived as more acceptable in the low than in the high severity predicament (Ms = 6.37, 3.92, respectively). The reverse was found for the justifications. They were perceived as more appropriate in the high (M = 4.71) than in the low severity predicament (M = 4.32), Severity × Account, $F(11, 1870) = 2.22$, $p < .01$. This pattern was also found with the offenders – The innocent partners, however, preferred apologies, justifications, and excuses in that decreasing order, regardless of severity –.

Also relevant is the defensive attribution study of Wilson and Jonah (1988), in which they assessed responsibility and penalty assignments in various cases of impaired driving resulting in an accident. They report that respondents with impaired driving histories (called DWI respondents) 'tended to vary their assignments of penalties across severity levels less than did non-DWI respondents; whereas non-DWI respondents assigned higher penalties with increased severity, DWI subjects actually assigned lesser penalties in the high, compared to the intermediate severity level. Thus the need for self-protection appears to be greatest when the consequences of an accident are most dire' (p. 580).

Finally, even if in general refusals and justifications lose out in comparison with excuses and concessions with increasing severity of offence, any remaining justificative elements, let alone refutational ones, may be particularly disturbing to opponents in cases of very serious failure events, and therefore they may still contribute markedly to an escalation of conflict as envisaged by our theory. Obviously, more work needs to be done with respect to the tentative hypotheses concerning the linkage between severity of failure and defensiveness of account.

7 Evaluation phase results

Let me now turn once more to the opponent's perspective, but this time to his or her postaccount evaluations of the account itself, of the failure event in the light of the account received, as well as of the actor's personality and the relationship between actor and opponent. In doing this I shall again observe the format suggested by the order of the relevant hypotheses in the theoretical chapter. So I shall start with the situational factors, that is with the effects of various types of account.

7.1 Defensiveness of accounts and negativity of evaluation

Our first evaluation phase study EPS I was strongly exploratory. At that time escalation theory was not yet fully developed and I did then entertain the hunch, compatible with hypothesis 3.1, that justifications would, as a rule, be considered by most people as more defensive than excuses, and hence be evaluated more negatively than the latter. However, there was this competing thought that in certain situations many people might prefer to hear a justification rather than an excuse to the extent that the justification would appear more helpful than an excuse in maintaining or restoring cognitions of an orderly, controllable world. With these competing hunches in mind we pitted excuses and justifications against each other in EPS I, after the presentation of a situation which in reality would be strongly conducive to a justificatory argument of self-defence.

Data from EPS I
Two excuses and two justifications were formulated for this study, one excuse and one justification with a predominantly internal orientation of the argument, the other two accounts with a predominantly external orientation. With a sample of 64 male students with fields other than psychology or law, each of these four account types was presented to 16 respondents in the opponent role after they had read the vignette Dubious Self-Defence. Several scales were offered for judgements of (1) the account, (2) the self-defensive act, (3) some personality traits of the actor and (4) the consequences the actor should or should not bear.

Table 15. Mean scores of unjustifiability accorded to the act of 'self-defence' after four types of accounts in EPS I

	Excuse	Justification
Internal	6.06	5.13
External	5.69	5.06

Note: Each cell contains 16 cases. The main effect of excuse vs justification is significant at $p < .02$.

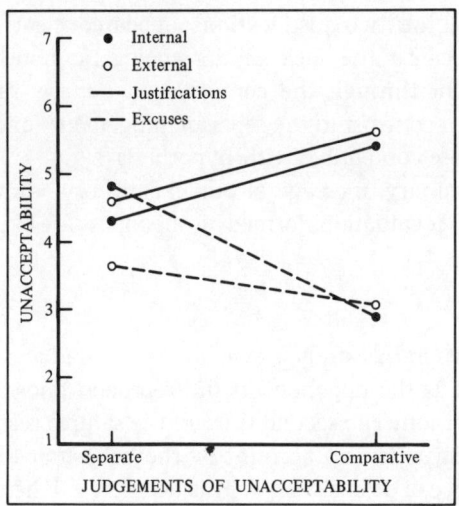

Figure 24. Separate and comparative mean judgements of unacceptability of four types of account in EPS I

Many of the comparisons of the four account condition groups on these dimensions did not yield significant differences, but in some instances data patterns relevant to hypothesis 3.1 did emerge. Table 15 presents mean ratings of the self-defensive act as to its justifiability. The higher the score, the more unjustified the act appeared to be.

These data clearly favour the justificatory accounts as being more efficient than the excuses in presenting the actor's case. However, the issue is not thereby closed. Towards the end of the interview each of the 64 respondents received all four accounts with the request to compare them and to rate each one with respect to its overall acceptability, again on a seven-step scale ranging from 'Very acceptable' to 'Not at all acceptable'. Figure 24 presents the results of these comparative judgements, together with the separate judgements of the four account types requested at the beginning of the questionnaire.

The separate and the comparative judgements juxtaposed in figure 24 are not strictly comparable. The four 'separate' data points are each based on the judgements of 16 different respondents. The four 'comparative' data points are each based on the judgements of all 64 respondents. Nevertheless, there is a clear message. An orthogonal 2 × 2 ANOVA to which the four 'separate' means were subjected did not yield any significant differences on the acceptability dimension among the four account types. A repeated-measures ANOVA with the 'comparative' judgements resulted in a highly significant ($p < .001$) main effect of excuses versus justifications. When compared directly with the excuses, the two justifications appeared clearly more unacceptable, possibly because the lack of an apologetic note in the justifications became salient through the comparisons. At any rate, the comparative judgements, in contrast to the separate judgements and to the results in table 15, are quite compatible with hypothesis 1.3.

Thus the main, if preliminary, message of our exploratory study EPS I seems to be that postaccount evaluations formed by opponents are likely to be highly context-dependent.

Data from EPS II
One-third of the respondents in this study, as we have seen, had to role-play the returning parent, that is the opponent in the reproach phase, of the situation Neglected Supervision. The second third of the sample received in addition to the general instruction an account by the babysitter that was marked by a very low degree of defensiveness. This account will henceforth be called the 'concessive account'. The remaining third of the respondents received a highly defensive account instead, henceforth called the 'refutational account'. Average CARDACOM values computed as measures of defensiveness from the codings of these two accounts by three independent, yet closely agreeing, raters were 3.33 for the concessive account and 16.67 for the refutational account.

Evaluative comments predominated in all three conditions, but significantly ($p < .001$) less so in the reproach condition than in the two account conditions combined. In the reproach condition 75% of the respondents offered at least one evaluative comment as compared to 95% in the concessive, and 97% in the refutational account condition. This result serves to underline the importance (and the correct labelling) of the 'evaluation phase'.

According to hypothesis 3.1 we expected that the actor with the concessive account would fare best in the judgements of the respondents. On some indices this proved to be the case, most clearly with the categories B 12 and B 13 for reassuring remarks about the unconditional or conditional continuation or restoration of a good relationship between actor and opponent. Significantly ($p<.004$) more respondents in the concessive account condition (16%) than in the refutational account condition (2%) made such remarks. The respondents of the reproach condition (6%) fell in between, differing from the concessive condition groups at the marginal level of $p<.10$.

On the summary index COMPREVAL, comprising all evaluative categories of the Taxonomy for Opponent Reactions, the average score in the concessive account condition (7.36) was lower and hence also more favourable to the actor than the average scores in the refutational account condition (8.36) and the reproach condition (8.89). However, none of the differences among these three means was significant.

Surprisingly at first sight, the refutational account did not elicit more negative evaluations than the reproach condition. On further reflection one may speculate that many respondents in the refutational account condition could not help but admit that the counter-reproach in that account – concerning the neglected cleaning fluid – had some validity and were therefore reluctant to judge the babysitter too negatively. One more result deserves attention in this context. Significantly ($p<.02$) more respondents in the concessive (30%) and the refutational (29%) account conditions combined minimized the damage incurred by the failure event (F 42) than respondents in the reproach condition (13%) did. I would guess that they did so for different reasons – the concessive account respondents to placate the actor, the refutational account respondents mainly to reassure themselves.

Data from EPS III

The evaluation phase statements turned out to be somewhat less negative than the immediate reactions in the reproach phase right after the confrontation with the Assault and Robbery event. This holds for both account conditions and for male as well as female respondents. The COMPREVAL mean for the reproach phase statements of all respondents ($N=123$) was 14.39. The corresponding mean for the evaluation phase statements, 13.73, was significantly ($p<.03$) lower on a t-test for repeated measures.

The adolescent's account, referring to his addiction, may have given cause to many respondents to reconsider the case and to react somewhat more moderately than before, whatever the tenor of the account. This is also mirrored in table 16. An appreciably large number of respondents in both account conditions who had previously reacted with uniformly negative statements, according to the comprehensive secondary codings, now offered more differentiated judgements or refrained from further evaluative comments.

Nevertheless, after the Assault and Robbery event, the two accounts had

Table 16. Perseverance and change of initial uniformly negative reactions to the Assault and Robbery event after the concessive and the refutational accounts in EPS III

	Account condition	
	Concessive	Refutational
Level of uniformly negative reactions *reached* after the account	5%	15%
Level of uniformly negative reactions *maintained* after the account	40%	45%
Level of uniformly negative reactions *abandoned* after the account	38%	20%
No uniformly negative reactions before or after the account	17%	20%
Total	100%	100%
(Number of cases)	(58)	(65)

Note: $\chi^2 = 6.79$, 3 df, $p < .08$.

Table 17. Main comprehensive secondary categorizations of the evaluation phase statements in various respondent groups of EPS III

	Account condition		
	Concessive	Refutational	Total
Uniformly negative statements (SW 12)			
Women	37%	55%	47%
Men	54%	67%	60%
All	45%	60%	
Ambivalent or non-evaluative statements (SW 15, 16, 17)			
Women	53%	24%	37% ⎤
Men	25%	15%	20% ⎦
All	39%	20%	
Number of cases (= 100%) in each cell			
Women	30	38	68
Men	28	27	55
All	58	65	123

Note: ⊔⊐ = $p < .05$; ⊔___⊐ = $p < .09$.

differential effects in agreement with hypothesis 3.1 (see tables 16 and 17). After the concessive account many more respondents ($p < .03$) than after the refutational account abandoned a uniformly negative judgement in favour of more differentiated ambivalent or non-evaluative statements. The difference between the COMPREVAL means for the refutational account condition

Defensiveness of accounts and negativity of evaluation

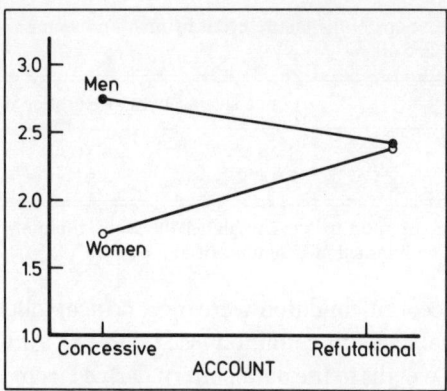

Figure 25. Mean scale evaluations of the two accounts in EPS III by male and female respondents. The higher the score the more negative the evaluation

(13.83) and the concessive account condition (13.63) is also in accordance with hypothesis 3.1, but is not significant.

A more complex data constellation, namely an intriguing interaction ($p<.01$) of gender of respondents and account version, emerged with the scale provided for the ratings of the account's acceptability after the respondent's free evaluation phase statements (see figure 25).

Men and women did not differ in their evaluations of the refutational account. Both average positions are close to the midpoint between the scores for the judgements 'An inadequate justification attempt' and 'Parts of it make you think, but as a whole not satisfactory'. However, men and women differed sharply in their evaluation of the concessive account. The female respondents rated it more positively than the refutational account, and this is in agreement with hypothesis 3.1. The males, on the other hand, rated the concessive account even more negatively than the refutational account.

With the benefit of hindsight, we can suggest that a number of males may have been disposed to doubt the credibility of the concessive account offered so shortly after the attack, and they may have also disliked its somewhat whining tone; so, with their attention directed to this account, they reacted rather negatively, whereas many females, more benevolent than the males, tended to accept the concessive account at least partly. The interpretation of the refutational account by men and women may also have differed. Men were perhaps somewhat impressed by the honesty of this account whereas women may have been frightened by it.

Probably due in part to an order effect, the scale for the judgement of the failure event, which immediately followed the scale for the account evaluation, produced a similar interaction pattern, significant at $p<.004$.

Table 18. Mean scale evaluations of the failure event by men and women in the two account conditions of EPS III

	Concessive account	Refutational account
Men	3.28	2.50
Women	2.52	2.97

Note: Cell frequencies range from 27 to 37. The higher the score, the more negative the evaluation. The interaction is significant at $p < .004$.

The men in the concessive account condition were most critical followed by the women in the refutational account condition (see table 18). Although I would tend to assign greater weight to the data pattern derived from the free statements, the lesson once more may be that account effects are likely to be highly dependent on context conditions, on the subjective interpretations of the accounts, and on the type of measurement one is able or willing to apply.

Related evidence

Several studies from other researchers can be cited in support of hypothesis 3.1 on the relationship between the defensiveness of accounts and the negativity of evaluations by opponents.

Blumstein et al. (1974), in their pioneering study on the honouring of accounts, assessed a multitude of potential determinants of such evaluations, and found as one important factor the proper ritual display of repentance in the accounts even with the relatively minor failure events which they used in their stimulus vignettes.

Felson and Ribner (1981) analysed the records of males incarcerated for serious crimes such as felonious assault, manslaughter and murder. They found that in cases of murder and first-degree assault, in which the intent of the offender had been established by the court, denial of guilt by the offender led to significantly higher sentences than admission of guilt.

Closest to our own approach are a series of studies conducted by McLaughlin and Cody together with various co-workers. McLaughlin, Cody and Rosenstein (1983) recorded dyadic conversations in 50 pairs of previously unacquainted students. The 176 account episodes which emerged in the course of these 50 conversations were coded for type of offence, type of reproach, account strategy and type of evaluation. Two evaluation types favourable for the actor, namely honouring and retreat, were likely to follow excuses (honouring) and concessions (retreat), respectively. The unfavourable evaluation types – reject, take issue or reinstatement of the reproach – were a likely consequence of justifications and refusals, as predicted. Comparatively often a justification also elicited a retreat from the original reproach position. I shall return to this point in chapter 8; at the moment I shall simply register the good overall agreement of these data too with hypothesis 3.1.

However, a number of qualifications have to be observed. First of all, there is the case of no differential effects. Shields (1979), in her study on various attributions in the case of a stolen cigarette lighter, reported that the account conditions excuse versus justification versus confession did not affect the amount of responsibility attributed to the stimulus person by the observers. Hence she tentatively concluded that 'students of the "account" . . . have tended to overestimate the ability of the account to "transform the meaning of the act"', but cautiously (and wisely, as we should say nowadays) she added that 'the results are, of course, preliminary and limited in generalizability' (p. 269).

While Shields' report does not seem to offer any clue as to why she did not obtain any differential account effects, there are other studies which allow for some speculation as to why they did not yield the expected results. (In some instances they in fact yielded the opposite of what was expected.) In all these cases, besides registering the cardinal category or type of the account, concession, excuse, justification or refusal, one must look at the account quality, and keep in mind two different kinds of 'quality'. There are accounts which are good or bad in practically all the circumstances in which they might be offered. Let me call such accounts inherently good and bad excuses, inherently good and bad justifications, etc. But there are also accounts which are good or bad depending on the context in which they are offered.

Hale's (1987) study furnishes an intriguing example of the first kind – inherently good and bad accounts. The undergraduate respondents in this study received the description of a student who had problems meeting the deadline for a course project, as well as four accounts, presumably offered by various students in such a predicament, together with requests for an extension. Speaker and request had to be evaluated on various scales. Eight accounts altogether were employed – a good- and a bad-quality account of each of the four types (confession, apology, excuse and justification). Quality had been assessed previously by 'an individual trained in the coding system but otherwise unconnected with the study' (Hale 1987, p. 124). A rating of high quality had to be accorded to an account if it did not only pay attention to the instrumental aspects, but also to the identity and interpersonal dynamics of the encounter.

Overall, justifications were most effective in creating a favourable definition of the failure event and the person who had committed that event. In general, the higher the quality of the account, the more likely the account was to elicit a positive response on the part of the reader. Contrary to expectations the low-quality excuse and low-quality justification, were, in general, judged the least and most favourable accounts respectively.

After a closer look at the accounts used in this study I find the results quite understandable. Low quality in the excuse case is hardly comparable to the reasonably acceptable low quality of the corresponding justification. In the low-quality excuse the speaker rather lamely explains that he was not sure what the professor was really asking and that he could not get hold of anybody else to explain it to him. To offer this argument so close to the deadline of the assignment must have sounded rather stupid to most if not all respondents. So it is not at all surprising that they rated the low-quality excuse rather unfavourably, and that thereby the mean ratings for both excuses combined also turned out to be comparatively negative. The low-quality justification, on the other hand, although not heeding the professor's wishes, presents a coherent and rather convincing case. The student explains that he had been away on a job interview trip and had just got back the night before, and he asks for an extension until the end of the week. Again, small wonder that this justification fared so well, and boosted the mean ratings for both justifications combined. It seems obvious that other aspects of quality than those envisaged by Hale played an important role in his study.

The second kind, the context-bound quality of accounts, is well illustrated by the work of Cody and McLaughlin. In contrast to the results quoted above from the dyadic conversation study by McLaughlin, Cody and Rosenstein (1983), two studies on traffic offences, one of patrolman–driver encounters (Cody and McLaughlin 1985) and the other of courtroom statements by traffic offenders (Cody and McLaughlin 1988), revealed that concessions were not effective in obtaining mitigated judgements; they were frequently followed by ticketing, fines and other penalties. Excuses, which had fared well in previous studies, also fared well in the patrolman–driver study, but not very well in the courtroom. In a subsequent study by McLaughlin, Cody and French (1989), in which traffic court accounts were presented to undergraduates, the mean rated likelihood of penalty across conditions was higher after excuses than after justifications or challenges.

Several further examples of various accounts widely differing in quality could be recruited from the studies of the Cody and McLaughlin group, for instance large differences in success rates between three subtypes of refusal in court; but the examples given must suffice. These studies strongly support a tentative conclusion I should like to draw at this point: hypothesis 3.1, relating negativity of evaluations to defensiveness of accounts, seems to hold its own rather well as a basic assumption, but it should be considered as a skeleton hypothesis upon which modifying predictions due to specific factors may be grafted. Inherent and context-bound qualities within the four cardinal account categories are likely to be of prime importance in this respect. Systematic assessments of those qualities are badly needed. The attributional analysis of excuse-giving (or account-giving, as I would say) by

Weiner et al. (1987) can only be seen as a beginning, although a very promising one.

7.2 Effects of gender on negativity of evaluation

Our first evaluative phase study EPS I did not allow for a test of hypothesis 3.2, which predicted that the final evaluations made by male opponents are likely to be more negative than the evaluations by female opponents. In this study only male respondents were addressed.

Data from EPS II
Our second evaluation phase study offers two gender aspects to be considered: the gender of evaluating respondents in the opponent role, and the gender of evaluated actors.

Gender of evaluating opponents. EPS II produced mixed results with respect to hypothesis 3.2. The percentages that follow are based on the six cell frequencies of the basic 2×3 design of this study (gender by reaction condition). These cell frequencies range from 31 to 34.

Some data from the primary codings of the opponent reactions are well in line with hypothesis 3.2. After a concessive account significantly ($p<.054$) more women (45%) than men (23%) indicated understanding of the actor's conduct during the failure event (F 34).

In both account conditions – concessive and refutational combined – women were more likely to make a full concession of the factual plausibility of the account (14%) than only a partial concession of such plausibility (5%). With men it was the other way round: only 9% conceded full plausibility and 14% just partial plausibility. This 2×2 contingency is marginally significant at $p<.08$.

Unexpected in view of hypothesis 3.2 was the fact that more men (35%) than women (15%) placated the actor (F 351) after receiving a concessive account ($p<.06$).

One result from the secondary codings clearly went against the hypothesis. In the two account conditions combined, significantly ($p<.05$) more women (20%) than men (8%) displayed uniformly negative judgement tendencies in their responses to the account (secondary category SW 12). On the other hand, significantly ($p<.02$) more men (15%) than women (3%) showed a transition from more positive to more negative judgement tendencies in the course of their responses to the account (SW 14).

A similarly mixed impression may finally be gained from the mean values of men and women in the three reaction conditions on the composite index COMPREVAL (see figure 26). In the reproach phase and the concessive account

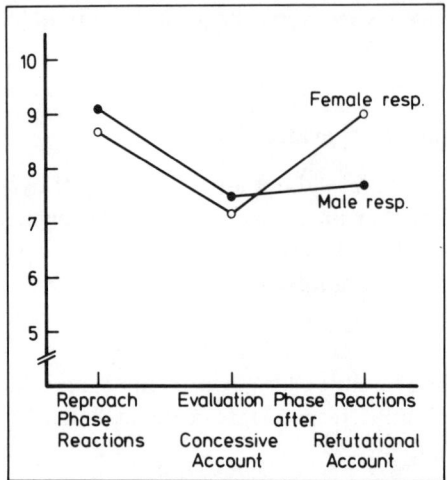

Figure 26. Mean COMPREVAL scores of male and female respondents in three reaction conditions of EPS II

condition the male scores slightly exceeded the female scores in the negative judgement direction. In the refutational account condition it was more clearly, but non-significantly, the other way round.

The data patterns just presented once more suggest the possibility that, in the student sample of the late 1980s addressed as respondents in EPS II, male–female differences in attribution and evaluation tendencies had diminished either generally with respect to account episodes or more specifically in failure situations of the Neglected Supervision type. Obviously, a more clearcut judgement on this issue must be postponed.

Gender of evaluated actors. Our male and female respondents were also similar in their judgements regarding the actor's gender. In general, the female babysitter was evaluated more positively than the male babysitter by both male and female students. The mean COMPREVAL scores for the female babysitter were 6.98 in the male respondent group and 8.22 in the female group. The corresponding scores for the male babysitter were 9.21 and 8.40, respectively. The overall means for the male (8.80) and the female babysitter (7.61) differ at $p < .09$. This main effect merits interest for two reasons: (1) it supersedes an interaction pattern, and (2) it stands in opposition to the corresponding result from RPS III. Let me comment on these two points in turn.

1 Figure 27 presents a 2 × 3 partition of the respondents according to the gender of the evaluated actor and the reaction condition (reproach phase,

Effects of gender

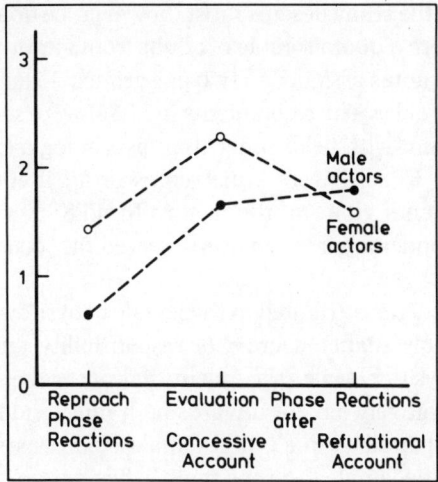

Figure 27. Mean number of positive themes mentioned in the judgements of male and female actors by the respondents in three reaction conditions of EPS II

concessive account, refutational account). The dependent variable is the mean number of categorized positive (friendly, favourable) themes mentioned by the respondents of a given group in their reactions.

The interaction visible in figure 27 is only marginally significant at $p < .09$. It is nevertheless noteworthy that only in two of the three conditions, reproach phase and concessive account, did the female babysitter fare better (and clearly so) than her male counterpart. With the refutational account strategy the obverse pattern emerged: the female babysitter elicited (nonsignificantly) fewer positive themes than the male babysitter, and male and female opponents again agreed on these judgements.

It is a reasonable guess that in the student population from which the respondents of EPS II were recruited, male and female judgement tendencies have converged in the 1980s on matters germane to our domain of discourse. However, it does not seem that traditional views of appropriate male and female behaviour have been completely eliminated in this process. Our data suggest that even among modern students, in judging women, concessions are honoured more and refutations are honoured less than in corresponding judgements of men.

2 The reproach phase condition of EPS II was a close replication of that condition of RPS III which contained the mild version of the failure event Neglected Supervision. The vignettes and the instructions were identical, and in both studies the babysitting actor was presented as a female to one half of the male and the female respondents and as a male babysitter to the other

half. Two differences between the study designs must, however, be noted. (1) The respondents in RPS III were a quota sample of adults from various cities in the Ruhr area, with equal quotas assigned to two age groups – those aged 18–35 and those aged 36 and older. The respondents in EPS II were students at the Ruhr-Universität Bochum with fields other than psychology. (2) The main dependent variables in RPS III were scale scores of attributions of responsibility, cost liability and guilt to the actor. In EPS II various categorizations of the respondents' free answers served as dependent variables.

In RPS III the female respondents attributed to the female babysitter in the mild failure version appreciably higher degrees of responsibility and cost liability than to the male babysitter. Male respondents did not make such a distinction; they were comparatively lenient towards both male and female babysitters. In EPS II the respondents, male and female alike, were more favourably disposed towards the female than the male babysitter on several indices derived from the categorizations.

For the time being one can obviously only attempt a guess as to the cause of this difference between the RPS III and the EPS II results. In further explorations of this issue I would probably first look into the sample differences between the two studies. The women in RPS III may have been relatively severe with the female babysitter because of more traditional views of what a woman may, and a man may not, be expected to know about the vicissitudes of babysitting. The respondents in EPS II may have been relatively lenient with the female babysitter, within the observed limits, possibly because of increasingly critical attitudes among students towards male prerogatives.

Over and above the differences observed between RPS III and EPS II it is noteworthy that in *both* studies the actors' gender played a role in determining the opponents' reactions in a presumably gender-sensitive situation.

Data from EPS III

As in EPS II, the results appeared mixed with respect to hypothesis 3.2, but on the whole they were clearly more favourable to the hypothesis. With the indices COMPREVAL and MEANEVAL no significant main effects of gender could be detected. But some comparisons of male and female reactions with respect to single categories were compatible with the prediction of more negative evaluations among men than among women.

Significantly ($p < .06$) more women (16%) than men (5%) showed concern for the culprit by emphasizing the bad consequences of his behaviour for himself (F 623).

Only women (9%), but no men (0%), expressed compassion with the actor (F 44). This difference is significant at $p < .05$ according to a Yates-corrected chi^2-test. On the other hand, an explicit denial of understanding for the actor's conduct (F 58) was voiced by 9% of the men and only 1% of the women. This difference fails to reach a conventional significance level in a Yates-corrected chi^2-test. The fourfold contingency table implied by these four percentages is significant at $p < .01$, one-tail, by Fisher's Exact Test.

The comprehensive categorizations of the evaluation phase statements of men and women, which have already been presented in table 17, are also in good accord with hypothesis 3.2. Significantly ($p < .05$) more women (37%) than men (20%), refraining from uniformly negative reactions, offered ambivalent or non-evaluative statements.

The more complex interactions of gender of respondents and account version on the two scales for judging the account and the failure event, respectively, have already been discussed in connection with figure 25 and table 18. Obviously the surprisingly lenient evaluation of the adolescent's attack by male respondents who had received the refutational account does not fit hypothesis 3.2. The male–female contrast in the concessive account condition is in good accord with the hypothesis. Further support for it may be inferred from a very interesting interaction of the gender and control needs of the respondents. This will be presented in section 7.3.

Discussion

Summarizing the results from the two studies EPS II and III leads to some optimism with respect to the viability of hypothesis 3.2 as a basic frame. But limiting conditions will have to be reckoned with, and careful research will be necessary to specify these conditions. For instance, it will not be easy to accommodate the baffling fact, if replicable in the future, that in both studies the male respondents in the refutational account conditions reacted comparatively mildly on some indices.

Our data so far seem to suggest that a majority of both men and women show similar reactions in the opponent role. Divergences between the two genders may mainly be due to a minority of men leaning towards the severity and negativity pole, and a minority of women tending rather strongly towards mildness and understanding. If this constellation should be confirmed it would still be a formidable task to ascertain the characteristics of these two minorities and the determinants and contextual conditions of their divergent reaction tendencies. The interaction of gender and control needs, to be reported in section 7.3 (see figure 30), may provide a first lead for such investigations.

Table 19. Some mean ratings of account, failure event and actor by respondents with low and high feelings of powerlessness in EPS I

	Feelings of powerlessness		p
	Low ($N=33$)	High ($N=31$)	
The account			
Not good	4.21	5.10	.04
Not acceptable	4.03	5.13	.02
Impudent	2.18	3.52	.01
The failure			
Not understandable	3.97	4.84	.05
Criminal	3.00	3.84	.05
The actor			
Not decent	4.70	5.55	.03
Mean	2.85	3.77	.03

7.3 Sense of control, self-esteem and negativity of evaluation

In the exploratory evaluation phase study EPS I we had not yet used the measures of desire for control and self-satisfaction which we employed in several of our later studies. Still, the moderator variables included in EPS I seem to be sufficiently close to the relationships predicted by hypothesis 3.3 to warrant an exploratory look at some exemplary data from this study.

Data from EPS I

The questionnaire of EPS I included our German version of Levenson's (1974) IPC scale as a measure of locus of control cognitions. A median split of the sample on the *P*-dimension, that is cognitions of powerlessness, yielded particularly clear and interesting results (see table 19).

All the ratings presented in table 19 were made on seven-step scales. The higher the score, the closer the mean rating to the pole stated in the table (i.e. Not good, Impudent, etc.). The p-values were derived from three-way analyses of variance with the factors 'justification versus excuse', 'internal versus external account', and 'low versus high powerlessness'. The listed main effects of powerlessness stand on their own. No significant interaction of powerlessness with any other factor emerged.

The data pattern is uniformly clear, and several pairs of means from other rating scales which point non-significantly in the same direction could be added. The stronger the feeling or conviction of his own powerlessness the more inclined, on average, was a respondent to judge severely and evaluate negatively the account, the failure event and the actor's personality.

Feelings of one's own powerlessness and the need to maintain control over self-relevant events are not identical; however, it seems plausible to assume for the time being that the two are positively correlated. It seems likely that feelings of powerlessness in many people sensitize or heighten the need for maintaining some form of control, even if secondary or vicarious. To the extent that this assumption will survive further testing the data in table 19 support hypothesis 3.3.

This hypothesis does not only relate the negativity of the opponent's final evaluations to his or her need to maintain control over self-relevant events, but also to the opponent's need for positive self-evaluation. Again, the EPS I questionnaire did not include a measure of self-esteem or self-satisfaction, but it did contain an instrument that may be, and has been, related to self-esteem, namely the Fenigstein–Scheier–Buss scales for measuring self-consciousness (in Heinemann's (1979) German translation).

Wicklund (1978), in an extension of the theory of objective self-awareness, drew parallels between the effects of externally stimulated directions of attention towards the self and habitual preoccupations with the self as measured by the private self-consciousness scale within the Fenigstein–Scheier–Buss instrument. It may be expected that in both cases discrepancies between accepted standards and one's own position on relevant dimensions become particularly salient, and usually elicit negative feelings. If no avoidance of such negative experiences is possible, various techniques of discrepancy reduction may be employed. For instance, 'when there is personal investment in a situation such that the self might be responsible for a real negative outcome, it is likely that the person will undertake self-esteem-protecting maneuvers' (ibid., p. 511).

Such statements support our tentative consideration of self-consciousness as a remote indicator of the need for positive self-evaluation, and we may formulate as a corollary of hypothesis 3.3 the following prediction: the higher the self-consciousness level of an opponent, the more negative, on average, will be his or her final evaluations in an account episode. Data relevant for this prediction are presented in table 20.

By a median split the sample had been divided into groups with low and high levels of self-consciousness. All the items on which these two groups differed significantly are listed in table 20. Again, several other items with near significant differences in the same direction could have been included. The mode of analysis was the same as for table 19 and, once more, no interaction of the factor 'excuse versus justification' with self-consciousness tainted the main effects of this latter factor which table 20 reports. In line with the prediction from our corollary, the highly self-conscious respondents were more negative in several of their evaluations than the respondents with low self-consciousness levels.

Table 20. Some mean ratings of account and actor by respondents with low and high levels of private self-consciousness in EPS I

	Private self-consciousness		
	Low (N=30)	High (N=34)	p
The account			
Untrustworthy	2.73	3.82	.03
The actor			
Brutal	3.43	4.53	.01
Mean	2.73	3.79	.01
Repulsive	3.13	4.21	.01

In the EPS I sample feelings of powerlessness and private self-consciousness were unrelated ($r = .03$). Although both factors had negativity effects, as predicted, a comparison of tables 19 and 20 shows that these effects manifested themselves mostly in different semantic domains. Only the judgement of the actor as more or less mean was affected by both powerlessness and self-consciousness. It is noteworthy that the highly self-conscious respondents focused their attention on the actor and were particularly harsh in their character judgements of him.

Data from EPS II

It should first be noted that this study supplements and supports an important result from the account phase study APS II. Restrained or conciliatory moves by the stimulus persons had particularly positive effects in both studies on those whose control needs were marked by a high level of desire for constancy.

If a respondent with a high desire for constancy in the babysitter's role in APS II had to answer a neutral question on the part of the returning parents rather than reply to a derogation of his or her self-esteem or sense of control, then this respondent's account was likely to show markedly little defensiveness. If, on the contrary, such a respondent was confronted with a derogatory reproach, then his or her account was likely to be markedly defensive, as figure 28 shows. The interaction between version of reproach and desire for constancy is marginally significant at $p < .10$, yet corroborated by significant ($p < .05$) a posteriori contrasts, for example NQ vs DS and NQ vs DC in the group with high desire for constancy. Apparently the restrained reaction of the parents who just asked for an explanation was particularly reassuring for respondents with high constancy needs. On the other hand, a reproach, especially one which derogated their sense of control, quickly aroused the defences of such respondents.

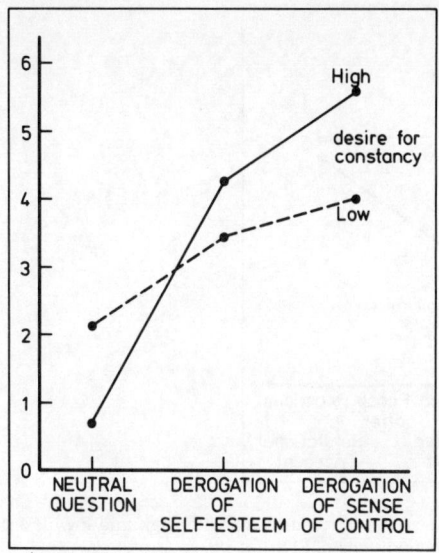

Figure 28. Mean CARDACOM values of respondents with high and low desire for constancy within three reproach settings of APS II

Let us now turn to EPS II. If a respondent with a high desire for constancy in the parent's role received a concessive account from the babysitter, then this respondent was most likely to react with a reasonably favourable evaluation compared with respondents with a low desire for constancy after a concessive account, and also compared with any respondent after a refutational account or a respondent still in the reproach phase (see the data pattern in figure 29). The 3×2 interaction is not significant, but single comparisons, warranted by the theoretical frame, showed the difference between reproach phase reactions and reactions after a concessive account of respondents with high constancy needs to be significant at $p < .03$. One may tentatively infer from this pattern that opponents with high needs for constancy react rather severely to a failure event in the reproach phase, but they seem to be quickly reassured in their need for constancy by a concessive account and honour this with mitigated judgements.

The corresponding data patterns from APS II and EPS II in figures 28 and 29 are encouraging in two respects: (1) they provide reinforcement for the combination of situational and dispositional variables in our domain of discourse and (2) they lend support to the vertical dimension of escalation theory, that is the prediction sequence concerning mitigation versus aggravation tendencies from the reproach phase via the actor's account to the opponent's final evaluation.

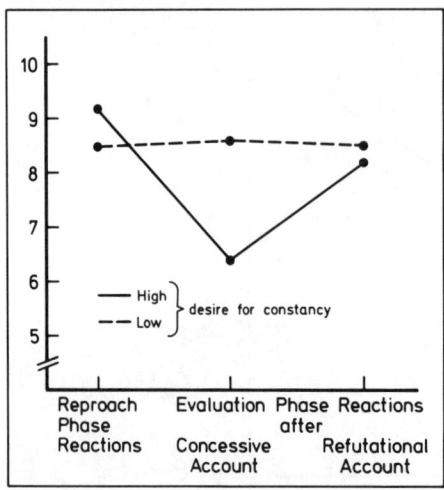

Figure 29. Mean COMPREVAL scores of respondents with high and low desire for constancy in three reaction conditions of EPS II

To save space I shall omit the evaluation data associated with desire for competence and with self-satisfaction. They are at least partly compatible with the results just presented and do not add any important information. But there is one aspect of the desire for competence which deserves a final word in this section.

In section 6.3 I already had reason to point out the double nature of the moderator variables, representing both enduring dispositions and momentary situational influences combined. If their measurement follows the experimental manipulation and assessment of the respondents' account episode behaviour, then the respondents' reactions to the moderator scales may well be somewhat influenced by this preceding experience. A split of the total EPS II sample closest to the median on the desire for competence dimension assigned 109 respondents to the high group and 84 respondents to the low group. Table 21 shows that these two groups are unequally distributed across the three reaction conditions. The frequencies of the two account conditions combined and contrasted with the frequencies of the reproach phase condition yielded a $chi^2 = 4.15$, $p < .05$.

The respondents with high desire for competence are overrepresented in the two account conditions and underrepresented in the reproach phase condition. Greater involvement in the account episode via exposure to the accounts apparently sensitized and heightened the competence needs of several respondents. This is in very good accord with escalation theory.

Table 21. Distribution of respondents with high and low desire for competence within the three reaction conditions of EPS III

Desire for competence	Reaction condition		
	Reproach phase	After concessive account	After refutational account
High	46%	62%	61%
Low	54%	38%	39%
Total	100%	100%	100%
(N)	(63)	(64)	(66)

Data from EPS III

In this study the desire for competence once more proved to be a strongly differentiating moderator variable. On all indices the same significant pattern in clear support of hypothesis 3.3 appeared. One example may suffice: on the COMPREVAL dimension the respondents with high desire for competence produced a significantly ($p<.001$) higher mean (14.38) and thus a more negative final evaluation than the respondents with low desire for competence (13.13). This pattern appeared in both account conditions and for men as well as for women. The correlations between the desire for competence scores and the COMPREVAL scores amounted to $r=.36$ ($p<.004$) for the male respondents and to $r=.27$ ($p<.02$) for the female respondents.

No such association, as has been shown, could be detected for the control need indices and the reproach phase reactions right after the confrontation of the respondents with the 'Assault and Robbery' vignette. It is my guess that the data patterns just reported from both studies, EPS II and III, point to essentially the same process. In some cases, so it seems, the opponents' control needs are not immediately activated to full force right after their confrontation with a failure event; thus they have at best partial and/or weak effects on the opponents' reproach phase reactions in those cases, and no effects at all if the failure event is sufficiently severe to push most respondents close to some ceiling of response severity. However, if the confrontation with the failure event continues, as with the presentation of an account by the actor and the requirement to deal with this account in some way, the control needs of some opponents are likely to rise beyond a salience threshold and are therefore likely to have an appreciable impact on opponent reactions in a subsequent evaluation phase. Needless to say, this speculation cannot rest on the currently available evidence. Careful tests are called for.

One more data constellation deserves attention in the present context. All the respondents of EPS III were grouped according to their position on *both* control dimensions, desire for competence and desire for constancy, divided

172 *Evaluation phase results*

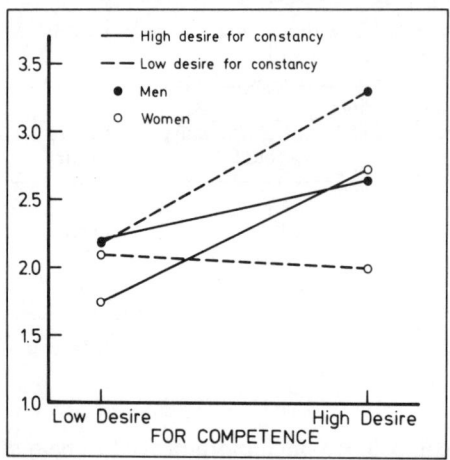

Figure 30. Mean scale evaluations of the accounts in EPS III by men and women with low versus high desire for competence, crossed with low versus high desire for constancy

by near-median splits. With a further division according to gender, eight groups resulted with cell frequencies ranging from 5 to 25; seven of the eight groups consisted of 10 or more respondents.[48]

From several analyses of variance, with gender, account version, desire for competence and desire for constancy as two-level factors and various indices of negativity of evaluation as dependent variables, an intriguing three-way interaction ($p < .03$) of gender, competence and constancy emerged with the account evaluation scale as negativity measure. This interaction is presented in figure 30.

The highest degree of negativity was produced by the male group with high desire for competence and low desire for constancy. The lowest degree of negativity appeared in the most opposite group: among the females with low desire for competence and high desire for constancy. This pattern fits well into the theoretical frame. Men who are mainly intent on asserting themselves and show little concern with the stability of their environment are those opponents we would expect to be most outspoken and aggressive in their evaluation of a misdeed and its perpetrator. Women who mainly desire that their environment remains non-threateningly constant, rather than wishing to assert their competence, may well be expected to be notably restrained in their evaluative reactions.

The data constellation in figure 30 suggests that the two aspects of control needs – desire for competence and desire for constancy – may acquire widely different functional meanings in the context of an account episode. This conclusion is most clearly supported by the four data points of the respondents with high desire for competence: men who also showed high desire for constancy reacted less negatively to the account than the competence-prone men who cared little about constancy. With the women the reverse pattern appeared. It seems that among the female respondents only the joint force of high need for competence *and* constancy produced markedly negative reactions.

Summary
The three studies EPS I, II and III differ in several respects in their designs, and somewhat different aspects of the needs for control and self-esteem became salient and influential in each study. Yet in all three cases the data fit well into the frame provided by escalation theory.

7.4 Severity of reproach and negativity of evaluation

This last section of the result chapters can be brief. Only one relevant study, EPS III, has so far been conducted, and its results are in clear agreement with hypothesis 3.4. A significant ($p < .001$) correlation of $r = .31$ between the respondents' ($N = 123$) COMPREVAL scores for their immediate reactions after the confrontation with the Assault and Robbery event and the corresponding scores for their postaccount evaluations supports the prediction that the greater the severity of an opponent's reproach phase reaction the more negative this opponent's final evaluation will tend to be. The strength of this association was almost identical for women ($r = .31$, $p < .01$) and men ($r = .30$, $p < .02$).

These correlations were supplemented by an analysis of variance, with COMPREVAL scores for the evaluation phase reactions as dependent variable and a high–low division determined by a median split on the COMPREVAL scores for the reproach phase reactions as a third factor, joining gender and account version. This analysis resulted in a highly significant ($p < .003$) and pervasive main effect of reproach phase severity, an effect that was not limited by any interaction. The overall means for the postaccount evaluations were 14.52 in the high-severity group and 13.23 in the low-severity group.

One may now ask to what extent the correlation between reproach phase and evaluation phase reactions is mediated by the intervening accounts and their reception by the respondents. At present an answer to this question can only be very tentative. The measurements used in EPS III and their sequence allow for the possibility that the evaluations focusing on the accounts did not clearly precede the (re-)evaluation of failure event and actor, but that the account evaluations themselves were at least partly determined by the very

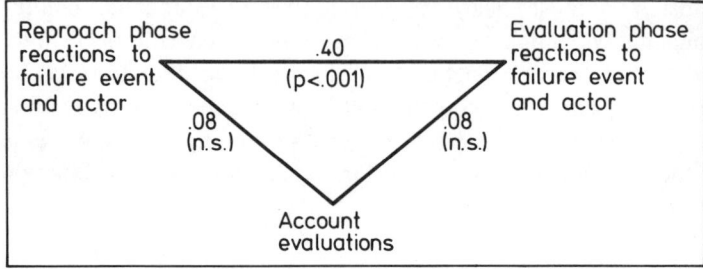

Figure 31. A pattern of correlations

evaluations of failure event and actor made during the reopened opportunity to consider once more crime and culprit. Such a state of affairs might spuriously increase the correlation between account evaluations and postaccount evaluations of failure event and actor. On the other hand, differences between the measure available for the assessment of account evaluations, that is the scale offered to the respondents after their free evaluation phase statements, and the summary indices derived from the categorizations of the pre- and postaccount reactions to failure event and actor may have led to method-based diminutions of the correlations in question.

Thus, only with due caution, and mainly with a heuristic intent, a triad of correlations is presented for the total sample (see figure 31). Essentially the same patterns emerge if the correlations are calculated separately for the concessive account condition and for the refutational account condition.

The tentative conclusion from this pattern is that the quasi direct association between pre- and postaccount evaluations remains fairly strong (partial correlation = .40) and it provides some support for individual predictions of postaccount evaluations. In contrast, the account evaluations seem to represent at best a very weak mediating role. It could be demonstrated that the accounts received by the opponents did influence their final evaluations (see tables 16 and 17), but such influences became manifest only as group effects. They did not attain a level that would allow person-to-person comparisons and predictions.

8 Inferences

It is time to take stock. It would be futile to attempt this by way of a statistical meta-analysis. The qualitative differences between the studies and the complexities of the results are prohibitive for such an enterprise. There is no way round careful multidimensional comparisons and comprehensive commentaries. To start with, a synopsis of the main characteristics of the data will be offered as an orientation guide. This will be followed by a discussion of the results along the prediction lines across the account episode phases. A listing of problems and challenges which remain or have emerged from our research programme, together with some proposals for future work, will conclude this final chapter.

8.1 Synopsis

Figure 32 offers an overview of altogether 35 tests of the 12 escalation network hypotheses in our 10 main studies, plus 1 case of some preliminary indications. The boxes and the arrows between them represent the hypotheses. The symbols placed alongside the arrows stand for the relevant evidence, that is each single symbol represents the results from a separate study, ordered from left to right and from top to bottom according to the chronological sequence in which the studies were treated in the result chapters. The symbols are to be read as follows:

- \+ Fairly strong support for the hypothesis from all or the predominant data patterns of the represented study.

- × Partial support, restricted to certain situational contexts or to specific interactions of the predictor variable with one or more other variables.

- * Evidence for both supportive main effects and interaction- or context-bound partial support.

- ⊥ Weak support from some isolated data patterns, not matched or contradicted by other data from the same study.

- − No support.

- ? Inconclusive preliminary evidence.

176 *Inferences*

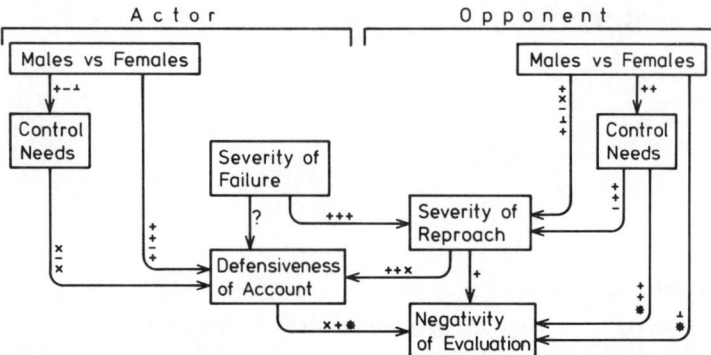

Figure 32. Synopsis of the main results. See text for explanation of symbols

Needless to say, many details and complexities have to be omitted in such symbolization. They will be supplemented verbally in section 8.2.

Four interconnected aspects of the empirical messages for the escalation theory may be inferred from figure 32.

1. The theory has stood up well to the tests, especially if it is considered as a framework with the heuristic function to allow for and invite specific modifications of its hypotheses. Only 5 of the 35 data patterns assembled in the diagram revealed no support at all.
2. In the theoretical chapter the hypotheses were presented as main-effect predictions, but with the cautionary proviso that they may well have to be modified in the light of restricted domains of applicability or limitations to joint effects of two or more predictors. This caution has proven to be fully justified.
3. The complexities due to such qualifications seem to increase in the course of events from the failure to the evaluation phase.
4. Prominently involved in these complexities are the control needs of the participants.

These general statements will be elaborated on in the following section.

8.2 Transphase perspectives

Each of the preceding result chapters concentrated on one particular phase. I shall now discuss the inferences that may be drawn from our findings for the interaction process across the four phases of an account episode.

The route from severity of failure to negativity of evaluation
The core part of the escalation theory consists of the hypotheses 1.1, 2.1, 3.1 and 3.4. Linking these hypotheses in a sequential order, the theory arrives at

its central escalation prediction. Given an appreciable degree of failure severity the probability is relatively high that an opponent's reproach phase reaction will be severe, that this will in turn elicit or facilitate defensive account phase reactions in the actor, and that such defensive reactions, meeting unfavourable response dispositions from the opponent's reproach phase reactions, will lead to fairly negative final evaluations by the opponent. With the opposition of a defensive account and a negative evaluation the foundering of the account episode is a likely outcome.

If we now link in a corresponding sequence the evidence pertaining to the four central hypotheses, the inference to be drawn is very encouraging for the escalation theory. All nine studies that are involved in this central test sequence provide at least some support, and seven of these studies do so quite firmly. Nevertheless, some qualifications have to be made.

Almost all the relevant data point the way, so to speak, from severity of failure via severity of reproach to defensiveness of account. Only the adolescent respondents in APS IV provided an exception that deserves closer attention. They too, according to expectation, were less willing to offer a concession in the face of a threatening reproach from the teacher, compared to their willingness to do so if confronted by a peer. However, unexpectedly they also seemed to refrain from defensive justifications and refutations of the teacher's reproach. Since this response pattern was particularly characteristic of the female adolescents I shall take it up again under the next subheading. At this point I just want to note a possible limitation of the validity range of hypothesis 2.1: under specific circumstances, especially when the reproach becomes really threatening, the monotonic relationship between severity of reproach and defensiveness of account may bend and reverse itself.

The most notable qualifications of the escalation sequence pertain to the nature and the impact of the accounts. Again, all three studies, EPS I, II and III, furnished evidence in accord with the prediction that defensive accounts would elicit or facilitate negative evaluations. However, these studies also provided several indications, in agreement with evidence from other sources quoted, that further characteristics of an account, apart from its defensiveness as measured by its placements on the dimension from concessions via excuses and justifications to refutations, may have an important influence on its reception by an opponent. Such an influence may derive from the specific content and structure of the argument which makes the account inherently more or less convincing. The influence may also depend upon, and be limited to, the context-bound persuasiveness of an account. Finally, an account may be influential only with opponents from a particular population, due to a specific match of account and opponent characteristics. There will be more about this last aspect in the next subsection.

Obviously there is much room for improving our understanding of these matters. Particular attention in this context should be paid to the ambivalent status of justifications.

The roles of gender

The theory invokes several reasons for the prediction that the escalation process towards final negative evaluations and an account episode's foundering is likely to be enhanced if at least one of the participants, actor or opponent, is a male, and that such an enhancement is particularly likely and will be pronounced if both actor *and* opponent are males. For instance, a male opponent's reproach phase reaction to a failure event is expected to be relatively severe (hypothesis 1.2) over and above the level of reproach severity induced by the severity of the failure event (hypothesis 1.1). If such a reproach is directed at a male actor, the likelihood of a particularly defensive reaction should be enhanced by the joint effects of that harsh reproach (hypothesis 2.1) and the actor's 'masculine' disposition to react defensively during an account phase (hypothesis 2.2). This in turn may be expected to intensify the male opponent's predispositions to react very negatively in the final phase.

Turning to the evidence, we may infer a number of data constellations in support of the proposed linkage of gender to an account episode escalation. Yet once more several qualifications have to be observed. Most important among them is the advice to restrict the validity range of the three gender-specific hypotheses 1.2, 2.2 and 3.2.

A synopsis of all our relevant studies, particularly regarding intra- and cross-study comparisons with respect to the severity of failure events and reproaches, strongly suggests that a differentiation of male from female response tendencies towards higher severity of reproach, more defensiveness of account, and for more negativity of evaluations is likely to occur only if the stimulating event is severe and if the male participant feels directly threatened by it. With the exception of APS III and its student sample all account phase studies produced clear support for the prediction in hypothesis 2.2 of higher male than female defensiveness. This result may in part be due to the fact that the opponent's reproach phase reactions in these studies were concrete utterances, unmistakably directed at the actor. Among the five studies investigating reproach phase reactions of opponents only the severe failure events Breach of Trust in RPS I and Assault and Robbery in EPS III produced equally clear evidence in accord with hypothesis 1.2 about masculine reproach phase severity. The vignette Assault and Robbery, with an adolescent throwing sand into the victim's face and dashing off with the handbag, had deliberately been designed as an attack primarily on masculine pride and feelings of control. The scenarios of the other failure events in the reproach phase studies may well have been experienced as less serious and less involving by male opponents, and thus leading only to marginal, if any, differences between male and female respondents.

The actor in the account phase plays a pivotal role in the course of the whole account episode. Thus the strength of hypothesis 2.2 on defensiveness differences between male and female actors deserves special attention. Two further phenomena attest to its viability.

1 Not only the three account phase studies, but also the reproach phase study RPS III, furnished corroborating evidence, namely a clearly more prevalent defensive, blame-avoiding attribution tendency between males than between females.

2 In APS IV the girls were quite defensive in the condition of a posited intermediate reproach severity, that is the teacher instead of the peer asking for an explanation. However, in the condition with the most serious reproach, namely the teacher not only asking for an explanation but also expressing disappointment with the actor and thereby attacking his or her self-esteem, many girls apparently shied away from a defensive account strategy. Nothing of that sort happened among the boys in this most severe reproach condition. On the contrary, they obtained the highest score of all male and female groups in this study on the defensiveness index CARDACOM (see figure 18).

Another qualification that has to be considered concerns the likelihood that in some cases a reproach or an account conveys, on average, different meanings to male and female participants. The male teacher's reproach just mentioned seems to be a case in point. Further indications may be derived from the evaluations subsequent to the accounts in EPS II and III. The concessive account in EPS III offers the clearest example. Male respondents, perhaps on second thoughts, evaluated it much less benevolently than the female respondents did. With no probing questions in this study we can only speculate; but it seems a plausible guess that the concessive account carried different connotations for men and women whereas the refutational account did so to a much smaller extent or not at all.

Finally, in trying to predict the course of an account episode, one should for each phase give thought to the gender of *both* actor *and* opponent. In two of our studies, RPS III and EPS II, we systematically varied these gender constellations. Although these two studies with samples from different populations point to opposite conclusions as to the relative liability of negligent male and female babysitters, both studies underline the importance of the actor's gender as a determinant of the opponent's reactions.

The interventions of the needs for control and self-esteem

Many data constellations also support the theoretical structure with respect to the predicted functions of the needs for control and self-esteem. However, again, several complexities in the data patterns also emerged and pointed to a number of intriguing qualifications that require and deserve further investigation.

Both male actors and male opponents showed higher needs for control, especially a stronger desire for competence, than their female counterparts. This accords well with one basic assumption of the theory.

The needs for control and self-esteem are said to be activated (or increased, or made salient) in the opponent by severe failures and defensive accounts, and in the actor by severe reproaches. Evidence for such activation may be inferred from three studies: APS IV, EPS II and III.

Strongly suggestive evidence for the mediating function in the escalation process of such activated or originally high needs for control or self-esteem resulted from the data patterns of six studies: RPS I, APS II and IV, and EPS I, II and III.

As far as the qualifications are concerned, it soon became clear that the desire for competence, the desire for constancy, and self-dissatisfaction, as measured by our instruments, do not always act in the same way at a given stage in an account episode. Furthermore, often enough the influence of one or other of these motivational factors manifested itself only in specific stimulus contexts, and only with male or only with female respondents. The following three constellations merit special consideration.

1 A high desire for competence predisposed many respondents, males in particular, to react markedly severely and negatively in the opponent role and defensively in the actor role, given an appropriate situational cue (failure event, reproach or account). With minimal stimulation, for example a neutral question instead of a derogatory reproach, the desire for competence, high or low, had little impact on the responses. A high desire for constancy, on the other hand, seemed to act as a polarizer. The data from EPS II and APS II suggest that a participant with high constancy needs, if confronted with a threatening event (failure event or reproach) in an account episode, is also likely to react very unfavourably, in a manner similar to that of a person characterized by a high desire for competence. However, if that participant with high constancy needs meets with a gentle, considerate reaction (neutral question or concessive account), he or she is likely to respond with a markedly favourable reaction, more so than a person with low constancy needs. Seeing this pattern in both actors and opponents is particularly interesting from a transphase perspective, because it points to one possible set of partial determinants for de-escalation processes and the accomplishment of account episodes.

Of course, this last statement is not to be construed as a general value judgement. There *are* situations in which excessive concern with constancy and subsequent acquiescence are highly detrimental.

2 Self-dissatisfaction and the desire for control, competence in particular,

correlate negatively. In many studies we found, originally to our surprise, that the majority of participants who desired competence were apparently fairly content with themselves and understood such desire as a self-assured claim. This fact gave rise to one of the most intriguing result patterns from our research programme. I refer to the joint effects of high versus low desire for competence, self-satisfaction versus self-dissatisfaction, gender of respondent, and type of reproach, on the actors' account phase behaviour in APS II (see figures 19, 20 and 21).

Most notable is the specific vulnerability and defensiveness of self-dissatisfied actors to direct attacks on their self-esteem, and of competence-claiming actors to direct attacks on their sense of control. These specific matches (or rather mismatches) of dispositions and instigations point once more to the importance and pivotal role of the account phase in the episode sequence.

3 Such multiple determination as a necessary condition for specifically unfavourable reactions to occur seems to be somewhat more characteristic for female than for male actors and opponents. Evidence for this hypothesis may be derived from three studies. Marked effects of self-esteem-threatening reproaches in eliciting defensive accounts from self-dissatisfied female actors apparently occurred not only among the female teachers in APS II, but also among the adolescent girls in APS IV (see table 14). Comparatively negative evaluations of the accounts were given only by those women in EPS III who voiced a high desire for both competence *and* constancy, but not by women with at most one of these desires.

It should be clear that several of the preceding statements in this section on transphase perspectives were found wanting. They were offered for heuristic reasons to stimulate the planning of future tests.

8.3 Tasks for the future

Many problems remained untouched and others emerged in the course of our research programme. They may be crudely classified as (1) challenges to meanings of the crucial events during an account episode, (2) challenges to influential characteristics of the participants, (3) challenges to unexplored factors that may contribute to beneficial outcomes of account episodes, and (4) challenges to gaps between theoretical aspirations and empirical realizations. Within the scope of this monograph I cannot attempt an exhaustive listing, let alone a comprehensive discussion, of all the problems that come to mind. But in concluding I should like to comment, at least briefly, on some of the problems and challenges that seem both urgent and amenable to some sort of a solution.

Context-free and context-bound persuasive qualities of reproaches and accounts

In the preceding section I have already referred to the fact that reproaches or accounts may carry degrees of conviction that are independent of the dimensions of severity and defensiveness. For instance, in EPS II, in the case of the Neglected Supervision, the refutational account, with its counter-reproach concerning the cleaning fluid left within reach of the child, elicited in many respondents acquiescent concessions of guilt and remorse.

In some cases such persuasive force seems to be largely context-free in the sense that it exerts its influence in many different situations. In other cases the persuasive force of a reproach or an account is context-bound, that is restricted to specific situations and/or special groups of addressees. It seems to me that further progress in the elucidation and prediction of account episode sequences would be enhanced by explorations and subsequent systematic investigations of such persuasive, and counterpersuasive, qualities done either apart from or in conjunction with the influences of severity of reproach and defensiveness of account. Special attention in such endeavours should be directed at any ambivalences of justifications.

In the pretests of the reproach and account versions used in our main studies we did not pay sufficient attention to these aspects. In the future questions that probe more deeply into the meanings of the statements to be used as stimulus material should be employed in the pretest stage, and such probes may well also be included in the main studies.

Besides characteristics of content, formal aspects such as length of utterance (Müller-Eckhard 1974) and narrative versus fragmented style (O'Barr 1982) may turn out to be influential in our domain of discourse too, which is close to these studies by O'Barr (courtroom behaviour) and Müller-Eckhard (reports on a case of juvenile delinquency). Supplementary analyses by Achim Studt of data from APS III revealed for male respondents an interesting negative correlation of $r = -.39$ ($p < .004$) between defensiveness of accounts as measured by the CARDACOM index and length of account as measured by the number of words. No such association appeared with the female respondents ($r = -.08$, n.s.).

A taxonomy of failure events

As far as I know no general-purpose multidimensional system for the classification of failure events exists. Category lists that have been published are restricted to specific domains such as the classification of problems reported by heterosexual couples in the studies of Kelley and his associates (Kelley 1979). Yet, considering the danger of idiographic dispersals in the wide field of studies of conflict involving reproaches and accounts, it seems highly desirable to supplement the taxonomies for reproaches and evaluations and for accounts with a similarly elaborated general classification system for failure events.

Such a taxonomy should facilitate the formation and testing of heuristic leads and predictions. Among other things it would probably be of considerable help in discerning the conditions in which the prediction of hypothesis A of an increase of account defensiveness with increasing failure severity would find support, and in which other conditions the obverse prediction of hypothesis A^1 would do so.

Some years ago, in a research seminar, we started to develop a failure event taxonomy based on the main superordinate categories of (1) type and degree of normative consensus, (2) type and degree of norm violations, (3) type and severity of consequences for victims and (4) type and degree of actors' involvement. But we had to discontinue this work and have not yet resumed it because of our other commitments.

The meanings and the interplay of motivational dispositions

Theoretical and empirical efforts should be directed at the joint effects of various dispositional (moderator) variables, both old and new, within the present scope of the escalation network. Both convergent and colliding forces should be envisaged in such endeavours. Even a specific sense of control such as the desire for competence might enhance two conflicting behaviour tendencies. For instance, an actor with strong competence needs might vacillate between the intention of contributing a concessive account and thereby steering the account episode towards a beneficial outcome and the intention of asserting competence via a mainly self-addressed justificative account. Such collisions may be even more likely if different aspects of the need for control, for example competence and constancy desires, point in different directions in certain situations.

Different sources should be explored in the search for theoretical refinement and greater precision. Julius Kuhl's theory of action control might prove to be helpful (see, for instance, his chapters and other contributions in Kuhl and Beckmann (1985)). It seems a plausible guess that Kuhl's concepts of action orientation and state orientation are related to desire for competence and desire for constancy, respectively. But, of course, careful work is called for to establish the validity of this speculation as well as the nature of these relationships.

Enlightenment may also come from the incorporation of other dispositions, notably social anxiety. In some of our studies we included measurements of social anxiety, and further work is envisaged for a separate report. Schönbach (1984) provides an interim statement. Social anxiety deserves interest in our context for two reasons.

1 It seems that a high degree of social anxiety in actors and opponents acts as a polarizer by enhancing both positive *and* negative reactions beyond levels manifested by persons with little or no social anxiety. But very little is as yet known about the conditions in which positive and negative polarizations occur.

2 Via its correlations with desire for competence (negative) and self-dissatisfaction (positive) social anxiety has shed light on the meaning and functioning of those variables. This heuristic potential should be further explored. The triangular association structure

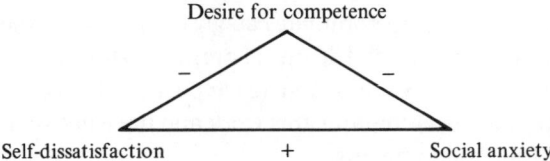

suggests for future studies the hypothesis that the dynamic complement of this structure may be a bidirectional positive feedback cycle.

Finally, we should be wary of, and search for, group-specific meanings of the motivational dispositions. For instance, the correlation matrices of the moderator variables calculated separately for male and female respondents suggested that, on average, the desire for competence carries more optimistic, but hence possibly also more vulnerable, connotations for males than for females.

Extant and latent characteristics of the participants

Gender. The last paragraph has already indicated a way of exploring gender-related dispositions. Another method would be to separate from the majority of male and female respondents two extreme groups, namely highly defensive (or severe) males and decidedly non-defensive (or lenient) females, and to look for characteristics which clearly differentiate these two extreme groups from each other as well as – more moderately perhaps – from their less extreme counterparts. A candidate high on the list of such characteristics to be tested should be 'masculinity' as measured by one of the existing instruments. A promising performance of this dimension in separating the two extreme and the middle groups should then lead to an assessment both of the type and degree of overlap with the already incorporated moderator variables, and of the joint effects – convergence or collision – of these variables on reproach severity, account defensiveness and negativity of evaluation.

Age and education. The data from RPS III showed very similar effects of age and educational status on reproach severity. Older respondents were more severe than younger ones and the less well-educated more severe than the better-educated respondents. This parallel of two main effects free from interactions suggests the possibility of a common underlying factor. My first attempt would be to look for a specifically vulnerable sense of control among many older and among many less well-educated persons, and to consider the likelihood that this latent characteristic requires the development of measures beyond the control scale we have used so far.

Obviously, there are many other characteristics that deserve attention, for instance the degree of intimacy between actor and opponent, the duration of their connection experienced before and expected after the account episode, and the status relationship between them. But for the moment I shall refrain from delving into these aspects.

Factors facilitating the accomplishment of account episodes
So far our main focus has been on the impediments and dangers which increase the probability that an account episode will founder. In the future a strong branch of research should be devoted to situational constellations and personal dispositions that may enhance the likelihood of a beneficial outcome. At present I am not prepared to say anything about such situational factors, but I should like to comment briefly on some dispositions that might merit further study.

The following three characteristics would be my prime candidates for systematic scrutiny: (1) the willingness to be guided by a solution-oriented concept of responsibility, (2) the capacity and motivation to empathize and (3) a communicative ability and inclination which Deborah Davis (e.g. 1982) has called 'responsiveness'. This latter characteristic might turn out to be of special interest. Davis defined the concept of responsiveness in terms of three contingencies: (a) the probability that a person will respond to the communications of an interaction partner, (b) the proportion of responses that are relevant to the preceding communications of the partner and (c) the proportion of responses that have a fitting format with respect to the preceding behaviour and the contingent expectations of the other, for example responses that are of the appropriate degree of elaboration.

Several studies by Davis and her associates have shown that highly responsive persons as compared to less responsive ones are clearly better liked and evaluated by their interaction partners. D. Davis and Perkowitz (1979) pointed out that A's responsiveness may have beneficial effects on B because it enhances A's predictability and B's feeling of control, and thereby reduces stress for B (with beneficial feedback for A as a likely consequence). Furthermore, A's responsiveness may be fundamentally rewarding for B because it ensures for B that his or her own behaviour makes a difference. Both the control needs and the self-esteem of B are thereby nourished.

Thus it stands to reason that an actor and an opponent who are both disposed to be responsive have a comparatively good chance of accomplishing an acceptable outcome in an account episode, given a minimal common interest in that respect. The task for future research with respect to this and other potentially beneficial respondent dispositions has two aspects: the assessment of the performance of the disposition and the assessment of the conditions which foster its development.

Gaps between theoretical aspirations and empirical realizations
My endeavours have been guided by a strong exploratory intention rather than by the ambition to carry out rigorous tests. Thus, instead of digging deeply at a particular spot, I have tried to cover ground and establish a fairly wide network of relationships, even if tenuous here and there. This heuristic strategy required a number of horizontally and vertically related studies, with restrictions on the time and energy that could be invested in any single study.

A great deal of effort went into the assessment of the reactions to failure events, reproaches and accounts, because in view of the heuristic intention it seemed crucial to allow for as much spontaneity of the respondents as possible. Hence the development of the taxonomies for the analysis of the free answers invited in the majority of our studies. But we had to simplify the experimental part of the studies by using written vignettes for the introduction of failure events, reproaches and accounts.

Our reliance on single-phase, albeit related, studies instead of longitudinal simulations of account episodes, and the employment of vignettes describing hypothetical situations, may invite the criticism of remoteness from social reality. Potter and Wetherell (1987, pp. 79–80) are particularly critical of this type of research: 'The problem with using vignettes . . . is that data are essentially dependent on participants' *theories* of how they would behave in the circumstances detailed in the vignette. The dependent measure is not what the participants *actually* do or say in a real situation but what they *imagine* they would do or say. And there may be all the difference in the world between being confronted with a situation in a vignette and in real life.' Potter and Wetherell also make the criticism that in experiments on accounts the participants, in contrast to real life, are usually strangers to one another, and that the presentation of accounts isolated from a normal sequence of events vitally impedes the understanding of their nature and use.

The situation may not be quite as bleak as Potter and Wetherell portray it. Fincham (1985, p. 211), examining three of his own studies on marital conflicts as well as a study by Madden and Janoff-Bulman (1981), concluded that the results showed no differences in attributions of blame between hypothetical vignettes of conflict situations and actual conflicts experienced.

My own view is that in strongly exploratory periods of research, such as

Tasks for the future

our programme so far, the use of vignettes and similar 'artificial' devices is fully justified, and I think that the yield of our studies with its heuristic leads bears me out on that. However, the problem of external validity remains and requires a supplementary strategy. Reality should be approximated step by step, and at each step one should carefully register to what extent the previously corroborated theoretical linkages can still be maintained.

The next stage might be a set of account episode simulations within a role-playing frame with instructions to an actor and an opponent to interact *in vivo* after a specified failure situation. Video-recordings should collect the raw data. One of the participants would be a true respondent, the other one a confederate of the investigator. In some studies this confederate would take the actor's role, in other studies the opponent's role, and he or she would act according to a standard repertoire of initiating comments and reactions designed to fit some experimental condition.

Such studies would require much pretesting and careful training of the confederates to preserve for the real respondent the impression of a spontaneous interaction; but I think it can be done. Our last study, EPS III, which may be seen as a first step towards such simulations, provides this encouragement: none of the respondents voiced any objection against the concessive or the refutational account as being strange or unnatural in the light of his or her own reproach phase statement.

Coda
Obviously, there is much to do, and some of the challenges are formidable. I hope that some readers will join in and carry on.

Appendix A
Taxonomy for reactions of actors during account phases

C	CONCESSIONS
C 110	**Peripheral concessions**
c 111	Willingness to report on the event in question without excuse, justification or refutational comment
c 112	Acknowledgement of *negative aspects of the failure event*, but no concession of own involvement
c 113	Acknowledgement of *opponent's right or reason* to question or reproach the actor, to be disturbed, disappointed or angry
C 120	**Admission of responsibility, guilt, mistake, shame, embarrassment**
c 121	*Partial admission* of *some responsibility*, guilt or mistake
c 122	*Full admission* of *responsibility*, guilt or mistake
c 123	Admission of responsibility, guilt, or mistake, and *explicit abstention* from excuse or justification
c 124	Admission of *shame* or embarrassment
C 130	**Expressions of regret**
c 131	Expression of *regret* concerning the failure event. *Focus of regret not specified or uncertain* (cf. c 710)
c 132	Expression of regret concerning *own role* in the failure event
c 133	Expression of regret concerning the *consequences* of the failure event for the victim(s). Hope for the victim's well-being
c 134	Expression of regret concerning *inability to provide* any (or sufficient) *restitution or compensation*
c 524	Announcement of *restitutions or compensations to be offered or already provided* in acknowledgement of own responsibility or guilt in connection with the failure event
c 710	Formal offer of *apology* or request for pardon or mercy, *addressed to the victim or other related persons* in acknowledgement of own responsibility for the occurrence of the failure event (cf. E 710)
c 999	Other concessions

E		**EXCUSES**
E 110–413		**Pleas for mitigation in judgement, based on claims of impairment of capacity and/or volition**
E 110		Claims of *impairment* of capacity and/or volition, *source* of impairment *unspecified or uncertain*
E 120		Claims of impairment due to *fatigue* or exhaustion
E 130		Claims of impairment due to *alcohol* or *drugs*
E 140		Claims of impairment due to *physical illness*
E 150		Claims of impairment due to *momentary affective or mental state* (e.g. intense rage or fear)
E 160		Claims of impairment due to *mental illness*
E 170		Claims of impairment due to *lack of training or lack of experience*
E 180		Admission of perplexity or helplessness as to what to say in view of the situation or the reproach
E 210		Claims of impairment due to *situational constraints*, e.g. stimulus overload, inscrutability or uncontrollability of the situation, unforeseeability of events
E 220		Claims of impairment due to *time pressure*
E 230		Claims of restriction of free course of action due to *loyalties* to higher-order *norms, values* or *standards*, implying a plea for mitigation in judging the failure event
E 240		Claims of restriction of free course of action due to *loyalties* to *specific other persons*, implying a plea for mitigation in judging the failure event
E 310		Claims of impairment due to *powerful agents*, e.g. denial of access to information or threat of punishment for disobedience
E 410		**Claims of impairment due to provocation**
E 411		Claims of impairment due to *provocation by the accuser*
E 412		Claims of impairment due to provocation by the *victim*
E 413		Claims of impairment due to provocation by *persons other than accuser and/or victim*
E 420–720		**Pleas for mitigation in judgement, based on arguments other than impairment claims**
E 420		**Appeal to participation of other co-actors in the failure event as frames of reference for mild judgements**
E 421		Appeal to the *participation of the accuser* as co-actor in the failure event, implying a claim of shared responsibility and hence a plea for mitigation in judgement
E 422		Appeal to the participation of the *victim* as co-actor in the failure event, implying a claim of shared responsibility and hence a plea for mitigation in judgement

E 423	Appeal to the participation of *persons other than the accuser and/or victim* as co-actors in the failure event, implying a claim of shared responsibility and hence a plea for mitigation in judgement
E 430	**Appeal to limitations, negative traits or misdeeds of other persons as frame of reference for mild judgements**
E 431	Appeal to *limitations, negative traits or misdeeds* of the *accuser* as frame of reference for the evaluation of the failure event, implying a plea for mitigation in judgement
E 432	Appeal to limitations, negative traits or misdeeds of the *victim* as frame of reference for the evaluation of the failure event, implying a plea for mitigation in judgement
E 433	Appeal to limitations, negative traits or misdeeds of *persons other than the victim and/or accuser* as frame of reference for the evaluation of the failure event, implying a plea for mitigation in judgement
E 510	**Plea for mitigation in judgement on the basis of assertions about actor's self, past or present**
E 511	Appeal to own *underprivileged past*, implying a plea for mitigation in judgement
E 512	Appeal to own *good record in the past*, apart from the failure event, implying a plea for mitigation in judgement
E 513	Appeal to own *present identity, role or status* in relation to other persons, implying a plea for mitigation in judgement
E 520	Plea for mitigation in judgement on the basis of assertions about actor's role concerning the failure event
E 521	Appeal to *conviction of the legitimacy* of the failure event, implying a plea for mitigation in judgement
E 522	Appeal to *good intentions* or lack of bad intentions in connection with the failure event, implying a plea for mitigation in judgement
E 523	Appeal to *effort and care* in connection with the failure event, implying a plea for mitigation in judgement
E 524	Appeal to *restitutions or compensations* offered or already provided, implying a plea for mitigation in judgement
E 525	Appeal to own *learning experience* in connection with the failure event and/or promise of avoidance of similar failures in the future, implying a plea for mitigation in judgement
E 610	**Plea for mitigation in judgement on the basis of assertions about characteristics of the future event**
E 611	*Minimization of the failure aspects* of the event, implying a plea for mitigation in judgement
E 612	*Denial of damage*, implying a plea for mitigation in judgement
E 613	*Minimization of damage*, implying a plea for mitigation in judgement

Taxonomy for account phases

E 614	Appeal to *positive consequences or side effects* of the failure event, implying a plea for mitigation in judgement
E 710	Expression of hope for understanding, pardon or mercy with respect to the failure event, and/or hope for the continuation or restoration of good relationship with the victim or other persons involved
E 711	Expression of concern with respect to the failure event and/or the damage done to the victim, offered in the hope of understanding, pardon or mercy, and/or hope of the continuation or restoration of good relationship with the victim, the opponent or other persons involved
E 999	Other excuses
J	JUSTIFICATIONS
J 210	Claims of *situational constraints* as fully or partly legitimizing own behaviour
J 220	Claims of *time pressure* as fully or partly legitimizing own behaviour
J 230	Appeal to *loyalties to higher-order norms, values or standards* as basis for explicit or implicit claims of legitimacy of own behaviour
J 240	Appeal to *loyalties to specific other persons* as basis for explicit or implicit claims of legitimacy of own behaviour
J 310	Claims of obedience to, or pressure by, *powerful agents* as fully or partly legitimizing own behaviour
J 410	**Claims of full or partial legitimacy in view of provocations by various agents**
J 411	Claims of full or partial legitimacy of own behaviour in view of *provocation by the accuser*
J 412	Claims of legitimacy of own behaviour in view of provocations by the *victim*
J 413	Claims of legitimacy of own behaviour in view of provocations by *persons other than the victim and/or accuser*
J 420	**Claims of full or partial legitimacy in view of participations of other agents in the failure event**
J 421	Claims of (full or partial) legitimacy of own behaviour in view of the *participation of the accuser* in the failure event
J 422	Claims of legitimacy of own behaviour in view of the participation of the *victim* in the failure event
J 423	Claims of legitimacy of own behaviour in view of the participation of *persons other than the victim and/or accuser*

J 430		**Claims of full or partial legitimacy of own behaviour in view of limitations, negative traits or misdeeds of other persons**
J 431		Claims of (full or partial) legitimacy of own behaviour in view of *limitations, negative traits or misdeeds* of the *accuser*
J 432		Claims of legitimacy of own behaviour in view of limitations, negative traits or misdeeds of the *victim*
J 433		Claims of legitimacy of own behaviour in view of limitations, negative traits or misdeeds of *persons other than the victim and/or accuser*

J 510 Appeals to the right of self-fulfilment

J 511   Claims of (full or partial) legitimacy of own behaviour in view of own *underprivileged past*. Appeal to the right of self-fulfilment

J 512   Claims of legitimacy of own behaviour in view of own *good record in the past*, apart from the failure event. Appeal to the right of self-fulfilment

J 513   Claims of legitimacy of own behaviour in view of *present identity, role or status* in relation to other persons. Appeal to the right of self-fulfilment

J 514   Appeal to the right of self-fulfilment, supported by *other arguments* or *without supporting argument*

J 520 Claims of full or partial legitimacy on the basis of assertions about actor's role in the failure event

J 521   Appeal to *conviction of the legitimacy* of the failure event as basis for explicit or implicit claim of full or partial legitimacy of own behaviour

J 522   Appeal to *good intentions*, or lack of bad intentions, in connection with the failure event, implying claim of full or partial legitimacy of own behaviour

J 523   Appeal to *effort and care* in connection with the failure event, implying claim of full or partial legitimacy of own behaviour

J 524   Appeal to *restitutions or compensations* offered or already provided, implying claim of full or partial legitimacy of own behaviour

J 610 Claims of full or partial legitimacy on the basis of assertions about characteristics of the failure event

J 611   *Minimization of the failure aspects* of the event, implying claim of full or partial legitimacy of own behaviour

J 612   *Denial of damage*, implying claim of full or partial legitimacy of own behaviour

J 613   *Minimization of damage*, implying claim of full or partial legitimacy of own behaviour

Taxonomy for account phases

J 614	Appeal to *positive consequences or side effects* of the failure event, implying claim of full or partial legitimacy of own behaviour
J 999	Other justifications
R	REFUSALS
R 110	**Refutation of allegation of a failure event or of actor's involvement in such an event**
R 111	*Denial of occurrence* of the alleged failure event
R 112	*Denial of own involvement* in the failure event
R 113	*Denial of opponent's right or reason* to question or reproach the actor, stated baldly, without supporting argument
R 114	*Refusal to concede guilt or responsibility* for the *occurrence* of the failure event
R 115	*Refusal to accept responsibility* for the *solution* of the problem created by the failure event. Denial of own contribution to restitution or compensation
R 116	*Refusal to accept* in the future a *task assignment* similar to the one for which the actor now has to bear the blame
R 117	*Refutation of a specific reproach or argument* as wrong or unjustified (regardless of actor's willingness or refusal to accept some or full responsibility for the failure event)
R 120	**Unrestricted attribution of responsibility for the failure event to other persons**
R 121	Unrestricted attribution of responsibility for the failure event to the *accuser*
R 122	Unrestricted attribution of responsibility for the failure event to the *victim*
R 123	Unrestricted attribution of responsibility for the failure event *to persons other than the victim and/or accuser*
R 130	**Evasions and mystifications**
R 131	*Deferral of account* to another time or occasion
R 132	*Referral of accuser* to another source of information
R 133	*Irrelevant talk*
R 134	*Silence*
R 139	*Other evasions or mystifications*
R 210	Denial of the right to question or reproach in view of the unforeseeability or unpreventability of the failure event due to *situational constraints*, or in view of the *immutability of the failure event* (It has happened and can't be changed, so stop complaining about it.)
R 220	Denial of the right to question or reproach in view of *temporal constraints* connected with the failure event

R 230 Denial of the right to question or reproach in view of *loyalties to higher-order norms, values or standards*
R 240 Denial of the right to question or reproach in view of *loyalties to specific other persons*
R 310 Denial of the right to question or reproach in view of obedience due to *authorities* or of pressure exerted by *powerful agents*

R 410 Denial of the right to question or reproach in view of provocations by various agents

R 411 Denial of the right to question or reproach in view of *provocations by the accuser*
R 412 Denial of the right to question or reproach in view of provocations by the *victim*
R 413 Denial of the right to question or reproach in view of provocations by *persons other than the victim and/or accuser*

R 420 Denial of the right to question or reproach in view of participation of other persons as co-actors in the failure event

R 421 Denial of the right to question or reproach in view of the *participation of the accuser* as co-actor in the failure event
R 422 Denial of the right to question or reproach in view of the participation of the *victim* as co-actor in the failure event
R 423 Denial of the right to question or reproach in view of the participation of *persons other than the victim and/or accuser* as co-actors in the failure event

R 430 Denial of the right to question or reproach in view of limitations, negative traits or misdeeds of other persons

R 431 Denial of the right to question or reproach in view of the *limitations, negative traits or misdeeds* of the *accuser*
R 432 Denial of the right to question or reproach in view of limitations, negative traits or misdeeds of the *victim*
R 433 Denial of the right to question or reproach in view of limitations, negative traits or misdeeds of *persons other than the victim and/or accuser*

R 510 Denial of the right to question or reproach based on self-relevant comments

R 511 Denial of the right to question or reproach in view of own *underprivileged past*
R 512 Denial of the right to question or reproach in view of own *good record in the past*, apart from the failure event
R 513 Denial of the right to question or reproach in view of present *own identity, role or status* in relation to victim, accuser or other persons
R 514 Denial of the right to question or reproach in view of the *right to self-fulfilment*, supported by *other arguments* or *without supporting argument*

R 520		**Refutation of the right to question or reproach on the basis of assertions about actor's role in connection with the failure event**
R 521		Appeal to *conviction of the legitimacy* of the failure event, implying a refutation of the right to question or reproach
R 522		Assertion of *good intentions* in connection with the failure event, implying a refutation of the right to question or reproach
R 523		Assertion of *effort and care* in connection with the failure event, implying a refutation of the right to question or reproach
R 524		Assertion of *restitutions or compensations* offered or already provided, implying a refutation of the right to question or reproach
R 610		**Refutation of the right to question or reproach on the basis of assertions about characteristics of the failure event**
R 611		*Minimization of the failure aspects* of the event, implying a refutation of the right to question or reproach
R 612		*Denial of damage*, implying a refutation of the right to question or reproach
R 613		*Minimization of damage*, implying a refutation of the right to question or reproach
R 614		Assertion of *positive consequences or side effects* of the failure event, implying a refutation of the right to question or reproach
R 999		Other refusals

Appendix B
Taxonomy for reactions of opponents during phases of reproach and evaluation

A	COMMENTS ON ACCOUNTS
A 10	**Relief of the actor from the obligation to render an account**
A 11	Relief of the actor from the obligation to render an account without further explanation
A 12	Relief of the actor from the obligation to render an account with reference to *aspects of the failure event*
A 13	Relief of the actor from the obligation to render an account with reference to characteristics of the *actor* or to his/her behaviour *before* or *after* the failure event
A 14	Relief of the actor from the obligation to render an account with reference to own characteristics, experiences or conduct of the *opponent*
A 15	Relief of the actor from the obligation to render an account with reference to characteristics, experiences or conduct of *victim(s)* other than or beside the opponent
A 16	Relief of the actor from the obligation to render an account with reference to characteristics, experiences or conduct of *other persons*
A 17	Postponement of the account with a friendly explanation
A 19	Relief of the actor from the obligation to render an account with other reasoning
A 20	**Questions about the causes, the course, or the consequences of the failure event**
A 21	Question about the *causes* or the *course* of the failure event *without* a reproachful innuendo or comment. Readiness to listen to a report from the actor's viewpoint
A 22	Question about the *causes* or the *course* of the failure event *with* a reproachful innuendo or comment
A 23	Question about the *consequences* of the failure event *without* a reproachful innuendo or comment
A 24	Question about the *consequences* of the failure event *with* a reproachful innuendo or comment
A 25	Question about *personal characteristics* of the actor *without* a reproachful innuendo or comment
A 26	Question about *personal characteristics* of the actor *with* a reproachful innuendo or comment

A 30		**Positive reactions to an explanation or account given by the actor**
A 31		Positive reaction to an explanation or account given by the actor without explanatory comment
A 32		Full concession of factual plausibility of the account
A 33		Partial concession of factual plausibility of the account
A 34		Full concession of moral acceptability of the account
A 35		Partial concession of moral acceptability of the account
A 36		Unconditional denial of the account with friendly reasoning
A 37		Partial denial of the account with friendly reasoning
A 39		Positive reaction to an explanation or account given by the actor with other reasoning or explanation

A 40 — **Criticism of the actor's account phase behaviour**

A 41 — Critique of the actor's deficient willingness to give information or render an account. Demand for a further or more detailed account or explanation
A 42 — Partial critique of the account for factual reasons
A 43 — Partial critique of the account for moral reasons
A 44 — Partial critique of the account as (possibly) insincere in parts (cf. A 54)
A 49 — Partial critique of the account with other reasoning

A 50 — **Refutation of the account rendered by an actor**

A 51 — Refutation of the account without explanation
A 52 — Refutation of the account as factually wrong
A 53 — Refutation of the account as morally untenable
A 54 — Refutation of the account as mendacious (cf. A 44)
A 55 — Refutation of the account with reference to own characteristics, experiences or conduct of the *opponent*
A 56 — Refutation of the account with reference to characteristics, experiences or conduct of *victim(s)* other than or beside the opponent
A 57 — Refutation of the account with reference to characteristics, experiences or conduct of the *actor*
A 58 — Refutation of the account with reference to experiences or conduct of *other persons*
A 59 — Refutation of the account with other reasoning

A 60 — **Refusal to listen to or otherwise receive an account about to be given or announced by an actor**

A 61 — Refusal to receive an account without explanation
A 62 — Refusal to listen to or otherwise receive an account about to be given or announced by an actor with reference to aspects of the failure event
A 63 — Refusal to listen to or otherwise receive an account about to be given or announced by an actor with reference to characteristics of the *actor* or to his/her behaviour *before* or *after* the failure event

Appendix B

A 64	Refusal to listen to or otherwise receive an account about to be given or announced by an actor with reference to own characteristics, experiences or conduct of the *opponent*
A 65	Refusal to listen to or otherwise receive an account about to be given or announced by an actor with reference to experiences or conduct of *victim(s)* other than or beside the opponent
A 66	Refusal to listen to or otherwise receive an account about to be given or announced by an actor with reference to characteristics, experiences or conduct of *other persons*
A 67	Postponement of the account with a hostile explanation or in a hostile mood without explanation
A 69	Refusal to listen to or otherwise receive an account about to be given or announced by an actor with other reasoning
A 99	Other comments on a specific account or on accounts in general
F	COMMENTS ON FAILURE EVENTS
F 10	**Inability, unwillingness or hesitation to comment on the failure event**
F 11	Explicit admission of inability to comment on the failure event
F 12	Attribution of responsibility for comment and judgement on the failure event to other persons or institutions (cf. F 655 and F 665)
F 13	Ambivalence of the opponent with respect to his/her own right to utter a reproach or with respect to the adequacy of reproaches or sanctions
F 14	Excuse or explanation with respect to the opponent role devolving upon or resting with the speaker
F 15	No direct address to the actor; he or she is listening to a statement addressed to another person by the opponent
F 19	Other signs or forms of inability, unwillingness or hesitation to comment on the failure event
F 20	**Attribution of guilt or responsibility for the occurrence of the failure event to persons other than the actor**
F 21	*Opponent's* admission of own *partial* guilt or responsibility for the occurrence of the failure event
F 22	*Opponent's* admission of *full or preponderant* guilt or responsibility for the occurrence of the failure event
F 23	Attribution of *partial* guilt or responsibility for the occurrence of the failure event to the *victim(s)* of this event, if not identical with the opponent (otherwise F 21)
F 24	Attribution of *full or preponderant* guilt or responsibility for the occurrence of the failure event to the *victim(s)* of this event, if not identical with the opponent (otherwise F 22)

F 25	Attribution of *partial* guilt or responsibility to *persons other* than the actor, victim or opponent
F 26	Attribution of *full or preponderant* guilt or responsibility to *persons other* than the actor, victim or opponent
F 30	**Positive comments on the actor's conduct during the failure event: exculpation, understanding, appeasement, friendly advice**
F 31	Denial that a failure event has occurred
F 32	Minimization of the norm violation by the failure event (cf. F 42)
F 33	Explicit statement of the opponent that he or she cannot or would not attribute guilt or responsibility for the occurrence of the failure event to the actor
F 34	Understanding of the actor's conduct during the failure event. Partial justification of the actor (e.g. 'This can happen to everybody), 'This has happened to me too' (cf. F 44)
F 351	Explicit appeasement or mollification of the actor
F 352	Humorous and calm comment on the failure event (cf. F 542, sarcastic irony)
F 361	Explicit concession of the actor's good intention or of the absence of evil intent on his/her part with respect to the occurrence of the failure event
F 362	Excusatory reference to limiting conditions for the capacity or volition of the actor to avoid the failure event
F 371	Friendly advice as to how to avoid failures in the future (cf. F 511, F 623)
F 372	Offers of help by the opponent for avoiding failures in the future (cf. F 46)
F 39	Other positive comments on the actor's conduct during the failure event
F 40	**Positive comments on the actor's liability for the consequences of the failure event: exoneration, waiving of claims, pardon, compassion, offers of help**
F 41	Exoneration of the actor from the liability for the damage caused by the failure event. Waiving of demands for restitution or compensation
F 42	Minimization of the damage caused by the failure event (cf. F 32)
F 431	Explicit statement of pardon
F 432	Explicit renunciation of punishment or revenge
F 44	Compassion for the actor with respect to his/her entanglement in the failure event and the resulting negative consequences for the actor (cf. F 34, F 623)
F 45	Acknowledgement of the actor's efforts during or after the failure event to prevent or minimize damage or to provide at least partial compensation

F 46	Offers of help by the opponent for restitution or compensation (cf. F 372)
F 49	Other exonerating comments on the actor's liability for the consequences of the failure event
F 50	**Negative comments on the actor's conduct during the failure event: reproach, critique, attribution of guilt, disappointment, warnings**
F 511	Admonition to avoid further entanglements in failure events. Amendment demands (cf. F 371, F 623)
F 512	Reproach that prior pertinent warnings have not been heeded
F 52	Appeal to the actor to admit guilt or responsibility for the occurrence of the failure event
F 53	Special disappointment that this very actor has been involved in the failure event
F 541	Emphasis of the normative violation by the failure event (cf. F 621)
F 542	Sarcastically ironic comment on the failure event (cf. F 352)
F 551	Explicit attribution of *partial* guilt or responsibility for the occurrence of the failure event to the actor
F 552	Explicit attribution of *full or preponderant* guilt or responsibility for the occurrence of the failure event to the actor
F 56	Extension of the guilt attribution or responsibility attribution to the actor. Inclusion of previous failures
F 571	Accusation of carelessness, negligence
F 572	Accusation of evil intent, malice
F 58	Explicit denial of understanding for the actor's conduct during the failure event (cf. F 64)
F 59	Other negative comments on the actor's conduct during the failure event
F 60	**Negative comments on the actor's liability for the consequences of the failure event: demands, threats, sanctions, dire predictions**
F 611	Hint at, or indirect phrasing of, a demand or expectation addressed to the actor for restitution or compensation of the damage caused by the failure event, or of some other sanction
F 612	Direct, open phrasing of a demand addressed to the actor for restitution or compensation of the damage caused by the failure event (cf. F 652)
F 613	Accusation of deficient readiness of the actor to provide compensation

Taxonomy for reproach and evaluation phases

F 621	Emphasis of actual or potential negative consequences of the failure event for the *opponent* (cf. F 541)
F 622	Emphasis of actual or potential negative consequences of the failure event for *victims* other than the opponent (cf. F 541)
F 623	Emphasis of actual or potential negative consequences of the failure event for the *actor* him- or herself (cf. F 44)
F 63	Ascertainment of the insufficiency of any restitution or compensation. A redemption of guilt is not possible
F 64	Explicit denial of compassion with the actor concerning the consequences of the failure event for him or her (cf. F 58)
F 65	Threat with a negative sanction, i.e.:
F 651	Limitation of range of autonomy
F 652	Enforcement of a compensation
F 653	Punishment
F 654	Revenge
F 655	Informing of agents legitimized to deal with the failure event
F 659	Other negative sanctions
F 650	Sanction not specified
F 66	Initiation or execution of a negative sanction, i.e.:
F 661	Limitation of range of autonomy
F 662	Enforcement of a compensation
F 663	Punishment
F 664	Revenge
F 665	Informing of agents legitimized to deal with the failure event
F 669	Other negative sanctions
F 660	Sanction not specified
F 67	Threat with physical violence
F 68	Execution of physical violence
F 69	Other incriminatory comments on the actor's liability for the consequences of the failure event
F 98	Comments of the opponent on his or her own involvement in the failure event, which are not covered by F 21 or F 22. (Coding according to the account phase taxonomy should be considered)
F 99	Other comments on the failure event, neither positive nor negative for the actor
P	COMMENTS ON THE ACTOR'S PERSONALITY
P 10	**Favourable comments on enduring characteristics of the actor**
P 11	Favourable evaluation of the actor's capabilities
P 12	Favourable evaluation of the actor's moral qualities
P 13	Favourable evaluation of other characteristics of the actor

P 20	**Unfavourable comments on enduring characteristics of the actor**
P 21	Unfavourable evaluation of the actor's capabilities
P 22	Unfavourable evaluation of the actor's moral qualities
P 23	Unfavourable evaluation of other characteristics of the actor
P 99	Other comments, neither positive nor negative, on the actor's personality
B	COMMENTS ON THE RELATIONSHIP BETWEEN ACTOR AND OPPONENT
B 10	**Favourable auspices for the relationship between actor and opponent**
B 11	Unconditional or conditional hope or confidence in an amelioration or intensification of the good relationship between actor and opponent
B 12	Unconditional assurance of the maintenance or restoration of a good relationship between actor and opponent
B 13	Conditional assurance of the maintenance or restoration of a good relationship between actor and opponent
B 20	**Unfavourable auspices for the relationship between actor and opponent**
B 21	Ascertainment or threat of a cooling or deterioration of the relationship between actor and opponent
B 22	Threat of rupture of the relationship with the actor
B 23	Rupture of the relationship with the actor
B 99	Non-evaluative comments, neither positive nor negative, on the relationship between actor and opponent
Z 99	Other comments of the opponent which do not fit into any of the superordinate categories A, F, P or B
Z 90	The opponent reacts with complete silence
	SECONDARY CODINGS
SV 10	**Tendency and differentiation of opponent comments during the reproach phase**
SV 11	Uniformly positive judgement tendencies
SV 12	Uniformly negative judgement tendencies
SV 13	Transition from negative to ambivalent or positive, or from ambivalent to positive judgement tendencies
SV 14	Transition from positive to ambivalent or negative, or from ambivalent to negative judgement tendencies
SV 15	Multiple change between positive and negative and/or ambivalent judgement tendencies
SV 16	Uniformly ambivalent judgement tendencies
SV 17	No positive, negative or ambivalent judgement tendencies can be recognized

SW 10	**Tendency and differentiation of opponent comments during the evaluation phase**
SW 11	Uniformly positive judgement tendencies
SW 12	Uniformly negative judgement tendencies
SW 13	Transition from negative to ambivalent or positive, or from ambivalent to positive judgement tendencies
SW 14	Transition from positive to ambivalent or negative, or from ambivalent to negative judgement tendencies
SW 15	Multiple change between positive and negative and/or ambivalent judgement tendencies
SW 16	Uniformly ambivalent judgement tendencies
SW 17	No positive, negative or ambivalent judgement tendencies can be recognized

Notes

1 My translations of the original 'Eine bis zur Unkenntlichkeit "geteilte" Programmverantwortung darf es nicht geben' and 'Aber diese Redaktionen konkurrieren mit genügend anderen, und diese Konkurrenz sorgt automatisch für wechselseitige Korrekturen.'
2 My translation of the original 'Die Unauffindbarkeit des Verantwortlichen ist, so gesehen, geradezu gespenstisch.'
3 'The other side should also be heard!'
4 The multidimensional concept 'responsibility' and its complex relationship to causal conditions has received attention in many intriguing discussions. I owe much to the treatments by Fauconnet (1928), Heider (1958), Fincham and Jaspars (1980) and Shaver (1985), to name but a few.
5 A particularly interesting, and distressing, case in point is the computer simulation game in Dörner et al. (1981), in which many subjects failed miserably in their much too simplistic directives as 'mayors' attempting to steer a community, 'Lohhausen', through the vicissitudes of interlocking events and crises.
6 It is amazing to see the vast expansion of the literature concerning evolutionary perspectives on epistemology during the last two decades. Scholars from various disciplines have addressed this topic (e.g. Riedl and Wuketits 1987), from psychology most notably Donald Campbell (e.g. 1974).
7 Lorenz (1973), Popper (1972) and Riedl (1981) proposed essentially equivalent concepts of innate facilitators of control-relevant learning.
8 Popper (1987, p.31) also stressed this point in a recent symposium on evolutionary epistemology (see Riedl and Wuketits 1987, p.31). A similar perspective on situational controllability versus personal control competence was presented by Oesterreich (1981).
9 A systematic treatment of this issue that was as intensive as our concern with the ten escalation hypotheses would have far exceeded our research capacity.
10 The original German versions of the vignettes may be obtained from the author.
11 Anne Heynen and Rudolf Schiffmann, who acted as research assistants in this seminar, contributed much towards the successful completion of this study. I gratefully acknowledge their excellent work as well as the highly motivated and competent participation of the following students who attended the seminar: Barbara Birkendorf, Regina Brandt, Susanne Bubber, Petra Kleibaumhüter, Ursula Lang, Delia Nixdorf, Ilona Prystav, Heidelinde Schindler, Michael Siebert, Joachim Studt and Dagmar Tonscheidt.
12 Wie groß ist der Anteil der Verantwortung Ihrer Freundin für den Vorfall?
13 Sie ist gar nicht verantwortlich. Sie ist voll und ganz verantwortlich!

Notes

14 Angenommen, die Kosten für Notarzt und Krankenhaus sind nicht durch eine Versicherung gedeckt. Soll die Freundin einen Teil der Kosten oder die gesamten Kosten tragen oder gar keinen Kostenbeitrag leisten?
15 Gar keinen Kostenbeitrag. Die gesamten Kosten.
16 Verantwortlich sein für etwas und schuldig sein daran, ist nicht immer dasselbe. Daher noch diese Frage: Hat Ihre Freundin bei dem Vorfall Schuld auf sich geladen?
17 Ja, die Freundin ist voll und ganz schuldig zu sprechen.

Ja, die Freundin hat einen erheblichen Anteil an Schuld auf sich geladen.

Der Fall liegt nicht so einfach; hier sind verschiedene Umstände zusammengekommen. Aber ganz freisprechen von Schuld kann man die Freundin auch nicht. Bis zu einem gewissen Grad hat sie sich schon schuldig gemacht.

Über die Verantwortung, die die Freundin zu tragen hat, kann man verschiedener Meinung sein. Aber von Schuld kann hier keine Rede sein.

18 See for instance R.M. Williams (1964) and from our own group the study by Heinemann and Schönbach reported in Schönbach et al. 1981, pp.74–87. For the difficulties of interpretation of 'age effects' and 'education effects' on hostile attitudes, see also J.A. Davis (1975) and Smith (1985).
19 Völlig unzuverlässig. Völlig zuverlässig.
20 A preliminary report on this project appeared in Schönbach and Kleibaumhüter (1989).
21 The original German text reads as follows:
  1 Die Eltern kehren zurück, erfahren schon auf der Treppe von dem Vorfall und fragen Sie nach einer Erklärung.
  2 Die Eltern kehren zurück, erfahren schon auf der Treppe von dem Vorfall und stellen Sie folgendermaßen zur Rede: 'Wie konnte Dir das nur passieren? Du warst wohl zu sehr mit Dir selbst beschäftigt?!'
  3 Die Eltern kehren zurück, erfahren schon auf der Treppe von dem Vorfall und stellen Sie folgendermaßen zur Rede: 'Warum hast Du das nicht verhindern können? Wir hätten nicht gedacht, daß Du so leicht den Überblick verlierst!'
22 Was glauben Sie, welche Wirkung hat Ihre Antwort auf die Eltern des Kindes?
  (a) Meine Antwort hat sie sehr milde gestimmt.
       ↓
  (b) Meine Antwort hat sie sehr ärgerlich gestimmt.
23 Wie gerechtfertigt erschien Ihnen der Vorwurf der Eltern in dieser Situation?
  (a) Der Vorwurf erschien mir völlig gerechtfertigt.
       ↓
  (e) Der Vorwurf erschien mir völlig ungerechtfertigt.
24 We are grateful to Delia Nixdorf and Ilona Prystav for having provided a first draft of a German translation of the desirability of control scale, which we adopted with minor modifications. Our version of the Burger and Cooper scale, as well as the interspersed items, may be obtained from the author upon request.
25 The original German version of these items and of other measurement instruments described in this chapter may be obtained from the author upon request.
26 See note 25.

27 This translation was based, with some modifications, on two earlier versions by Krampen (1979) and Mielke (1979). Levenson's IPC scale was used in this study since the data of RPS I and APS I suggested that Schopler's (1973) scale lacked discriminatory power in our settings.
28 I gratefully acknowledge the splendid assistance provided by Petra Kleibaumhüter in this seminar and a subsequent one, from which EPS III emerged. I am also very grateful to the following co-workers and students who participated as interviewers and coders in one or both of these seminars: Ingrid Andrecht, Dirk Bergmann, Barbara Birkendorf, Susanne Bubber, Volker Bussmann, Joannis Economou, Silke Erkens, Jörg Kleine, Udo Kluttig, Annerose Rieger, Sabine Rund, Christoph Saft and Heike Stuhrmann-Berg.
29 See note 25.
30 See note 25.
31 See note 25.
32 I am aware of the fact that many linguists (e.g. Halliday 1970) use the terms 'theme' and 'rheme' in the sense of 'topic' and 'comment', which implies the equation theme = topic. It is just for lack of a better term in the present context that I have chosen 'theme' to denote 'topic-and-comment'.
33 Wolfgang Heinemann drew my attention to this interesting possibility.
34 I gratefully acknowledge the support and stimulation provided by Petra Flaßhove as seminar assistant and Rudolf Schiffmann as student participant and subsequent co-worker.
35 See note 28 for my expression of gratitude to the core group of participants in the taxonomy project. Many other students, too numerous to mention, had also helped much in collecting and analysing the pilot study data during the 1987 seminar, and I thank them too very much.
36 Coding instructions for the Opponent Taxonomy exist in German in mimeographed form. They will be sent to interested readers upon written request as long as the supply lasts.
37 The German version of the categories is as follows:
 1 Kein Schuldvorwurf.
 2 Schuldvorwurf mit Einschränkung.
 3 Schuldvorwurf ohne Einschränkung in ruhigem Ton.
 4 Schuldvorwurf ohne Einschränkung in scharfem Ton – Beschimpfung.
38 This sign test was based on the imbalance that 82 of the 120 respondents were more severe in their blame attributions to the actor in Breach of Trust than in their attributions to the actor in Neglected Supervision, whereas only 38 respondents were either equally severe in both situations or less severe in Breach of Trust. This imbalance is significant at $p < .0001$.
39 Unless stated otherwise, significance levels reported in this book are those obtained in multifactor analyses of variance. For RPS II the ANOVAs included four two-level factors, namely severity of failure, and gender, age and educational status of the respondents, and as a fifth factor four levels of the respondents' social anxiety. Four-way and higher interactions were ignored.
40 Fincham and Shultz (1981) also obtained data consistent with the entailment model Cause (C)→Blame (B)→Restitution (R). However, they, as well as Fincham and Jaspars (1980), point out that such data are also consistent with two different orders, that is R→B→C and $B \rightleftarrows {}^C_R$. For different reasons I shall also have to offer a cautionary comment on the entailment model in section 5.3.

41 The two significance levels resulted from analyses of variances using difference measures as dependent variables, namely responsibility minus cost liability attributions, and responsibility minus guilt attributions, with a linear transformation of the guilt scores to equalize the two scales with respect to the zero point and the potential range.
42 These significance levels resulted again from t-tests admittedly less justifiable than those applied to the replication part of the data, that is attributions to the female babysitter by male and female respondents. The second-order interactions in ANOVAs involving all eight data points failed to reach conventional criteria of significance. On the responsibility scale the one deviating gradient for female attributions to female actors did produce a $p < .11$ for the first-order interaction of gender of respondent by gender of actor.
43 Again, a t-test was employed on the predictive basis of the preceding data from the study part devoted to the situation Neglected Supervision.
44 Each mean value in figure 11 is based on all respondents from RPS III within the corresponding cell. The eight cell frequencies range from 18 to 24. Responses to the vignette Neglected Oil Puddle were included regardless of its position in the order of vignettes. Thus one-third of the raw data that entered into the mean values represented in figure 11, that is those for the Oil Puddle situation in first position, are identical with one-third of the raw data base for table 4.
45 This secondary coding was done in my research seminar in the winter of 1987–8. See note 28 for my acknowledgements. The participants had some knowledge of the answers given in EPS II and in a preceding extensive pretest; but they did not learn about the respondents' gender until all the primary and secondary codings had been completed. Individual codings of the participants were compared in the seminar plenum, and consensus agreements were reached by discussion.
46 These are our German versions of the five chance conviction items from Schopler's Internal–External Scale:

Item 2. Wenn man jemanden trifft, der wirklich Erfolg hatte, dann war meistens Glück bei ihm im Spiel.

Item 7. Das Leben ist in der Hauptsache ein Glücksspiel.

Item 15. Immer, wenn ich etwas Kreatives zu tun versuche, z.B. ein Bild zu malen, habe ich nur Glück, wenn etwas Gutes dabei herauskommt.

Item 17. Einige der schönsten Dinge, die mir in meinem Leben passiert sind, hat mir das Glück beschert.

Item 18. Viele Ereignisse, die das Leben eines Menschen beeinflussen, liegen außerhalb seiner Kontrolle.

47 Non-parametric ordinal test proposed by Raatz (1966).
48 These cell size inequalities are mainly due to the fact that desire for competence and desire for constancy correlated fairly strongly in the male respondent group ($r = .43, p < .001$); the corresponding correlation for the female respondents was negligible ($r = .09$, n.s.). The smallest group ($N = 5$) was formed by males with low desire for competence and high desire for constancy, the largest group ($N = 25$) by males high on both dimensions.

References

Abramson, L.Y., Seligman, M.E.P. and Teasdale, J. (1978) Learned helplessness in humans: Critique and reformulation. *Journal of Abnormal Psychology*, 87, 49–74.

Adler, A. (1929) *Menschenkenntnis*, 3rd edn. Leipzig: Hirzel.

Anderson, N.H. (1968) Likableness ratings of 555 personality-trait words. *Journal of Personality and Social Psychology*, 9, 272–9.

Anon. (1977) Justification and excuse in the Judaic and common law: The exculpation of a defendant charged with homicide. *New York University Law Review*, 52, 599–629.

Arkin, R.M. and Baumgardner, A.H. (1986) Self-presentation and self-evaluation: Processes of self-control and social control. In R.F. Baumeister (Ed.), *Public self and private self*, pp. 75–97. New York: Springer.

Aronson, E. and Bridgeman, D. (1981) Jigsaw groups and the desegregated classroom: In pursuit of common goals. In E. Aronson (Ed.), *Readings about the social animal*, 3rd edn, pp. 329–40. San Francisco: Freeman.

Austin, J.L. (1961) A plea for excuses. In J.D. Urmson and G. Warnock (Eds.), *Philosophical papers*, pp. 123–52. Oxford: Clarendon Press.

Bandura, A. (1977) *Social learning theory*. Englewood Cliffs, N.J.: Prentice-Hall.

Bartlett, F.C. (1932) *Remembering*. Cambridge: Cambridge University Press.

Bauer, R.A. (1961) Problems of perception and the relations between the United States and the Soviet Union. *Journal of Conflict Resolution*, 3, 223–9.

Becker, E.W. and Lesiak, W.J. (1977) Feelings of hostility and personal control as related to depression. *Journal of Clinical Psychology*, 33, 654–7.

Bem, S.L. (1974) The measurement of psychological androgyny. *Journal of Consulting and Clinical Psychology*, 42, 155–62.

Bennett, W.L. (1980) The paradox of public discourse: A framework for the analysis of political accounts. *Journal of Politics*, 42, 792–819.

Bergemann, N. and Johann, G.K. (1985) Zur Erfassung von Selbstakzeptanz und Akzeptanz anderer: Eine deutschsprachige Version der Berger-Skalen. *Diagnostica*, 31, 119–29.

Berscheid, E. (1985) Interpersonal attraction. In G. Lindzey and E. Aronson (Eds.), *Handbook of social psychology*, Vol. 2, *Special fields and applications*, pp. 413–84. New York: Random House.

Berten, G. (1981) Zusammenhänge zwischen Internalität, Selbstaufmerksamkeit, Geschlecht und Vorwurfsmustern: Vorwürfe nach einer unzulänglich erfüllten Aufsichtspflicht. Unpublished diploma thesis. Ruhr-Universität Bochum.

Birkendorf, B., Bubber, S. and Tonscheidt, D. (1987) Attributionen in Vorwurfsphasen durch Männer und Frauen. Unpublished joint diploma thesis. Ruhr-Universität Bochum.

Blumstein, P.W., Carssow, K.G., Hall, J., Hawkins, B., Hoffman, R., Ishem, E., Maurer, C.P., Spens, D., Taylor, J. and Zimmerman, D.L. (1974) The honoring of accounts. *American Sociological Review*, 39, 551–66.
Brickman, P., Rabinowitz, V.C., Karuza, J., Coates, D., Cohn, E. and Kidder, L. (1982) Models of helping and coping. *American Psychologist*, 37, 368–84.
Brown, P. and Levinson, S.C. (1987) *Politeness*. Cambridge: Cambridge University Press.
Burger, J.M. (1981) Motivational biases in the attribution of responsibility for an accident: A meta-analysis of the defensive-attribution hypothesis. *Psychological Bulletin*, 90, 496–512.
Burger, J.M. and Cooper, H.M. (1979) The desirability of control. *Motivation and Emotion*, 3, 381–93.
Calicchia, J.P. and Pardine, P. (1984) Attributional style: Degree of depression, respondent's sex, and nature of the attributional event. *Journal of Psychology*, 117, 167–75.
Campbell, D.T. (1974) Evolutionary epistemology. In P. Schilpp (Ed.), *The library of living philosophers: The philosophy of Karl Popper*, Vol. 1, pp. 413–63. La Salle, Ill.: Open Court.
Carver, C.S. and Scheier, M.F. (1981) *Attention and self-regulation: A control-theory approach to human behavior*. New York: Springer.
Cody, M.J. and McLaughlin, M.L. (1985) Models for the sequential construction of accounting episodes: Situational and interactional constraints on message selection and evaluation. In R.L. Street and J.N. Cappella (Eds.), *Sequence and pattern in communicative behaviour*, pp. 50–69. London: Edward Arnold.
Cody, M.J. and McLaughlin, M.L. (1988) Accounts on trial: Oral arguments in traffic court. In C. Antaki (Ed.), *Analysing everyday explanation: A casebook of methods*, pp. 113–26. London: Sage.
Council on Environmental Quality and the US State Department (1980) (Eds.) *The Global 2000 Report to the President*. Washington: US Government Printing Office.
Cupach, W.R., Metts, S. and Hazleton Jr., V. (1986) Coping with embarrassing predicaments: Remedial strategies and their perceived utility. *Journal of Language and Social Psychology*, 5, 181–200.
Damerow, G. (1982) Bewertung verschiedener Typen von Rechenschaften nach einer 'Notwehrhandlung'. Unpublished diploma thesis. Ruhr-Universität Bochum.
Davis, D. (1982) Determinants of responsiveness in dyadic interaction. In W. Ickes and E.S. Knowles (Eds.), *Personality, roles and social behavior*, pp. 84–139. New York: Springer.
Davis, D. and Perkowitz, W.T. (1979) Consequences of responsiveness in dyadic interaction: Effects of probability of response and proportion of content-related responses on interpersonal attraction. *Journal of Personality and Social Psychology*, 37, 534–50.
Davis, J.A. (1975) Communism, conformity, cohorts, and categories: American tolerance in 1954 and 1972–73. *American Journal of Sociology*, 81, 491–513.
De Man, A., Simpson-Housley, P. and Curtis, F. (1985) Assignment of responsibility and flood hazard in Catahoula County, Louisiana. *Environment and Behavior*, 17, 371–86.

Dittes, J.E. (1959) Attractiveness of group as function of self-esteem and acceptance by group. *Journal of Abnormal and Social Psychology*, **59**, 77–82.
Dörner, D., Kreuzig, H.W., Reither, F. and Stäudel, T. (Eds.) (1983) *Lohhausen: Vom Umgang mit Unbestimmtheit und Komplexität*. Bern: Huber.
Dressler, J. (1984) New thoughts about the concept of justification in the criminal law. A critique of Fletcher's thinking and Rethinking. *UCLA Law Review*, **32**, 61–99.
Fauconnet, P. (1928) *La Responsabilité*. Paris: Alcan.
Feather, N.T. (1985) Masculinity, femininity, psychological androgyny, and the structure of values. *Journal of Personality and Social Psychology*, **47**, 604–20.
Felson, R.B. and Ribner, S.A. (1981) An attributional approach to accounts and sanctions for criminal violence. *Social Psychology Quarterly*, **44**, 137–42.
Fenigstein, A., Scheier, M.F. and Buss, A.H. (1975) Public and private self-consciousness: Assessment and theory. *Journal of Consulting and Clinical Psychology*, **43**, 522–7.
Festinger, L. (1957) *A theory of cognitive dissonance*. Evanston, Ill.: Row, Peterson.
Festinger, L. (1981) Human nature and human competence. *Social Research*, **48**, 306–21.
Festinger, L. (1983) *The human legacy*. New York: Columbia University Press.
Fincham, F.D. (1985) Attributions in close relationships. In J.H. Harvey and G. Weary (Eds.), *Attribution: Basic issues and applications*, pp. 203–34. Orlando, Fla.: Academic Press.
Fincham, F.D. and Jaspars, J.M. (1980) Attribution of responsibility: From man the scientist to man as lawyer. In L. Berkowitz (Ed.), *Advances in experimental social psychology*, Vol. 13, pp. 81–138. New York: Academic Press.
Fincham, F.D. and Shultz, T.R. (1981) Intervening causation and the mitigation of responsibility for harm. *British Journal of Social Psychology*, **20**, 113–20.
Flaßhove, P. (1981) Zusammenhänge zwischen Internalität, Selbstaufmerksamkeit, Geschlecht und Rechenschaftstendenzen: Rechenschaften im Falle einer unzulänglich erfüllten Aufsichtspflicht. Unpublished diploma thesis. Ruhr-Universität Bochum.
Fletcher, C. (1978) *Rethinking criminal law*. Boston: Little-Brown.
Ford, M.R. and Lowery, C.R. (1986) Gender differences in moral reasoning: A comparison of the use of justice and care orientations. *Journal of Personality and Social Psychology*, **50**, 777–83.
Freedman, J.L., Carlsmith, J.M. and Sears, D.O. (1970) *Social Psychology*. Englewood Cliffs, N.J.: Prentice Hall.
Gilligan, C. (1977) In a different voice: Women's conceptions of self and of morality. *Harvard Educational Review*, **47**, 481–517.
Goffman, E. (1971) *Relations in public: Micro-studies of the public order*. Harmondsworth: Penguin.
Goodstadt, B.E. and Hjelle, L.A. (1973) Power to the powerless: Locus of control and the use of power. *Journal of Personality and Social Psychology*, **27**, 190–6.
Greenawalt, K. (1984) The perplexing borders of justification and excuse. *Columbia Law Review*, **84**, 1897–1927.
Greenberg, J., Pyszczynski, T. and Solomon, S. (1986) The causes and consequences of a need for self-esteem: A terror management theory. In R.F. Baumeister (Ed.), *Public self and private self*, pp. 189–212. New York: Springer.

Hale, C.L. (1987) A comparison of accounts: When is a failure not a failure? *Journal of Language and Social Psychology*, **6**, 117–32.
Hall, P.M. and Hewitt, J.P. (1970) The quasi-theory of communication and the management of dissent. *Social Problems*, **18**, 17–27.
Halliday, M.A.K. (1970) Language structure and language function. In J. Lyons (Ed.), *New horizons in linguistics*, pp. 140–65. Harmondsworth: Penguin.
Hamilton, V.L. (1978) Who is responsible? Toward a social psychology of responsibility attribution. *Social Psychology*, **41**, 316–28.
Hart, H.L.A. (1968) *Punishment and responsibility*. Oxford: Clarendon Press.
Heider, F. (1958) *The psychology of interpersonal relations*. New York: Wiley.
Heinemann, W. (1979) The assessment of private and public self-consciousness: A German replication. *European Journal of Social Psychology*, **9**, 331–7.
Henderson, M. and Hewstone, M. (1984) Prison inmates' explanations for interpersonal violence: Accounts and attributions. *Journal of Consulting and Clinical Psychology*, **52**, 789–94.
Hewitt, J.P. and Stokes, R. (1975) Disclaimers. *American Sociological Review*, **40**, 1–11.
Hockett, C.F. (1958) *A course in modern linguistics*. New York: Macmillan.
Holland, B. (1981) Zusammenhänge zwischen Internalität, Selbstaufmerksamkeit, Geschlecht und Vorwurfsmustern: Vorwürfe nach einem Vertrauensbruch. Unpublished diploma thesis. Ruhr-Universität Bochum.
Hormuth, S.E. and Lalli, M. (1986) Eine Skala zur Erfassung der bereichsspezifischen Selbstzufriedenheit. Unpublished manuscript. University of Heidelberg.
Howard, J.A. (1984) Societal influences on attribution: blaming some victims more than others. *Journal of Personality and Social Psychology*, **47**, 494–505.
Hupka, R.B., Jung, J. and Silverthorn, K. (1987) Perceived acceptability of apologies, excuses and justifications in jealousy predicaments. *Journal of Social Behavior and Personality*, **2**, 303–14.
Hyland, M.E. (1987) Control theory interpretation of psychological mechanisms of depression: Comparison and integration of several theories. *Psychological Bulletin*, **102**, 109–21.
Janis, I.L. (1972) *Victims of groupthink: A psychological study of foreign-policy decisions and fiascoes*. Boston: Houghton Mifflin.
Janis, I.L. (1982) *Groupthink: Psychological studies of policy decisions and fiascoes*, revised and enlarged edn. Boston: Houghton Mifflin.
Janis, I.L. (1986) Problems of international crisis management in the nuclear age. *Journal of Social Issues*, **42**, 201–20.
Janis, I.L. and Mann, L. (1977) *Decision making: A psychological analysis of conflict, choice, and commitment*. New York: Free Press.
Jaspars, J., Fincham, F.D. and Hewstone, M. (1983) *Attribution theory and research: Conceptual, developmental and social dimensions*. London: Academic Press.
Jonas, H. (1979) *Das Prinzip Verantwortung: Versuch einer Ethik für die technologische Zivilisation*. Frankfurt am Main: Insel.
Jones, E.E. and McGillis, D. (1976) Correspondent inferences and the attribution cube: A comparative reappraisal. In J.H. Harvey, W.J. Ickes and R.F. Kidd (Eds.), *New directions in attribution research*, Vol. 1, pp. 389–420. Hillsdale, N.J.: Erlbaum.
Jones, E.E. and Nisbett, R.E. (1971) The actor and the observer: Divergent perceptions of the causes of behavior. In E.E. Jones, D.E. Kanouse, H.H. Kelley, R.E. Nisbett, S. Valins and B. Weiner, *Attribution: Perceiving the causes of behavior*, pp. 79–94. Morristown, N.J.: General Learning Press.

Jones, E.E. and Pittman, T.S. (1982) Toward a general theory of strategic self-presentation. In J. Suls (Ed.), *Psychological perspectives on the self*, Vol. 1, pp. 231–62. Hillsdale, N.J.: Erlbaum.

Kanekar, S., Pinto, N.J.P. and Mazumdar, D. (1985) Causal and moral responsibility of victims of rape and robbery. *Journal of Applied Social Psychology*, **15**, 622–37.

Kelley, H.H. (1979) *Personal relationships: Their structures and processes*. Hillsdale, N.J.: Erlbaum.

Kleibaumhüter, P. (1988) Rechenschaftsäußerungen von Lehrerinnen und Lehrern auf verschiedene Vorwurfsarten. Unpublished diploma thesis. Ruhr-Universität Bochum.

Kleinke, C.L. (1977) Assignment of responsibility for marital conflict to husbands and wives: Sex stereotypes or a double standard? *Psychological Reports*, **41**, 219–22.

Krahé, B. (1985) Die Zuschreibung von Verantwortlichkeit nach Vergewaltigungen: Opfer und Täter im Dickicht der attributionstheoretischen Forschung. *Psychologische Rundschau*, **36**, 67–82.

Krampen, G. (1979) Differenzierungen des Konstruktes der Kontrollüberzeugungen. *Zeitschrift für experimentelle und angewandte Psychologie*, **26**, 573–95.

Krampen, G. (1982) *Differentialpsychologie der Kontrollüberzeugungen*. Göttingen: Hogrefe.

Kuhl, J. and Beckmann, J. (Eds.) (1985) *Action control: From cognition to behavior*. Berlin: Springer.

Langer, E.J. (1983) *The psychology of control*. Beverly Hills, Calif.: Sage.

Lerner, M.J. (1980) *The belief in a just world: A fundamental delusion*. New York: Plenum Press.

Levenson, H. (1974) Activism and powerful others: Distinctions within the concept of internal–external control. *Journal of Personality Assessment*, **38**, 377–83.

Lloyd-Bostock, S. (1983) Attributions of cause and responsibility as social phenomena. In J. Jaspars, F.D. Fincham and M. Hewstone (Eds.), *Attribution theory and research: Conceptual, developmental and social dimensions*, pp. 261–89. London: Academic Press.

Lorenz, K. (1973) *Die Rückseite des Spiegels: Versuch einer Naturgeschichte menschlichen Erkennens*. Munich: Piper.

Maccoby, E.E. and Jacklin, C.N. (1974) *The psychology of sex differences*. Stanford: Stanford University Press.

McGraw, K.M. (1987) Guilt following transgression: An attribution of responsibility approach. *Journal of Personality and Social Psychology*, **53**, 247–56.

McHugh, P. (1968) *Defining the situation*. Indianapolis: Bobbs-Merrill.

McLaughlin, M.L., Cody, M.J. and French, K. (1989) Account-giving and the attribution of responsibility: Impressions of traffic offenders. In M.J. Cody and M.L. McLaughlin (Eds.), *The psychology of tactical communication*, pp. 244–67. Clevedon: Multilingual Matters.

McLaughlin, M.L., Cody, M.J. and O'Hair, H.D. (1983) The management of failure events: Some contextual determinants of accounting behaviour. *Human Communication Research*, **9**, 208–24.

McLaughlin, M.L., Cody, M.J. and Rosenstein, N.E. (1983) Account sequences in conversation between strangers. *Communication Monographs*, **50**, 102–25.

Madden, M.E. and Janoff-Bulman, R. (1981) Blame, control, and marital satisfaction: Wives' attributions for conflict in marriage. *Journal of Marriage and the Family*, **43**, 663–74.

Maynard, D.W. (1984) *Inside plea bargaining: The language of negotiation.* New York: Plenum.
Mielke, R. (1979) *Entwicklung einer deutschen Form des Fragebogens zur Erfassung interner vs. externer Kontrolle von Levenson (IPC).* Bielefeld Studies in Social Psychology 46. University of Bielefeld.
Mills, C.W. (1940) Situated actions and vocabularies of motive. *American Sociological Review,* 5, 904–13.
Mischel, W. (1973) Toward a cognitive social learning reconceptualization of personality. *Psychological Review,* 80, 252–83.
Mitchell, C.L. (1987) Relationship of femininity, masculinity, and gender to attribution of responsibility. *Sex Roles,* 16, 151–64.
Müller-Eckhard, E. (1974) *Äusserungslänge und Eindrucksbildung.* Bochum: Brockmeyer.
Nixdorf, B.D. and Prystav, I. (1988) Rechenschaften von Jungen und Mädchen nach einer Verfehlung. Unpublished joint diploma thesis. Ruhr-Universität Bochum.
North, R.C., Holsti, O.R., Zaninovich, M.G. and Zinnes, D.A. (1963) *Content analysis: A handbook with applications for the study of international crisis.* Evanston, Ill.: Northwestern University Press.
O'Barr, W.M. (1982) *Linguistic evidence: Language, power and strategy in the courtroom.* New York: Academic Press.
Oesterreich, R. (1981) *Handlungsregulation und Kontrolle.* Munich: Urban and Schwarzenberg.
Osnabrügge, G., Stahlberg, D. and Frey, D. (1985) Die Theorie der kognizierten Kontrolle. In D. Frey and M. Irle (Eds.), *Theorien der Sozialpsychologie,* Vol. 3, *Motivations- und Informationsverarbeitungstheorien,* pp. 127–72. Bern: Huber.
Penfold, P.S. (1985) Parents' perceived responsibility for children's problems. *Canadian Journal of Psychiatry,* 30, 255–8.
Petronio, S. (1984) Communication strategies to reduce embarrassment: Differences between men and women. *Western Journal of Speech Communication,* 48, 28–38.
Popper, K. (1966) *Of clouds and clocks: an approach to the problem of rationality and the freedom of man.* St Louis, Mo.: Washington University.
Popper, K. (1972) *Objective knowledge.* Oxford: Clarendon Press.
Potter, J. and Wetherell, M. (1987) *Discourse and social psychology: Beyond attitudes and behaviour.* London: Sage.
Powers, W.T. (1973) *Behavior: The control of perception.* Chicago: Aldine.
Raatz, U. (1966) Wie man den White-Test bei großen Stichproben ohne die Verwendung von Rängen durchführen kann. *Archiv für die gesamte Psychologie,* 118, 86–92.
Riedl, R. (1981) *Biologie der Erkenntnis: Die stammesgeschichtlichen Grundlagen der Vernunft,* 3rd edn. Berlin: Parey.
Riedl, R. (1984) *Evolution und Erkenntnis: Antworten auf Fragen aus unserer Zeit.* Munich: Piper.
Riedl, R. and Wuketits, F.M. (1987) *Die evolutionäre Erkenntnistheorie: Bedingungen, Lösungen, Kontroversen.* Berlin: Parey.
Rothbaum, F., Weisz, J.R. and Snyder, S.S. (1982) Changing the world and changing the self: A two-process model of perceived control. *Journal of Personality and Social Psychology,* 42, 5–37.
Rothman, M.L. and Gandossy, R.P. (1982) Sad tales: The accounts of white-collar defendants and the decision to sanction. *Pacific Sociological Review,* 25, 449–73.

Rotter, J.B. (1966) Generalized expectancies for internal versus external control of reinforcement. *Psychological Monographs*, **80** (No. 609).

Runge, T.E., Frey, D., Gollwitzer, P.M., Helmreich, R.L. and Spence, J.T. (1981) Cross-cultural stability of masculine (instrumental) and feminine (expressive) traits. *Journal of Cross-Cultural Psychology*, **12**, 142–62.

Sanders, J. and Hamilton, V.L. (1987) Is there a 'Common Law' of responsibility? The effect of demographic variables on judgements of wrongdoing. *Law and Human Behavior*, **11**, 277–98.

Schank, R.C. and Abelson, R.P. (1977) *Scripts, plans, goals, and understanding*. Hillsdale, N.J.: Erlbaum.

Schellenberg-van Holt, H.-J. (1981) Zusammenhänge zwischen Geschlecht, Internalitätsneigung, Selbstaufmerksamkeit und Rechenschaftsstrategien: Rechenschaften nach einer Gegenwehr in einer Bedrängnissituation. Unpublished diploma thesis. Ruhr-Universität Bochum.

Schlenker, B.R. (1980) *Impression management: The self-concept, social identity, and interpersonal relations*. Monterey, Calif.: Brooks-Cole.

Schmalt, H.D. (1986) Das Machtmotiv und Verantwortlichkeitsattribution für interpersonale Ereignisse. *Psychologische Beiträge*, **28**, 533–50.

Schönbach, P. (1972) Likableness ratings of 100 German personality-trait words corresponding to a subset of Anderson's 555 trait words. *European Journal of Social Psychology*, **2**, 327–34.

Schönbach, P. (1980) A category system for account phases. *European Journal of Social Psychology*, **10**, 195–200.

Schönbach, P. (1984) Kontrollbedürfnisse und Schwierigkeiten der Verständigung in Rechenschaftsepisoden. In J. Engelkamp (Ed.), *Psychologische Aspekte des Verstehens*, pp. 165–84. Berlin: Springer.

Schönbach, P. (1985) A taxonomy for account phases: Revised, explained and applied. Unpublished report. Ruhr-Universität Bochum.

Schönbach, P. and Kleibaumhüter, P. (1989) Severity of reproach and defensiveness of accounts. In M.J. Cody and M.L. McLaughlin (Eds.), *The psychology of tactical communication*, pp. 229–43. Clevedon: Multilingual Matters.

Schönbach, P., Bucher, E., Heinemann, W., Lackmann, M. and Regelmann, S. (1979) Sprachstrukturelle Einflüsse auf Personenbeurteilungen. *Zeitschrift für experimentelle und angewandte Psychologie*, **26**, 621–42.

Schönbach, P., Gollwitzer, P., Stiepel, G. and Wagner, U. (1981) *Education and intergroup attitudes*. London: Academic Press.

Schopler, J. (1973) Personal orientation scale: 11/73 revision. Personal communication.

Schwitalla, J. (1979) Nonresponsive Antworten. *Deutsche Sprache*, **7**, 193–211.

Scott, M.B. and Lyman, S.M. (1968) Accounts. *American Sociological Review*, **33**, 46–62.

Secord, P.F. and Backman, C.W. (1961) Personality theory and the problem of stability and change in individual behaviour: An interpersonal approach. *Psychological Review*, **68**, 21–32.

Semin, G.R. and Manstead, A.S.R. (1983) *The accountability of conduct: A social psychological analysis*. London: Academic Press.

Shaver, K.G. (1970) Defensive attribution: Effects of severity and relevance on the responsibility assigned for an accident. *Journal of Personality and Social Psychology*, **14**, 101–13.

Shaver, K.G. (1985) *The attribution of blame: Causality, responsibility, and blameworthiness*. New York: Springer.

Shaw, M.E. and Sulzer, J.L. (1964) An empirical test of Heider's levels in attribution of responsibility. *Journal of Abnormal and Social Psychology*, **69**, 39–46.

Shields, N.M. (1979) Accounts and other interpersonal strategies in a credibility detracting context. *Pacific Sociological Review*, **22**, 255–72.

Shultz, T.R. and Schleifer, M. (1983) Towards a refinement of attribution concepts. In J. Jaspars, F.D. Fincham and M. Hewstone (Eds.), *Attribution theory and research: Conceptual, developmental and social dimensions*, pp. 37–62. London: Academic Press.

Shultz, T.R., Schleifer, M. and Altman, J. (1981) Judgements of causation, responsibility, and punishment in cases of harm-doing. *Canadian Journal of Behavioral Science*, **13**, 238–54.

Smith, A.W. (1985) Cohorts, education, and the evolution of tolerance. *Social Science Research*, **14**, 205–25.

Snyder, C.R., Ford, C.E. and Hunt, H.A. (1985) Excuse making: A look at sex differences. Paper presented at the APA convention in Los Angeles, August.

Snyder, C.R. and Higgins, R.L. (1988) Excuses: Their effective role in the negotiation of reality. *Psychological Bulletin*, **104**, 23–35.

Snyder, C.R. and Higgins, R.L. (1989) Reality negotiation and excuse-making: President Reagan's March 4, 1987 Iran Arms Speech and other literature. In M.J. Cody and M.L. McLaughlin (Eds.), *The psychology of tactical communication*, pp. 207–28. Clevedon: Multilingual Matters.

Snyder, C.R., Higgins, R.L. and Stucky, R.J. (1983) *Excuses: Masquerades in search of grace*. New York: Wiley.

Spence, J.T. and Helmreich, R.L. (1978) *Masculinity and femininity: Their psychological dimension, correlates, and antecedents*. Austin: University of Texas Press.

Spence, J.T., Deaux, K. and Helmreich, R.L. (1985) Sex roles in contemporary American society. In G. Lindzey and E. Aronson (Eds.), *Handbook of social psychology*, Vol. 2, 3rd edn., pp. 149–78. New York: Random House.

Steininger, M. and Colsher, S. (1980) Beliefs about freedom and responsibility. *Journal of Social Psychology*, **110**, 143–4.

Stokes, R. and Hewitt, J.P. (1976) Aligning actions. *American Sociological Review*, **41**, 838–49.

Studt, J. (1988) Rechenschaften von Studenten auf Vorwürfe verschiedener Schärfegrade. Unpublished diploma thesis. Ruhr-Universität Bochum.

Tajfel, H. and Turner, J. (1979) An integrative theory of intergroup conflict. In W.G. Austin and S. Worchel (Eds.), *The social psychology of intergroup relations*, pp. 33–47. Monterey, Calif.: Brooks-Cole.

Taylor, S.E. (1983) Adjustment to threatening events: A theory of cognitive adaptation. *American Psychologist*, **38**, 1161–73.

Tedeschi, J.T. and Norman, N. (1985) Social power, self-presentation, and the self. In B.R. Schlenker (Ed.), *The self and social life*, pp. 293–322. New York: McGraw-Hill.

Tedeschi, J.T. and Reiss, M. (1981) Verbal strategies in impression management. In C. Antaki (Ed.), *The psychology of ordinary explanations*, pp. 271–309. London: Academic Press.

Teichgräber, R. (1981) Zusammenhänge zwischen Internalität, Selbstaufmerksamkeit, Geschlecht und Rechenschaftstendenzen: Rechenschaften im Falle eines Vertrauensbruches. Unpublished diploma thesis. Ruhr-Universität Bochum.

Thornton, B., Robbins, M.A. and Johnson, J.A. (1981) Social perception of the rape victim's culpability: The influence of respondents' personal–environmental causal attribution tendencies. *Human Relations*, **34**, 225–37.

Wagner, U. and Schönbach, P. (1984) Links between educational status and prejudice: Ethnic attitudes in West Germany. In N. Miller and M.B. Brewer (Eds.), *Groups in contact: The psychology of desegregation*, pp. 29–52. Orlando, Fla.: Academic Press.

Walster, E. (1966) Assignment of responsibility for an accident. *Journal of Personality and Social Psychology*, **3**, 73–9.

Weiner, B., Amirkhan, J., Folkes, V.S. and Verette, J.A. (1987) An attributional analysis of excuse giving: Studies of a naive theory of emotion. *Journal of Personality and Social Psychology*, **52**, 316–24.

White, R.W. (1959) Motivation reconsidered: The concept of competence. *Psychological Review*, **66**, 297–333.

Whitehead, G.I. and Hall, A.E. (1984) Sex differences in the assignment of responsibility for an accident. *Sex Roles*, **11**, 787–98.

Whitehead, G.I. and Smith, S.H. (1986) Competence and excuse-making as self-presentational strategies. In R.F. Baumeister (Ed.), *Public self and private self*. New York: Springer.

Wicklund, R.A. (1978) Three years later. In Berkowitz, L. (Ed.), *Cognitive theories in social psychology*, pp. 509–21. New York: Academic Press.

Wicklund, R.A. and Gollwitzer, P.M. (1982) *Symbolic self-completion*. Hillsdale, N.J.: Erlbaum.

Williams, C.B. and Vantress, F.E. (1969) Relation between internal–external control and aggression. *Journal of Psychology*, **71**, 59–61.

Williams, J.E., Best, D.L., Voss, H.G., Tilquin, C., Bjerke, T., Keller, H. and Baarda, B. (1981) Traits associated with men and women: Attribution by young children in France, Germany, Norway, the Netherlands, and Italy. *Journal of Cross-Cultural Psychology*, **12**, 327–46.

Williams, R.M. (1964) *Strangers next door: Ethnic relations in American communities*. Englewood Cliffs, N.J.: Prentice Hall.

Wilson, R.J. and Jonah, B.A. (1988) Assignment of responsibility and penalties for an impaired driving incident. *Journal of Applied Social Psychology*, **18**, 564–83.

Zimbardo, P. and Radl, S. (1981) *The shy child*. New York: McGraw-Hill.

Index of names

Abelson, R.P., 5
Abramson, L.Y., 20
Adler, A., 20
Altman, J., 97
Amirkhan, J., 161
Anderson, N.H., 4
Andrecht, I., 206
Arkin, R.M., 22
Aronson, E., 21
Ashby, W.R., 9
Austin, J.L., 79

Baarda, B., 33
Backman, C.W., 4
Bandura, A., 21
Bartlett, F.C., 2
Bauer, R.A., 7, 8
Baumgardner, A.H., 22
Becker, E.W., 119
Beckmann, J., 183
Bem, S.L., 30, 33
Bennett, W.L., 5
Bergemann, N., 57, 137
Bergmann, D., 206
Berscheid, E., 149
Bertalanffy, L.V., 9
Berten, G., 49, 87
Best, D.L., 33
Birkendorf, B., 52, 204, 206
Bjerke, T., 33
Blumstein, P.W., 10, 86, 94, 158
Brandt, R., 204
Brickman, P., 10, 41, 114
Bridgeman, D., 21
Brown, P., 12
Bubber, S., 52, 204, 206
Bucher, E., 58
Burger, J.M., 33, 57, 59, 119, 137, 138, 139, 205
Buss, A.H., 50, 51, 52, 53, 57, 61, 62, 167
Bussmann, V., 206

Calicchia, J.P., 137
Campbell, D.T., 22, 23, 204

Carlsmith, J.M., 4
Carssow, K.G., 10, 86, 94, 158
Carver, C.S., 21, 22
Coates, D., 10, 41, 114
Cody, M.J., 6, 10, 35, 76, 86, 122, 127, 150, 158, 160
Cohn, E., 10, 41, 114
Colsher, S., 41
Cooper, H.M., 57, 59, 119, 137, 138, 139, 205
Council on Environmental Quality and the US State Department, 25
Cupach, W.R., 136
Curtis, F., 42, 111, 114

Damerow, G., 60, 61
Davis, D., 185
Davis, J.A., 205
De Man, A., 42, 111, 114
Deaux, K., 30
Dittes, J.E., 149
Dörner, D., 20, 204
Dressler, J., 83, 84, 85

Economou, J., 206
Erkens, S., 206

Fauconnet, P., 40, 204
Feather, N.T., 30
Felson, R.B., 150, 158
Fenigstein, A., 50, 51, 52, 53, 57, 61, 62, 167
Festinger, L., 23, 30
Fincham, F.D., 40, 76, 186, 204, 206
Flaßhove, P., 50, 54, 206
Fletcher, C., 83, 84, 85
Folkes, V.S., 161
Ford, C.E., 136
Ford, M.R., 42, 111, 114
Freedman, J.L., 4
French, K., 10, 160
Frey, D., 24, 30, 33

Gandossy, R.P., 135
Gilligan, C., 41, 114

Index of names

Goffman, E., 13, 76
Gollwitzer, P.M., 23, 27, 30, 33, 42, 43, 106, 205
Goodstadt, B.E., 119
Greenawalt, K., 84, 85
Greenberg, J., 22

Hale, C.L., 159, 160
Hall, A.E., 111
Hall, J., 10, 86, 94, 158
Hall, P.M., 14
Halliday, M.A.K., 206
Hamilton, V.L., 115
Hart, H.L.A., 40
Hawkins, B., 10, 86, 94, 158
Hazleton Jr., V., 136
Heider, F., 40, 96, 204
Heinemann, W., 42, 50, 51, 57, 58, 61, 205, 206
Helmreich, R.L., 30, 33
Henderson, M., 150
Hewitt, J.P., 12, 13, 14, 76
Hewstone, M., 76, 150
Heynen, A., 116, 204
Higgins, R.L., 13, 17, 21, 76, 78, 79, 136
Hjelle, L.A., 119
Hockett, C.F., 81
Hoffmann, R., 10, 86, 94, 158
Holland, B., 49, 87
Holsti, O.R., 75, 115
Hormuth, S.E., 57, 137
Howard, J.A., 112
Huff, C.W., 41, 115
Hunt, H.A., 136
Hupka, R.B., 122, 137, 150
Hyland, M.E., 21, 22

Ishem, E., 10, 86, 94, 158

Jacklin, C.J., 33
Janis, I.L., 8, 25, 27
Janoff-Bulman, R., 119, 186
Jaspars, J.M., 40, 76, 204, 206
Johann, G. K., 57, 137
Johnson, J.A., 111
Jonah, B.A., 102, 150
Jonas, H., 26
Jones, E.E., 7, 76
Jung, J., 122, 137, 150

Kanekar, S., 34
Karuza, J., 10, 41, 114
Keller, H., 33
Kelley, H.H., 25, 76, 86, 182
Kidder, L., 10, 41, 114
Kleibaumhüter, P., 55, 76, 204, 205, 206
Kleine, J., 206
Kleinke, C.L., 111

Kluttig, U., 206
Kohl, H., 1
Kohlberg, L., 41
Krahé, B., 111
Krampen, G., 119, 206
Kreuzig, H.W., 20, 204
Kuhl, J., 183

Lackmann, M., 58
Lalli, M., 57, 137
Lang, U., 204
Langer, E.J., 24
Lerner, M.J., 3, 25, 32, 85
Lesiak, W.J., 119
Levenson, H., 61, 62, 166, 206
Levinson, S.C., 12
Likert, R., 44, 55
Lloyd-Bostock, S., 40
Lorenz, K., 22, 204
Lowery, C.R., 42, 111, 114
Lyman, S.M., 15, 20, 76, 79, 80, 86, 125

Maccoby, E.E., 33
McGillis, D., 7
McGraw, K.M., 117
McHugh, P., 13
McLaughlin, M.L., 6, 10, 35, 76, 86, 122, 127, 150, 158, 160
Madden, M.E., 119, 186
Mann, L., 8
Manstead, A.S.R., 76, 79
Maurer, C.P., 10, 86, 94, 158
Maynard, D.W., 13
Mazumdar, D., 34
Metts, S., 136
Mielke, R., 206
Mills, C.W., 13
Mischel, W., 38
Mitchell, C.L., 42, 114
Müller-Eckhard, E., 58, 182

Nisbett, R.E., 7
Nixdorf, B.D., 58, 204, 205
Nixon, R., 27
Norman, N., 22
North, R.C., 75, 115
Null, C.H., 41, 115

O'Barr, W.M., 182
Oesterreich, R., 204
O'Hair, H.D., 10, 76, 86, 122, 150
Osnabrügge, G., 24

Pardine, P., 137
Penfold, P.S., 111, 136
Perkowitz, W.T., 185
Petronio, S., 137
Pinto, N.J.P., 34

Index of names

Pittman, T.S., 76
Popper, K., 22, 23, 204
Potter, J., 186
Powers, W.T., 21
Prystav, I., 58, 204, 205
Pyszczynski, T., 22

Raatz, U., 207
Rabinowitz, V.C., 10, 41, 114
Radl, S., 21
Räuker, F.W., 2, 3
Reagan, R., 8, 13
Regelmann, S., 58
Reiss, M., 76
Reither, F., 20, 204
Ribner, S.A., 150, 158
Riedl, R., 9, 22, 25, 26, 204
Rieger, A., 206
Robbins, M.A., 111
Rosenstein, N.E., 6, 10, 35, 86, 158, 160
Rothbaum, F., 24
Rothman, M.L., 135
Rotter, J.B., 119
Rund, S., 206
Runge, T.E., 30, 33

Saft, Ch., 206
Sanders, J., 115
Schank, R.C., 5
Scheier, M.F., 21, 22, 50, 51, 52, 53, 57, 61, 62, 167
Schellenberg-van Holt, H.J., 50, 54
Schiffmann, R., 204, 206
Schindler, H., 204
Schleifer, M., 40, 97
Schlenker, B.R., 26, 76
Schmalt, H.D., 42, 114
Schönbach, P., 4, 42, 43, 56, 58, 61, 75, 76, 85, 106, 183, 205
Schopler, J., 50, 118, 206, 207
Schreiber, M., 3
Schwitalla, J., 86
Scott, M.B., 15, 20, 76, 79, 80, 86, 125
Sears, D.O., 4
Secord, P.F., 4
Seelman-Eggebert, R., 2
Seligman, M.E.P., 20
Semin, G.R., 76, 79
Shaver, K.G., 10, 33, 40, 41, 54, 98, 101, 111, 112, 115, 204
Shaw, M.E., 40
Shields, N.M., 159
Shultz, T.R., 40, 97, 206
Siebert, M., 204

Silverthorn, K., 122, 137, 150
Simpson-Housley, P., 42, 111, 114
Smith, A.W., 205
Smith, S.H., 149
Snyder, C.R., 13, 17, 21, 76, 78, 79, 136
Snyder, S.S., 24
Solomon, S., 22
Spence, J.T., 30, 33
Spens, D., 10, 86, 94, 158
Stahlberg, D., 24
Stäudel, T., 20, 204
Steininger, M., 41
Stiepel, G., 42, 43, 106, 205
Stokes, R., 12, 13, 14, 76
Stucky, R.J., 21, 76, 78, 79, 136
Studt, J., 58, 182, 204
Stuhrmann-Berg, H., 206
Sulzer, J.L., 40

Tajfel, H., 15
Tandler, G., 1
Taylor, J., 10, 86, 94, 158
Taylor, S.E., 21
Teasdale, J., 20
Tedeschi, J.T., 22, 76
Teichgräber, R., 50, 54
Thornton, B., 111
Tilquin, C., 33
Tonscheidt, D., 52, 204
Turner, J., 15

Vantress, F.E., 119
Verette, J.A., 161
Voss, H.G., 33

Wagner, U., 42, 43, 106, 205
Walster, E., 31
Weiner, B., 161
Weisz, J.R., 24
Wetherell, M., 186
White, R.W., 20
Whitehead, G.I., 111, 149
Wicklund, R.A., 23, 27, 167
Wiener, N., 9
Williams, C.B., 119
Williams, J.E., 33
Williams, R.M., 205
Wilson, R.J., 102, 150
Wuketis, F.M., 204

Zaninovich, M.G., 75, 115
Zimbardo, P., 21
Zimmermann, D.L., 10, 86, 94, 158
Zinnes, D.A., 75, 115

Subject index

Concepts with ubiquitous appearance are selectively indexed.

accommodation, 24
account episodes
  accomplishment of, 16–17, 180, 185–6
  foundering of, 16–17
  functions of, 5, 13–16
  as scripts, 5
  structures of, 10–13, 29
account phase, 11, 39–40, 54–60, 121–51
accountability, 3, 5, 83
accounts
  concessions, 12, 39, 65, 76–8, 154–8
  defensiveness of, 29, 35, 39, 63, 121–60, 177
  egocentric, 27
  excuses, 12, 61, 76–80, 82–5, 152–4, 159
  intervening role of, 173–4
  justifications, 12, 61–2, 76–7, 80, 82–5, 152–4, 159
  quality of, 159–60, 177, 182
  refusals, 12, 36, 65, 76–7, 80, 154–8
action control theory, 183
actor, 11–13, 17
age, 42–3, 103–5, 184–5
aligning actions, 13–15
altercasting, 15
assimilation, 24
attribution tendencies, 7

basic assumptions, 22, 27
basic categories, *see under* categories
basic question, 16–17

CARDACOM index, 133–5
cardinal aspects, *see* categories, cardinal
categories
  analytic, 70–1
  and aspects, 76–83
  basic, 76, 85–6
  cardinal, 78–83, 122–9
  cross-cardinal, 78–83
  hierarchies of, 71–2
  intracardinal, 78–83
  subdivisions of, 86
  superordinate, 78–85
  synthetic, 70–1
  targets of, 88–9
  themes of, 76–83, 85–6
category systems, 68–90
  construction principles of, 18, 68–75
  for failure events, 18, 182–3
  for reactions of actors, 18, 75–86
  for reactions of opponents, 18, 86–90
causal thinking
  linear, 6–8, 25–6
cause, *see under* responsibility
chance, *see* control, locus of
coding reliability, 74–5
coding strategies
  dimensional coding, 73, 90
  frequency coding, 74
  interpretive context of, 74–5
  occurrence coding, 74
  primary coding, 72–3
  résumé coding, 73, 90
  secondary coding, 72–3, 90, 108–10
  superordinate coding, 72–3
competence
  desire for, 20, 24, 57, 119–20, 138–9, 142, 145, 171–3, 180
COMPREVAL index, 108–10, 119–20
concessions, *see under* accounts
conflict, 14–15
  escalation of, 27–40, 175–8
consonance, *see* dissonance theory
constancy
  desire for, 23–4, 30, 57, 138–9, 168–9, 171–3, 180
control, *see also* competence *and* constancy
  desire (need) for, 3–4, 32, 35, 57, 117–20, 137–49, 166–73, 179–81
  evolution of, 22–3
  locus of, 50, 62, 118–19, 166–7
  measurement of, 57
  and self-esteem, 20–2, 34, 36, 57–8, 138–9
  and vulnerability, 27
coping, 20, 25

Subject index

cost liability
  attribution of, 51–2, 91–114
cross-cardinal themes, *see* categories, cross-cardinal

defensive attributions
  and avoidance of blame, 98, 101–3, 111–13
  and avoidance of harm, 101
  hypothesis of, 33–4, 101, 111–13
defensiveness, *see under* accounts
depression, *see* helplessness
dissonance theory, 30, 37

educational status, 105–7, 184–5
egocentric accounts, *see under* accounts
empathy, 185
escalation, *see under* conflict
evaluation phase, 11, 36–7, 60–5, 152–74
evaluations
  negativity of, 29, 36–7, 152–74, 176–8
evolutionary perspectives, 9, 22–3, 25
excuses, *see under* accounts

failure events, 11, 39–40
  severity of, 29, 31–2, 39–40, 91–5, 149–51, 176–8
females, *see* gender effects

gender effects, 178–9
  on account phase behaviour, 35, 127–37
  on evaluations, 36, 161–5
  gender of evaluated actors, 162–4
  on need for control, 41, 139–41
  on reproach phase behaviour, 32–4, 95–103, 109–13
  on responsibility concepts, *see under* responsibility
  on self-dissatisfaction, 140–1
guilt attribution, 52, 91–114

helplessness, 20–1

identity
  negotiation of, 15
idiographic degeneration, 18
impairment claims, 79, 86
inborn teaching masters, 25–6
intracardinal themes, *see* categories, intracardinal

judgements
  targets and themes of, 88–9
  tendencies of, 88–9
just world, 3, 5, 32, 85
justice, *see* just world
justifiability, 5
justifications, *see under* accounts

locus of control, *see under* control

males, *see* gender effects
masculinity, 29–30, 33, 184
misalignment, *see* aligning actions
moderator variables
  associations among, 138–9
motive talk, 13

negativity, *see under* evaluations
nomothetic ambition, 18

opponent, 11–13, 17, 31–4, 36–7
  status of, 60

powerlessness, *see* control, locus of
predicaments, 26

quasi-theorizing, 14

readiness, 23
refusals (refutations), *see under* accounts
remedial interchanges, 13
reproach phase, 11, 31–4, 49–54, 91–113, 117–20
reproaches
  egocentric, 27
  quality of, 182
  severity of, 29, 31–6, 91–113, 117–27, 173–4
responsibility
  attribution of, 51, 91–114
  cause and, 3–10, 40–1
  diffusion of, 3, 6
  gender-specific notions of, 41–2, 66–7, 113–17
  meaning of, 10, 26, 40–2, 65–7, 113–17, 185
responsiveness, 185–6

scripts, *see under* account episodes
secondary coding, *see under* coding strategies
self-completion, 23–4
self-confidence, *see* self-esteem
self-consciousness, 50, 62, 167–8
self-dissatisfaction, *see* self-esteem *and* gender effects
self-esteem, 20–1, 30–1, 43, 57, 137–49, 166–8, 179–81
  and control, *see under* control
  maintenance of, 15, 21
  measurement of, 57
self-handicapping, 21
severity
  of failure, *see under* failure events
  of reproach, *see under* reproaches
shyness, 21

situation
  definition of, 14
social anxiety, 50, 62, 138–9, 183
social change, 14
social stability, 14
social status, 42–3

targets, *see under* categories
tasks for the future, 181–7

taxonomies, *see* category systems
themes, *see under* categories
theoretical guidance, 18, 20–7, 175–6
transphase perspectives, 87, 176–81
trustworthiness, 4

utterance length, 182

vignettes, 45–9, 186–7